1954

Adventures

In

New York

A young man makes his way in a city that temps at every turn.

Neal P. Gillen

The author in 1954

1954 Adventures In New York

All rights reserved. No part of this book shall be reproduced or transmitted in any form or by any means, electronic, mechanical, magnetic, or photographic including photocopying, recording of any information storage and retrieval system, without prior written permission of the author. No patent liability is assumed with respect to the use of the information contained herein. Although every precaution has been taken in the preparation of this book, the author and distributor assume no responsibility for errors or omissions. Neither is any liability assumed for damages resulting from the use of the information contained herein.

Printed in the United States of America

Published September 2012

Copyright © 2012 by Neal P. Gillen

All rights reserved.

ISBN-13:978-1479268351
ISBN-10:1479268356

Also
By
Neal P. Gillen

Sugar Time

Capitol Punishment

Dinner in Bordeaux

Kitty's Rules

Slamming the Close

The Night Clerks

Altar Boy

Lonely No More

1954 Adventures In New York

This story is dedicated to those who in 1954 helped to lead me in

the right direction.

"Live all you can; it's a mistake not to. It doesn't so much matter what you do in particular so long as you have your life. If you haven't had that what have you had?"

The Ambassadors by Henry James

Harper and Brothers, 1903

Introduction

In the latter stages of my career in the world cotton trade, the International Cotton Advisory Committee, an inter-governmental organization, appointed me as its permanent representative to the United Nations Commission on International Trade Law (UNCITRAL), a position I still hold. This prestigious assignment took me to New York twice a year to participate in a five-day conference with legal experts from around the world tasked to update the United Nations' Model Arbitration Law.

The "One World Café," the cafeteria in the UN Headquarters Building, is one of the best places to eat in Manhattan. In addition to its excellent food and cut rate prices, it offers a spectacular view of the East River, the 59th Street Bridge, and the rapidly changing Queens and Brooklyn shore lines. I always take a seat near the floor-to-ceiling rear window so I can look out and watch the river traffic and reminisce about my first job out of high school in a red brick building on Vernon Boulevard that is visible from the cafeteria.

I was doing just that, when a young Asian woman, pointing to the vacant seat across from me, asked in broken English, "May I sit here?"

I smiled at her, "Of course you may."

"Hello, my name Nguyen. I am intern."

"Where are you from?"

"Vietnam. Did you fight there?"

"No. My military service was in the late 1950's."

"Were you soldier?"

"No. Sailor. I was in the Navy."

She was charming, and all through the meal she chattered away about life in Hanoi, her studies at the University of Missouri, and her desire to be an international diplomat. Along with her quick mind came a great sense of humor. She was also quite perceptive. Whenever the conversation lulled she would ask me why I always looked over at Queens. When I told her that is where I was born and raised, she shook her head in disbelief – "Not possible, you from Queens. Everybody there Spanish, Korean, and Chinese." I laughed at first and then explained how at one time it was mostly Irish, German, Italian, and other European derivations. "Where all the people go?" she asked. I told her that they died after their children moved on. I explained that New York continually recycled itself. That new people were always coming, and that the City, especially Queens, was always in transition.

I asked her where she lived, and she told me that she lived with a Spanish family in Flushing, noting it was one of the few remaining Spanish families in Flushing, which had become predominantly Asian. I pointed to the red-brick building across the river where I used to work, telling her that many years ago, in 1954; I once made women's hats. She laughed and questioned my credibility. "How could you work in that kind of place, and now be speaking at meetings in the Trusteeship Council Room?"

"It's a long story," I told her. "That was the year I began to change my life around."

"That's what I like about Americans," she said. "They can forget quickly and do, what you say, 'The right thing?'"

"Yes, you could say I did the right thing, but it took some time."

I did not have time to tell her this story. J. D. Salinger I am not; therefore the story does not follow the rule he set out in the 16-year-old voice of Holden Caulfield in the brilliant opening sentences of *Catcher in the Rye:*[1]

"If you really want to hear about it, the first thing you'll probably want

---

[1] 1951, Little, Brown and Company.

to know is where I was born and what my lousy childhood was like, and how my parents were occupied and all before they had me, and all that David Copperfield kind of crap, but I don't feel like going into it, if you want to know the truth. In the first place, that stuff bores me, and in the second place, my parents would have about two hemorrhages apiece if I told anything pretty personal about them."

Well, my childhood wasn't boring – it was fun, and, well, you could say it was adventurous. My parents were interesting if not difficult. And, this story about a pivotal year in my life and the characters who made it possible are far from boring. I do agree, however, that my parents would have multiple hemorrhages were they to read this.

New York City In 1954

In 1774, on his first visit to New York, John Adams was excited with the great potential of this bustling city. At that time, its 25,000 inhabitants were crowded together at the tip of Manhattan Island, though a handful of English and Dutch farmers were making a go of it north of City Hall in Manhattan, the Bronx, Queens, Brooklyn, and Staten Island. A long neglected cemetery from that era, located on 54th Street near 32nd Avenue in Woodside, contains headstones evincing that this area of Queens was settled in the latter part of the 1600s, but even then, Manhattan was considered "The City," and the "in" place to live.

Once the colonists defeated the British and secured their independence, it did not take long for New York to grow up and out from the tip of Manhattan Island. Its rapid growth soon made it a polyglot of different tongues and customs flavoring each neighborhood with a multitude of European influences. Within 100 years it had become the largest city in the world.

At the turn of the 20th Century, Byron Rufus Newton, a journalist for the *New York Herald Tribune*, penned, "Owed to New York," a tongue-in-cheek poem, that some might say is still an appropriate description of New York at the turn of the 21st Century. Newton described her as:

Vulgar of manner, overfed
Overdressed and underbred
Heartless, Godless, hell's delight,
Rude by day and lewd by night
Purple-robed and pauper clad,
Raving, rotting, money-mad;
A squirming herd in Mammon's mesh,

A wilderness of human flesh;
Crazed with avarice, lust and rum,
New York, thy name's Delirium.

F. Scott Fitzgerald said of New York, "that anything was possible," and by 1954 the City reigned supreme, still enjoying the afterglow of victory in World War II. It was said to be the greatest experiment in business and in civil and political democracy. Without question, it was the capitol of the universe since London's government- controlled and lackluster economy was still struggling to recover from the damage inflicted by German V2 rockets. Paris, though unscarred by the war, was politically unstable and experiencing a new government every few months. Rome was just beginning to show life in its post war recovery. Berlin was still littered with the detritus resulting from the Allied air strikes and recovery was far off. Tokyo, like Berlin, was starting to find its way with considerable assistance from Uncle Sam.

In 1954, other U.S. cities could not compare with New York. Philadelphia was a vaudeville joke, Miami a quiet beach town, Chicago was still the stockyards and a few years from the growth associated with the Daley era, during which it would become home to great skyscrapers. Dallas and Houston were cotton, oil, and cow towns. Los Angeles was smog ridden and just beginning its great growth and San Francisco was a tolerant port town waiting to become a tourist Mecca and the home of thousands of free spirits.

The New York City that I was caught up in had a vibrant beat in 1954. This city of endless re-composition was then in its post-World War II/Korean War stage of life. It was a city infatuated with itself and a far different place than it is today. Its ever-changing population was comprised primarily of first and second generation Americans of European extraction, mostly Irish and Italian followed by Germans, Poles and other Eastern Europeans. At that time it housed more Irish than all of Ireland's major cities except Dublin, more Italians than the combined populations of Florence and Venice, more Germans than Bonn, and more Poles than Gdansk.

The city's rhythms and nuances echoed the influences of the western world. The migration from the Caribbean Islands, led by Puerto Rico, was in its infancy, and only beginning to effect housing conditions in upper Manhattan and the East Bronx. In Manhattan, blacks were isolated in Harlem as well as the Bedford-Stuyvesant, Fort Greene, and the East-New York sections of Brooklyn, and in Corona and South Jamaica in Queens. The City's color was white and its religion Catholic. Catholics went to Mass every Sunday, ate fish on Friday out of fear of going to hell, and religiously attended movies that did not adhere to the recommendations of the church's "Legion of Decency." What the legion recommended we not see, we saw.

The subway was clean and safe and taxis were efficient and relatively inexpensive. The 3rd Avenue El would function for another two years and the trolleys were still running in Brooklyn and across the 59th Street Bridge. We had double-decker buses on 5th Avenue that were a thrill to ride on, if you lucked out and found a seat on the upper deck. A ride on the subway and a draft beer cost 15 cents. Bars in Manhattan offered bowls of complimentary peanuts and pretzels along with free-lunch offerings of saltine crackers, inexpensive cold cuts, pickled herring in sour cream, and sardines. The legal drinking age was 18; therefore, drinking at the age of 16 was a given – it was deemed the Irish age of consent. Smoking was appropriate and advertised as sophisticated. Virtually every male smoked, as did many females, though it was considered inappropriate for women to smoke on the street. My parents gave me permission to smoke when I was 13.

One could dine at many of the city's better restaurants for $5. An adequate meal complete with coffee and apple pie in a Horn & Hardart Automat cost $1, while the slightly fancier Schraft's might cost an additional 25 cents. You could get a plate of spaghetti at Romeo's on 42nd Street for 33 cents. A cup of coffee and a piece of apple pie would cost you a quarter. Movies at Radio City Music Hall, the Paramount or Roxy Theatres in Times Square cost $1.25 to $1.50 and included top name entertainment like Bob Hope, Dean Martin and Jerry Lewis, or Johnny Ray. New York had three baseball teams, the New York Yankees in the American League and the New York Giants and the Brooklyn Dodgers in the National League. A seat in the bleachers at Ebbets Field, the Polo Grounds, or Yankee Stadium was 50 cents, and you could see a basketball or hockey game in the cheap seats at Madison Square Garden for 75 cents.

Housing was affordable and readily available even in Manhattan. The price disparity between many parts of Manhattan and the outer boroughs did not exist in 1954. Eastside one bedroom walkups went for $50 dollars a month, while Westside walkups were less expensive. Aristocratic inhabitants of Manhattan used to snub the West side, often noting, "I only go there when I'm taking the steamer to Europe." Nice apartments in the outer boroughs of the Bronx, Queens, Brooklyn, and Staten Island were available at no higher than the West side rates. Our commodious, rent-controlled, three-bedroom apartment in Woodside was $75 a month. There were a number of single-occupancy furnished rooms available in Manhattan for $25 a month and many families in the boroughs rented rooms to boarders at similar rates.

Jobs were plentiful as New York City was the capitol of corporate

America. An estimated 140 of the largest corporations were headquartered in Manhattan. Aside from the white-collar job opportunities in corporate America, it also was a working-class city offering well-paid jobs in manufacturing, machine tooling, shipbuilding and repair, construction, warehousing, stevedoring, and truck driving. There were more than a million industrial jobs in the City in 1954.

High school graduates entered the job market at weekly salaries as high as $45, while college graduates would start at $75. Middle-management salaries ranged from $125 to a $150 per week with senior executives averaging $200 to $250 per week. The annual salary of corporate CEO's ranged from $25,000 to $50,000.

World War II veterans with college degrees financed by the G.I. Bill of Rights were now part of the work force, while Korean Veterans were beginning their college educations. The economy was booming with Detroit selling new cars as soon as they moved off the assembly lines. New homes were springing up like weeds in the suburbs of New York, resulting in a number of my friends leaving the neighborhood as their parents were lured to suburbia. New appliances were the rage. Households were acquiring washing machines, dryers, refrigerators, freezers, and televisions in record numbers. New and improved were the sales catch words. America had unleashed its purchasing power, too long pent-up by the price controls of the Korean War.

New York seemed to be everyone's destination. The piers in Brooklyn, Manhattan, and Hoboken were thriving as ships were backed up all the way to the Ambrose Lightship in the outer harbor, waiting to load or unload their cargoes. Every day a passenger liner from the numerous European ports would discharge and load passengers coming from or going to the Continent. La Guardia Airport was busting at its seams while Idlewild, a new airport, was under construction in Jamaica Bay. Like the great city it serves, Idlewild, now known as J.F.K. International Airport, continues to recreate itself – it's an ongoing construction site. Trains were still popular and service was excellent. Penn Station routed railroad traffic to and from the south and southwest, while Grand Central Station served the northern and western routes. New York was a funnel for people and goods bound in every direction.

Dwight D. Eisenhower, who led us to victory in Europe, himself a New Yorker during his brief tenure as President of Columbia University, was in his second year as president of the United States. The shooting in the Korean War ended in July 1953, but the tense negotiations of the Armistice Agreement would be ongoing until November 1954. Viet Nam was then called French Indo China, where the French would soon suffer a bloody defeat in a place called Dien Bien Phu. The British Empire was further diminished by its withdrawal from Egypt after a 72-year occupation.

Though America was at peace, we gave the Soviet Union a dire warning by revealing our successful and secret testing of a Hydrogen Bomb in 1952, which exceeded all test expectations. Instead of the four to eight megatons, it was measured at 15 resulting in the obliteration of part of Eniwetok, a small atoll in the South Pacific. Dr. J. Robert Oppenheimer, the man credited with fathering the Atom or "A" Bomb, would be punished for his intellectual opposition to the development of the "H" bomb by being stripped of his security clearance by an Atom Energy Commission Review Board.

While the economy lost some of its zip early in the year, it picked up considerably by the end of the summer when I began to spend the bulk of my meager income. Over 573 million shares would trade on the New York Stock Exchange, the largest number of shares traded since the low point in 1933. Two brothers from Manchester, New Hampshire, Dick and Maurice McDonald, sold the franchising rights to their successful

McDonald's hamburger and milk shake restaurant in San Bernardino, California to their Mix Master salesman, Ray Kroc, who would expand this new fast food concept a thousand fold within 10 years. Kemmons Wilson, a Memphis, Tennessee homebuilder, foresaw a demand in accommodations for families traveling by car and decided to expand his highly successful Memphis area motel operation, giving rise to the rapid growth of a nationwide system of Holiday Inns. America was literally on the move.

General Electric would hire Ronald Reagan, a fading actor, to host the "G.E. Theatre" on network television and to tour its plants and lecture on the virtues of free enterprise and the American way. Though unaware of his dress size, Americans worshipped FBI Director J. Edgar Hoover.

A new polio vaccine was developed by Dr. Jonas Salk, a true-to-form, stereotypical, aggressive Brooklyn-born doctor/researcher, who, knowing that speed was vital to save lives, discarded the time-consuming "live vaccine" theory and pushed ahead over the opposition of the distinguished researcher Albert Sabin. Instead, Salk pursed a "kill the virus" technique that increased the level of polio antibodies resulting in the successful vaccine that was tested on Pittsburgh area children.

The Supreme Court of the United States issued its landmark ruling in *Brown v. Kansas City Board of Education*, the seminal beginning of meaningful racial change in the United States. Convicted perjurer and suspected Soviet agent Alger Hiss finished his 42-month prison term. Marilyn Shepard, the wife of a doctor in Cleveland, Ohio was murdered. Soon the public would begin a five-decade focus on whether Dr. Sam Shepard was guilty or innocent. A legend began to take shape when Elvis Presley, a young truck driver from Tupelo, Mississippi, cut his first record in the Sun Records studio in Memphis, Tennessee. So too, the dawn began to rise on the myth of Camelot. Photos of a newly married couple, John

Fitzgerald Kennedy, a 34-year-old U.S. senator from Massachusetts and a shy 24-year-old socialite and *Washington Post* reporter, Jacqueline Bouvier, were featured in a *Look Magazine* article.

America's baseball hero, Joe DiMaggio, surprised the world by marrying screen goddess Marilyn Monroe, though eight months later she surprised Joe by leaving him for playwright Arthur Miller. Lucille Ball and Desi Arnaz, Milton "Uncle Miltie" Berle, Jackie Gleason, Ed Sullivan, Loretta Young, and Danny Thomas were the dominant television personalities. Steve Allen and his zany guests "Gypsy" Boots and Jim Moran in the original *Tonight* show, put us to bed, while Dave Garroway and a chimpanzee named J. Fred Muggs started our mornings on the *Today* show.

From Here to Eternity won the Oscar for best film. William Holden was voted best actor for his role in *Stalag 17*. Audrey Hepburn, a young woman who the world would admire for the next 45 years was named best actress for her role in *Roman Holiday* opposite Gregory Peck. Frank Sinatra and Donna Reed won the best supporting Oscars for their roles in *From Here to Eternity*.

George P. Metesky, aka "The Mad Bomber," a vengeful, former Con Edison employee, remained on the loose, terrorizing New York City by setting off explosive devices in Grand Central Station, the Port Authority Bus Terminal, Radio City Music Hall and other locations. A boorish, but powerful U.S. senator from Wisconsin, Joseph McCarthy, dominated the news with accusations of Communist Party infiltration into sensitive positions in the U.S. Government. Five Puerto Rican Nationalists fired 25 shots from the Visitors' Gallery of the U.S. House of Representatives and wounded five members during a congressional session. The uproar following this event almost equaled that achieved by Dr. Alfred Kinsey, when his second controversial report, *Sexual Behavior in the Human*

Female, revealed the sexual proclivities of women. Hugh Hefner, a young Chicago magazine promoter, capitalized on this sexual uproar by launching *Playboy Magazine*. Its first issue, in December 1953, revealing Marilyn Monroe's principal attributes, could be found in many New York barbershops well into 1954.

Hurricanes "Carol" in September and "Hazel" in October battered the East Coast from the Carolinas through Canada, killing more than 300 people and causing damage losses exceeding $100 million. The Navy launched the first nuclear submarine, "The USS Nautilus," ushering in a new era in marine warfare and soon thereafter christened the largest ship ever constructed, "The USS Forrestal," a 60,000 ton aircraft carrier.

Rocky Marciano reigned supreme as boxing's heavyweight champion by decisively defeating Ezzard Charles in two fights. Bill Vukovich won the Indianapolis 500 for the second consecutive time, his car averaging 130.8 miles per hour. A year later, going for three in a row, he lost his life in the same race. All-American Tom Gola led Philadelphia's La Salle College to the NCAA Basketball Championship over highly touted Bradley University. The Minneapolis Lakers continued their domination in the NBA by beating the Syracuse Nationals four games to one for the championship. San Diego's Maureen "Little Mo" Connelly won the Women's Singles title at Wimbledon, and Determine won the Kentucky Derby. In professional football, Otto Graham would lead the Cleveland Browns in a wholesale 56 to 10 slaughter of the Detroit Lions in the NFL Title Game.

Baseball was undisputedly American's pastime in 1954 when Henry Aaron began his brilliant career with the Milwaukee Braves and his quiet quest to surpass Babe Ruth as the all-time home run leader with 755 round-trippers. Another great career in sports took life in the form of a magazine venture called *Sports Illustrated*.

The Cleveland Indians dominated the American League, winning a record breaking 111 games and the Pennant, only to lose the World Series in four straight games to the New York Giants. The country was stunned by this incredible and unexpected World Series upset that featured the famous over-the-shoulder catch by Willy Mays of Vic Wertz's massive shot to right center field in the Polo Grounds and the home run hitting heroics of a virtual unknown, James Lamar "Dusty" Rhodes. Lawrence "Yogi" Berra, winning the first of his three American League Most Valuable Player awards, made it easier for Yankee fans to accept the humility of defeat that year. But all of these athletic feats seemed to pale in comparison to the accomplishment of a reed thin English medical student, Roger Bannister, who became the first person to break the four-minute mile barrier.

It was a fabulous time and place. Buck O'Neil, a player and manager of the Kansas City Monarchs and Baseball Hall of Fame member, best described it as "That was New York City when it was New York City."

It's when I began to come of age in a city, an iconic city, bursting with life and adventure. It was a time that began in my harshest of winters and transitioned into a year of wonder, enlightenment, levity, and eventually the realization, given the advice of friends and one very observant teacher, that it was time to shape up and get on with life.

It was the time where Billy Joel begins his hit song, "We Didn't Start The Fire." While I didn't start it, I certainly felt its warmth that year. I was a crazy kid in a hurry to do everything – including some bad things.

1

Arrested Development

I was still dressed in the brown tweed suit, blue shirt, and a paisley maroon tie that I wore to Mass that morning. I can recall that today because there it is in my faded mug shot. While comfortable and warm in such garb, I quickly learned I was overdressed for the routine of the next few days. My alleged accomplice and I were driven to the 114th Precinct in Astoria and taken upstairs to the second floor detective room – the same place where I was questioned the previous Sunday. In the large dimly lit room, we were seated across the desk from Detective Allmendinger, who played the role of the good cop. Pacing about and making accusations was Detective Horan, quite comfortable in the role of bad cop. Despite our vigorous denials of involvement, we were booked for "Grand Larceny Auto" and fingerprinted adjacent to a wire mesh holding cage. Thereafter, we were placed in a so-called "paddy wagon" and driven to the 110th Precinct in Elmhurst for an overnight stay.

As we were booked into the Elmhurst Precinct, the desk sergeant noted my friend's Irish name and in a mocking Irish brogue said, "Descendent of the kings, I see. Well, the fucking king should see you now!"

The sergeant's displeasure was clearly evident in his sarcasm. The predominantly Irish members of the N.Y. Police Department had little patience with "their own kind" being arrested. He was used to jailing African Americans and Italian Americans in the 110th Precinct. Standing before him that Sunday evening were two-well dressed, clean-cut Irish Catholics spoiling his quiet night.

"I've two altar boys who will be spending the night with us," he said to the approaching officer who led us to the holding cells. That carried a harsh ring of truth, since I had been an altar boy at Corpus Christi Church for almost five years. All those cold mornings trudging off to serve the seven o'clock Mass. Where had it gotten me? Also, I had attended Mass and Communion on nine consecutive First Fridays, the equivalent of winning the trifecta on three horses with great odds. In Catholicism, this feat held the promise that I would go to my final reward with the opportunity to confess all. I had figured that the worst-case scenario was to do time in purgatory before moving up to heaven. If the 110th Precinct was purgatory, I thought that where we were headed might not exactly be a joy ride to heaven.

Following a late night snack of greasy White Castle hamburgers, my alleged accomplice and I attempted to sleep on a wooden bench. About the time we figured it out, we heard loud noises outside the cell-block area, doors slamming, and then approaching footsteps. It was my friend's father – a hard-working, kind, and quiet man. He was tall, strong as an ox, and at that moment in a high state of perturbation – he was really pissed.

"I suppose you expect me to mortgage the house to get you out of here?" he asked. "Well we're not going to do that, son. There's a lesson to be learned." They exchanged a few words and suddenly he was gone.

My friend, though a tough-minded individual, was embarrassed and distraught. It then dawned on me that this was serious stuff. What would happen in the morning? Was this it? Obviously a court appearance and then we would get to go home, I thought, or at least I hoped that would be the case. Adding to my puzzlement was my father's failure to protest when the detectives came to the house, and the fact that I didn't get a visit. I surmised that Dad was working on something or had something already worked out.

The next morning, we were handcuffed together and loaded into another paddy wagon. The 110th Precinct was close to Newtown High School, where Myrna Goodzeit, a girl I had recently stopped seeing, went to school. The weather that Monday morning was beautiful. It was sunny and warm. As we stopped for a light, on a street appropriately named Justice Avenue, Myrna suddenly appeared, her coat draped over her arm, wearing a sweater and a tight skirt highlighting her dynamite figure. It was like an apparition – Myrna in the flesh crossing the intersection on her way to school, hugging her books to her remarkably ample chest. A terrible feeling overcame me, and I was too ashamed to call out to her. Tears came to my eyes. Could it get any worse?

In 15 minutes we arrived at what was to be our initial destination, the Ridgewood Felony Court. We were photographed and placed in a holding room with an assortment of characters. One of them, sensing our newness to the process, was kind enough to advise us on what to expect procedurally. Our respective families had front row seats, looking on with strained and indifferent faces. We assumed that we would be released, but our parents knew what was about to happen – a different type of fix was in.

When our case was called, the Assistant DA approached the bench. "This arraignment is being held-over on the agreement of defense counsel."

"Is that agreeable to you, Mr. O'Connor? I mean Senator O'Connor," the judge asked our attorney.

"Yes, your honor."

"Does the County have a bail recommendation?"

"Your honor, the agreement stipulates that the parties will be held over until arraignment, and that they not be released on bail," the assistant DA responded.

1954 Adventures In New York

A quizzical look on his face, the judge looked directly at Senator O'Connor, who nodded his concurrence. The judge hesitated for a moment and then slammed down his gavel – "So ordered!"

My eyes closed as my head slumped over. I turned to look at my parents as we were led away. Mother was crying and Dad, his jaw clinched tightly, was shaking his head. This can't be happening to me, I thought. What's the point of all of this? I had stopped joyriding in cars. Our freedom would wait. This was a lesson being taught, but I had already learned my lesson. I want to go home, I thought. We were being given an extended stay as the guests of Queens County. Stunned, we were led off to a corridor, chained to yet another selection of new associates, very bad guys, and packed into a larger van for transport for our next place of residence.

Arriving at Long Island City Prison[2] in Court House Square, we formed a conga line and shuffled into a large barred pen. We were unshackled, given wire baskets, and told to strip and deposit our clothes and valuables into the baskets. Thereafter, I experienced my first strip search and an examination of my rectal cavity. "Spread those cheeks real wide for me boys," the guard said before examining the inner regions of our anatomy with the beam of a large flashlight. Following this embarrassing moment, my clothes were returned. This gave me hope, since most of the other prisoners were given dungaree pants and shirts.

I was separated from my friend and led by a guard through a myriad of passageways in this 19th-century brick building. We passed through

---

[2] Prior to our arrival, Willy "The Actor" Sutton was housed in Long Island City Prison in early 1953. Willy specialized in escaping from jails and robbing banks. He was hiding out on Staten Island when he was arrested for robbing the Manufacturer's Hanover Sunnyside Branch Bank on Queens Boulevard. A young Brooklyn man, Arnold Schuster, recognized Sutton, on the subway, and informed the police. To prove the adage that no good deed goes un-rewarded, Schuster's reward was two shots to the back of his skull, administered, reportedly on the orders of Mafia boss Albert Anastasia, as he made his way home from work. New Yorkers didn't seem to care since Willy "The Actor" was a folk hero. His reputation lives on for a quotation that has stood the test of time. When asked by a reporter why he robbed banks, Sutton replied, "Because that's where the money is."

secured checkpoints and up four flights of stairs to the far end of the structure. I was assigned to Cellblock 'C' high up in a tier with an excellent southerly view of Long Island City, Greenpoint, the United Nations Building and the East side of Manhattan. The guard assured me that I would be safe in this area of the prison. Safe? Jesus, what kind of place is this? I wondered, never realizing my vulnerability to a physical attack or sexual assault. There were four other cells within the pale green walls of the cellblock, all occupied by young black men in their 20's, recently transferred from the Raymond Street Jail in Brooklyn. Safe? I don't think so, I thought. Much to my relief, they immediately sized me up as a kid that didn't know the score – someone who didn't fit into what they knew as the justice system.

"What you in for, dude?"

"Riding in a stolen car."

"Man, they don't arrest people for riding in stolen cars. They arrest people for stealing cars."

I proceeded to explain the circumstances of my joy riding. "Well, we really weren't stealing them. You know, we would drive the cars around for an hour or so and then park them back where we found them. We never damaged them or anything like that."

"Man, that shit's not stealing them – you put them back," one of them opined.

"What kind of cars you take? You get any Cadillac's?" another asked.

I laughed at that. "There were few of them in my neighborhood, but we did take a real nice Olds one night. I never saw so much chrome on a car."

One of them said laughingly, "You wanna find a Caddie you best come over to Bed-Sty (Bedford-Stuyvesant), that's what all the poor folks there drive."

Their questions and comments quickly put me at ease.

"Man, you don't belong in here," I was told as they attempted to provide me assurances that it had to be a mistake.

"You should've been bailed out in Ridgewood. You can't be in here for that car shit."

"First arrest, you had a lawyer – a Senator. You denied that shit, and you're here, sounds funny to me man."

"Someone's jiving you, man – filling you with jive-ass shit!"

"They set you up. You some kind of chump."

"Sure sounds funny – doesn't jive, man."

"White boy, when you going home?" was the first thing I heard each morning in my two days of penance in Long Island City. I occupied the days and nights listening to jail talk, stories of lovemaking, abusive families, school failures, and the tough life in the Clinton Hill, Bedford-Stuyvesant and East-New York sections of Brooklyn. Though hardened young men, they were nice to me, and continually encouraged me with reassurance that everything would soon be all right.

When their constant chatter subsided that first day, I began to think about what was happening to my life. That night, I found myself dozing in and out of a light sleep. The grinding wheels of the passing Main Street, Flushing/Times Square (now the '7') elevated trains coming in and out of the adjacent Court House Square station, the heavy traffic on Jackson Avenue, and the shrill sound of the sirens from ambulances coming to and from nearby St. John's Hospital precluded sleep. I sat up on my bunk and looked down at my body. I felt as if I was outside of myself, an observer watching another person inhabiting my body and venting his anguish over his failures in life. I didn't like being me. Here I was one step removed from that me, that other person - a loser. I had finally come to realizing that my options would be severely limited if I didn't straighten myself out. I was a cocky kid riddled with self-doubt given my prior school experience and being told, especially in recent days, that I wouldn't amount to anything. I was constantly criticized by my mother for just about everything I did or may have failed to do. My shortcomings were always compared to someone else who was doing a particular thing better. Some of it was probably deserved. She was hoping for the perfect son, but that was not to be. Simply put, I was a complete fuck-up, a kid prone to do reckless things for the attention and the thrill that came with it, like setting fire to the high weeds on the railroad trestle, throwing rocks at passing trains and cars, pulling fire alarms, getting into fights, walking along the roof ledges of the Boulevard Gardens, and finally stealing cars.

Self-discovery is slow in coming. Sixteen is a young age. Those who reach it are full of themselves believing they have learned all there is to know in life. That certainly was my mindset. I learned in my confinement with four young black men who lacked my options in life that I best change my ways if I expected to take advantage of the opportunities life offered. I didn't realize what those opportunities were, but I knew that unless I shaped up, the door would soon be closed, and the full potential for a meaningful future gone.

Early Wednesday morning, my fourth day of incarceration, I looked out at the winter curtain shrouding Long Island City – its shade of gray seemingly holding little promise. I sat on my bunk wondering what would become of me as the gray curtain gradually gave way to streaks of reddish orange and blue. Daybreak might hold some promise, I thought, as a guard opened the cell block door and called out my name. "Gillen, you're traveling today."

The guys in the cell block were happy for me. They wished me well. "You're going to court, man. Good luck."

The prison guard escorting me out of the cell block to a shower room seemed surprised at how well I had bonded with my new cell-block friends. Looking at me intently, he asked, "They try any shit on you?"

"No," I responded in surprise.

"Fucking losers from Brooklyn – we're getting all the shit from the Raymond Street Jail."

"They were nice guys. They're pulling for me."

He shrugged and smiled. "They were pulling more than that, kid."

After I showered and shaved, he led me down the narrow stairs to the main receiving area adjacent to the garage, where I was reunited with my neighborhood friend, and informed we were being taken to Ridgewood Felony Court. Freedom was apparently at hand. Yet, the question remained: at what cost?

We were escorted into the courtroom where Senator O'Connor greeted us in a friendly fashion. Our mothers, though timid and ashamed, were smiling this time, while our fathers looked on in total disgust. Judge Lo Piccolo, who, five years later would interview me for membership in the Benevolent Protective Order of Elks, Lodge 878, inquired of Senator O'Connor, "Frank, what are you doing here?"

"I represent the defendants in this matter, your honor. I wish to inform the Court that the complaining witness has withdrawn the complaint on which the charges are based."

"Is the complaining witness present?" Judge Lo Piccolo asked.

"No, your honor, he resides in Montgomery County, in the State of Maryland. He has submitted this notarized affidavit withdrawing his complaint."

"Was the vehicle in question registered in Maryland?"

"Yes, your honor."

After reviewing the document, Lo Piccolo said, "Does the county agree with a disposition of dismissal?"

The young Assistant DA nodded his head in agreement.

Banging his gavel, Judge Lo Piccolo said, "This case is dismissed!"[3]

In the hallway outside the courtroom, there were hugs from our mothers, but hell to pay from our fathers. Frank O'Connor's dignity and status were the only things that saved me from the wrath of my father in the courthouse that day.[4]

I had reached the low point in my young life. I had always craved attention, as it was hard to come by with a father with two jobs and a mother with five children and now she too was working. A little praise here and there would have helped immeasurably. The lack thereof impelled me to find it elsewhere.

As a child, the first born, I received a lot of attention due to frequent bouts with asthma – a debilitating lung condition that I gradually conquered. There was a time that Mother used to take me to the movies every few weeks and after the show we'd go for an ice cream soda at this neat ice cream shop on Steinway Street near the Lowe's Triboro Theatre. Those trips were special, especially when she said I was her "little man." Dad used to take me to the Elks Club on Saturdays where we would play handball and swim. Being with him and his friends was a great ego booster. But those days were long past – they had little time for me now. As the oldest, I was pretty much on my own. I had serious doubts about myself.

---

[3] Two ironic coincidences to note here: in 1966, I joined Frank O'Connor in resigning our memberships from Elks Lodge 878 given its failure to admit people of color, and I have resided continually in Montgomery County, Maryland since 1971. Also of note, when the Secretary of the Elks Lodge received my letter of resignation, he informed my father who told him to ignore it. Unknown to me, Dad continued to pay my Elks Club dues until he died in 1975.

[4] A year later, through Mr. Thomas Carroll of the Youth Counsel's Office, my fingerprints and mug shots were returned and my record cleared.

Doing adventurous things had garnered me the attention and admiration of my peers. Subconsciously, I was seeking praise from others for doing the wrong things. Somehow I had to figure out how to do things right.

There was not much said when we got home that day from the Ridgewood Felony Court other than Dad's statement, "I hope you've learned your lesson." Mother was worried that I had missed three days of school. She had called Delehanty's and told them I had the flu. Dad made it clear that I would go to school in the morning and immediately come home and catch up on my homework. I had no problems with that as I was too embarrassed to see anyone. I wouldn't miss my fellow idle minds standing outside of the Greeks' Luncheonette or Mr. Green's candy store across the street from P.S. 151 thinking about things to do – troublesome things. My sisters were fielding all sorts of question from their friends, but they had little to say. The word had spread throughout the neighborhood and to some friends at school. I begged my friends at school to keep it quiet so I wouldn't get expelled. I avoided people in the neighborhood by walking quickly, with my head down, on a circuitous route to and from the subway on my way to and from school. Mother and Dad also avoided people in the neighborhood, but when they did encounter people they found them to be supportive.

I didn't call anyone or talk to anyone on the street until after Christmas. I was not anxious to see anyone. I still felt the shame. My arrest and confinement was only part of my ordeal. My expected rehabilitation would be the ultimate test of whether I had it in me to turn things around. The first thing I had to do was to fully prepare for my final examinations, something I had not been diligent about in previous efforts.

2

The Boulevard Gardens

My formative years were spent in a large Queens apartment complex called the Boulevard Gardens, which, looking back, was an extraordinary place for a young boy or girl to begin life. The neighborhood, once the homeland of the Delaware Indians, is located near La Guardia Airport at the northwestern edge of Woodside, wedged between Astoria to the west and Jackson Heights to the east.

The Boulevard Gardens and its surrounding land is steeped in history. Cornelius Rapelye, a descendant of Joris Jansen de Rapalie, a French Huguenot who arrived in New York in 1623, farmed this area during the Revolutionary War and is credited with fathering the first Christian child born in the Dutch Colonies.[5]

Growing up there in the 1940s and 50s, I didn't have a clue about the property's history. Had the kids known about the Delaware Indians, it would have added meaning to the games of cowboys and Indians we played on the vast lawns and in the thick evergreen hedges bordering the walkways between the apartment buildings.

At one time this area was known as North Woodside, or Charlotteville.[6] The street on which my sister Carol still lives, 32nd Avenue, was named Charlotte Avenue until the Borough of Queens dropped the street names in 1915 for a numeric system. The community is well planned, ideally located, and efficiently serviced by public transportation. The Northern Boulevard subway station is two blocks away and only six stops

---

[5] *"Woodside, Queens County, New York – A Historical Perspective 1652-1994,"* at page 22, by Catherine Gregory, Woodside On The Move, Inc., 1994.
[6] Id at page 56.

(15 minutes) from Manhattan. A myriad of bus systems move people quickly into the surrounding Queens neighborhoods of Astoria, Jackson Heights, or out to Flushing.

My mother, Rose McPartland Gillen, and my father, Patrick Aloysius Gillen, were original tenants when this federally financed experiment of garden apartments sprung to life in 1935. A wealthy property owner and diplomat, Cord Meyer,[7] developed the land and built the Boulevard Gardens and many of the private homes in the surrounding neighborhood. A quality builder, he had also developed Forest Hills Gardens, a unique and exclusive oasis.

Meyer and his co-developer, J. Henry Dick, along with the residents of the Gardens, became the beneficiaries of the largesse of President Franklin Delano Roosevelt's "New Deal." The Federal Government initiated a housing program that provided Meyer and his partner with a loan equal to 87 percent of the $3.7 million construction cost at the generous interest terms of four percent payable over 25 years. The building corporation was limited to a yearly profit, not to exceed six percent, and the original rents were capped at $11 per room.[8]

The Gardens opened in 1935, with 2,548 residents, mostly second, but some first- generation Irish with a sprinkling of Germans and Italians who had emigrated across the 59th Street Bridge from the melting pot neighborhoods of Manhattan. All were hard working; many of the fathers in the 960 families held down two jobs. The blue-collar workers toiled in the construction trades, the Brooklyn Navy Yard, and the West Side docks.

---

[7] His son Cord Meyer, Jr. would distinguish himself as a CIA covert operative. His daughter in-law, Mary Pinchot Meyer, was also an under the covers operative. She was mysteriously murdered on the C & O Canal towpath in Georgetown in 1964. Shortly thereafter, James Jesus Angelton, a CIA colleague of Meyer was observed attempting to break into her house, presumably seeking her diary later discovered by her sister revealing an extended and torrid affair with President John F. Kennedy. The crime remains unsolved.

[8] *"Woodside, Queens County, New York – A Historical Perspective 1652-1994,"* at page 146.

They drove delivery trucks or buses, were printers or pressmen at one of the seven New York newspapers, installed and repaired telephones, or did utility work for Brooklyn Union Gas or Con Edison. Some were bartenders, waiters, and waitresses.

The white-collar workers were middle managers, salesmen, supervisors, clerks, telephone operators and secretaries in insurance companies, banks, Wall Street brokerage houses, Railway Express, Western Union, Bell Telephone, and the Madison Avenue advertising agencies. There were also shoe salesmen and department store buyers along with a multitude of civil service clerks, policemen, and fireman, and also, teachers, engineers, nurses, journalists, and musicians. Overall, 120 separate occupations were represented.

Our parents had survived tough circumstances growing up in the harsh neighborhoods of Manhattan in the early part of the 20th Century. Unlike many others of that era, they had a sense of optimism. Yes, there were problems. After all, for the most part we were Irish Americans. Understandably, such a heritage came with some baggage.

We did not, however, suffer as much as the author Joe Queenan, who grew up a few years later in Philadelphia. In Queenan's words, with my parentheticals: "We told great stories, we had an odd, unsettling sense of humor (true in both instances), we were fiercely devoted to our mothers without actually enjoying their company (some truth there), we wished our fathers were dead (occasionally), we spent most of our lives being depressed (sounds familiar), we drank ourselves to early graves (I saw some of that), we were Irish."[9]

Early each weekday morning a parade of workers would emerge from their apartments and funnel out of the complex through the arch in the center of 'A' Building and down Hobart Street on its west side and 31st

---

[9] "Closing Time – A Memoir," by Joe Queenan, Viking, 2009.

Avenue on the south side. The times they departed and the uniforms they wore reflected their occupations. The blue-collar workers were the first and the white-collar crowd took up the rear of this march down 54th Street to the Northern Boulevard subway station. The order was reversed in the evening, as was the parade route, which took the marchers to their favorite taverns. The blue-collar workers turned right on 31st Avenue for the "Garden Grill" or cut across the triangular park to the "Shannon," while the suited, white-collar crowd turned left for "Murphy's" or the "Colony Tavern," as it was originally called.

There were 240 children when the families first moved in and soon there were many more in the 10 apartment buildings spread across the 12-acre hillside adjacent to the north-south line of the New York, New Haven & Hartford Railroad. Mollie Coor, an Irish immigrant and beloved Gardens resident, was often heard to remark that it was the noisy 2 a.m. train that helped to maintain the birth rate. When I was about 10 years old, Molly found a group of us smoking in the basement of her building. She lectured us on the evils of smoking by reciting a poem that I still remember:

> *Tobacco is a weed*
> *And from the devil it does proceed*
> *It robs your pockets*
> *And burns your clothes*
> *And makes a chimney out of your nose*

The Boulevard Gardens complex was a vast expanse of well-maintained lawns bordered by shrubs, flowerbeds, conifers and tall oak trees – connected by an intricate system of walkways. It also had a large population of well-fed squirrels dashing about the lawns and up the trees. The local bartenders would attest that the behavior of some of the residents on their best days could be described as squirrelly. In many respects we were all alike – happy and unhappy at times, much like the opening of Tolstoy's Anna Karenina,[10] "Happy families are all alike; every unhappy family is unhappy in its own way."

The Gardens retained its own private police force composed of three old timers who worked in shifts. They wore gray uniforms and were led by Mr. Taylor who delighted in reporting kids for playing on the grass – a serious infraction. The parents of repeat offenders like me were often warned and sometimes threatened with eviction.

Every day after school I would race home to play in the large playground at the edge of the complex near the railroad trestle. It had a wading pool, swings, monkey bars, a basketball hoop, and a huge sandbox for the younger children. "Lefty" Wellman supervised the playground and organized the daily punch ball and basketball games. Dedicated parents and residents who taught us the fundamentals of football, basketball, and baseball assisted Lefty at the playground and in nearby Queens Park. Lefty was also the coach of the 34th Avenue Boys – a baseball team from Astoria that featured a left-handed first baseman nick-named "Whitey," who pitched every few games. Edward "Whitey" Ford signed with the New York Yankees as a pitcher when he graduated from high school and went on to win 236 games, a career high for Yankee pitchers, and secured a place in the Baseball Hall of Fame in Cooperstown, New York.

Our team, the Boulevard Gardens Grasshoppers, usually took the field at Queens Park after the 34th Avenue Boys finished their game. I sat in the dugout during their games dozens of times. I'm one of the few Yankee fans who saw Whitey Ford play first base. We were also privileged to have as one of our coaches another Baseball Hall of Fame member, Walter

---

[10] "Anna Karenina," by Leo Tolstoy - published in serial installments from 1873 to 1877 in the Russian periodical, *The Russian Messenger*.

"Rabbit" Maranville, who played shortstop for five, of the then eight, National League teams.

The Rabbit was my father's close friend and drinking companion, and he lived one floor below us in 'J' Building. I spent a considerable amount of time with him, much to my delight. I wish I could have seen him play during his 23-year Major League career. In 1914, during his first season in the majors with the Boston Braves, the so-called "Miracle Braves" won the World Series. He also played for the Chicago Cubs, Pittsburgh Pirates and St. Louis Cardinals, and was the player manager of the Brooklyn Dodgers when his career came to an end.[11]

Many a Saturday morning, I would awaken to find the Rabbit with his face resting on our Formica kitchen table or stretched out on our plastic covered living room couch as he slept off the activities of the previous evening. The Rabbit and I soon developed a system. Once I revived him, he'd hand me a $5 bill and I'd run down to Sam's candy store and purchase the *N.Y. Daily News* and the *N.Y. Daily Mirror*. Then, I'd proceed to Wintermeyer's bakery for warm kaiser rolls and crumb buns. Upon my return I'd find the Rabbit freshly shaved by my father's razor and ready to sneak downstairs and surprise a skeptical Mrs. Maranville with the morning papers and fresh baked goods, but not before giving me a quarter for my role in his deception.

With room to field two baseball, softball, and football teams, the line was long in the playground and the neighboring P.S. 151 schoolyard for pick-up stickball, softball, and basketball games. There were Cub Scouts and Boy Scouts, Brownies and Girl Scouts, a Men's Club and a Women's Club, a Young People's Club, and movie cartoons every Wednesday

---

[11] In 23 seasons, all in the National League, he played in 2,670 games, with 2,605 hits, 177 triples, 291 stolen bases, hitting .258. His 5,139 putouts remains the all-time record for shortstops. He led the NL in putouts 6 times, and double plays 5 times.

afternoon in the 'H' Building Assembly Room, where more than 100 children gathered each week. We even had a credible weekly paper, *The Boulevard Gardens Beacon*, which is still in publication.

Although there were definite advantages to growing up in the Gardens, a few of the residents thought they were a step above the rest, which caused resentment from time to time, particularly from the 1,350 families who settled into the Woodside Housing Project in 1949. The Project was built by the New York Housing Authority on the site of the 22.5-acre "Wanderer's Field," next to Bryant High School.[12]

Wanderer's Field had been a place of adventure for the young boys from the surrounding neighborhoods. We choose up sides and played war games during World War II. We camped overnight on occasion and had endless fun exploring its vast undulating terrain. It was also a haven for pets – dog owners would let them run loose to play with the other neighborhood dogs. During the winter months the residue water at the bottom of a large gully adjacent to Broadway would freeze over, providing the neighborhood with an ice skating venue that on Saturdays and Sundays was mobbed with people. While not exactly Currier and Ives, the crowd of onlookers atop the gully warming themselves with pints of Rye Whiskey near strategically located fires burning in oil drums created a picturesque scene. Every spring and fall, a traveling carnival set up at the southwest side of Wanderers' Field, adjacent to 48th Street. It provided enjoyment to children and parents alike. When the housing project was built, though it took away the adventures of the Wanderer's Field, it brought forth new friends and interesting people.

With the loss of the Wanderer's Field as a venue for play and social activity, the three-block commercial complex between the Gardens and the Projects become the social hub for young and old alike. The area was

---

[12] *"Woodside, Queens County, New York – A Historical Perspective 1652-1994,"* at 179.

known as "down front." It was divided in part by a small triangular shaped park bordered with benches.[13] During the day, young mothers sat on the benches and gossiped while their infant children slept close by in baby carriages. Retired people gathered there to read the paper and discuss the pending issues of the day. During the evening it became a gathering place for teenagers.

Three taverns thrived with one on each block down front, the Garden Grill, Murphy's, and the Shannon. Dad and the Rabbit frequented Murphy's, but on occasion could be found in the Garden Grill.

The Shannon was the grittiest of the three bars, attracting a young and boisterous crowd that was shunned by those at Murphy's and the Garden Grill, where a more civil code of conduct was strictly enforced, particularly in Murphy's.

The Shannon was small in size, about 20-feet deep and 15 feet wide. The floor was covered in a square pattern of dark linoleum and up against the right wall were three green naugahyde booths. The bar on the opposite wall had 10 stools also covered in green naugahyde. Aside from the elegant art deco chrome coat hooks affixed to the side of each booth, the only other memorable décor was the red neon Rheingold Beer sign in each window and the display of bottles of mediocre brands of rye, scotch, gin and vodka stacked on glass shelving fronting a dusty mirror. At the front of the bar near the door the bartender or the customer sitting on the corner stool had an excellent view of the entrance to the Boulevard Gardens and the triangular shaped park that split the traffic on Hobart Street. From that vantage point one could see who was coming and going or lurking about the neighborhood. Many a day or night a customer was alerted that his wife or girlfriend was approaching. A sufficient warning often allowed the errant party to beat it out the back door and make his escape by way of 50th Street.

---

[13] The site is now known as Stripoli Square.

In contrast, Murphy's and the Grill were corner bars that were cleaner, more commodious in size with longer bars and seating areas where people could congregate and socialize. Each establishment attracted an older and more civil crowd where people felt comfortable taking their wives or lady friend. Fights in these two bars were rare events compared to the Shannon, where the patrons frequently did battle. The Shannon was a place where after a certain time you felt on edge waiting for something to happen. And when it did, you hoped that you were not part of the action.

On many occasions Mother would send me out to locate Dad. "Find your father, and tell him that dinner will be ready in 20 minutes." Not wanting to miss one of my favorite programs on the radio, I was often reluctant to go. Sometimes I had to check all three bars down front or run through the P.S. 151 schoolyard and over to 30th Avenue to find him at another one of his favorite haunts, the Shillelagh Tavern or Nickel Will's, where beer was only five cents a glass in those days.

When I found him, he knew he was in trouble. "Is she angry?"

"She'll be all right if we get home on time, Dad. She's cooking roast beef. You don't want to miss it. There's baked potatoes too."

"Roast beef and potatoes," he'd exclaim licking his lips and patting his stomach. "We better get going, son. You're right – we don't want to miss that."

He'd toss down his beer, wave goodbye to his friends, and take off at a fast clip, motioning with his arm for me to get in step with his brisk walk.

The two candy stores, Sam's, and Mr. Green's, sold cigarettes, ice cream, newspapers, greeting cards, and toys. Mr. Green lost an arm in World War I, but that never seemed to be a handicap. He could make an ice cream sundae or pack a carton of loose ice cream as fast as any person with two good arms. I can still visualize the large red Coca-Cola cooler packed with chopped ice and cold soda that stood outside his store dripping with beads of condensation. I would run from the P.S. 151 schoolyard to that cooler on hot summer days to slake my thirst with cold bottles of Mission Orange soda.

Sam's holds different memories – the savory taste of egg creams and the thick malteds he concocted. When I was 11, Sam gave me my first job inserting the comics and magazine sections into the Sunday morning papers. I would do this on a Saturday night for $2 and a free malted.

Our two bakeries, Wintermeyer's and Benkert's were exceptional. I would often gaze longingly at the mouth-watering éclairs, napoleons, cakes and pies in their windows.

Charlie the butcher ran an old fashioned store with sawdust on the floor. He and his brother chopped and cut the meat on huge butcher blocks in full view of their customers. If I were ever in need of money on a Friday or Saturday night, Charlie would gladly slip me a five or ten from the register, and put it on Mother's account. It never got by her. She was very good with numbers, and soon I would have to cough-up the money.

Two drug stores were available for the medical supplies of the neighborhood and two beauty parlors kept the neighborhood women confined in a row of chairs under humming, Martian-like hoods until somehow the latest hairdos were revealed.

Our other necessities were met by a shoe repairman, a gift shop with greeting cards and books, a jewelry store, fresh produce market, two liquor stores, hardware store, and two barber shops. In the larger of the two, the House of Mirrors, a Marilyn Monroe calendar hung on the back of the bathroom door. The other essential services – dry cleaning and laundry were provided by Bob's Dry-Cleaning & Tailor shop and Sam Lee's Hand Laundry, where Sam, his wife, and numerous children washed and ironed shirts and sheets in a small store front, the back of which also served as their home.

Just next door to a great Danish delicatessen that made potato salad, pickled herring, and fish cakes to die for, was the Pickwick Supermarket, which did a substantial business. Our hangout was a luncheonette known as the Greek's, and for entertainment we had the Hobart Theatre. I spent countless hours in the Greek's and the Hobart. Above the Hobart was a dancing school and the residence and office of Dr. Yarry, a dentist also known as "Yank'em Yarry." He had an attractive and talented daughter, Lynn, who danced on Broadway into her 50s, and a son, who for many years masqueraded as a physician, until apprehended by the authorities.

Mom & Dad

Despite the advantages of living in the Gardens, there were other influences and temptations that caused some of us to stray off course. The lack of parental supervision came into play, particularly for those in their mid-teens. In the spring of 1950, my father re-injured an eye, weakened years before during his professional boxing career. It was a freak accident in the locker room at one of his jobs, with the Department of Maintenance & Ways of the Independent Subway System (IND), the newer of the three subway lines then running in New York City.

The injury occurred when he was reaching into his locker. Due to the vibrations caused by passing trains, the adjoining locker door swung open and caught and tore the lens of his eye. Once his eye was surgically removed, Mother decided she would have to return to work, given that my sisters Carol, Rose, Patricia, and I were attending Catholic schools. It also required that someone look after our two-year-old brother, Jimmy. While the disability payments were generous, and Dad was physically fine and derived good income through his other job with the Operating Engineer's Union, Mother's strong will prevailed – soon she was working as a switchboard operator at Triboro General Hospital.

Having lost her mother as a young girl, she was raised by her aunt and then lived through and survived the Great Depression. Hard times were part of her basic composite. Working was her way to overcome the economic insecurity she had experienced in her early life – it was something she feared, and a job was necessary to protect herself and her family should something happen to Dad. Unfortunately, he didn't see it that way.

Dad was furious and a battle royal ensued at dinner.

"No wife of mine's going to work. What will people think? I'll tell you what they'll think – that I can't support my family."

"Pat, be reasonable about this."

"I won't allow it, Rose. You'll ruin my reputation. I can't have that – I won't have that."

"There are plenty of women, my age, going back to work."

"You don't have to. There's enough money coming in."

"There is now, but what if something should happen to you."

"End of story – you're not working."

In short order, my father's pride and his political connections ended her career at Triboro General Hospital – a big-time mistake on his part, since it immediately deprived him of his conjugal rights and other privileges of the household, namely civility. Home became a war zone.

Once determined to do something, Rose Gillen would roll over you like a Mack truck. If she had any doubts about working, Dad gave her all the inspiration a wronged woman needed – she was not his chattel – she was one determined person. Mother was a feminist, a super mom of sorts, and was not afraid to take on anyone including my father, unions, the Catholic Diocese of Brooklyn, school principals, corrupt hospital officials, or health care providers holding back on payments. It didn't take her long to find another job at Lexington Hospital in Manhattan. She would work in hospitals for another 43 years to within a year of her death from cancer at the age of 85. Hospitals became her home away from home for the remainder of her life, either as a patient or an employee.

Like many women during that time she was viewed as somebody's wife, and Dad considered himself that somebody. Married to someone who experienced success as an athlete and in union politics, it was difficult for her to accomplish anything in her own right. Dad assumed he was the head of the household – that he had the right to come and go as he pleased, drink whenever he pleased, expect a hot meal when he walked in the door, and that Mom would always be receptive to the needs of his libido.

When we were younger, and she was struggling with five rambunctious children in a crowded apartment, she often would take out her frustrations on us when we had done something wrong. Mother had her "Mommie Dearest"[14] – Joan Crawford moments. When she cracked, the punishment was swift and often harsh. She had no preferred choice of weapon. Metal or wooden hangers if handy, a hair brush, and sometimes the vacuum's electric cord would do. There were also occasional enemas of one or two siblings to determine who had eaten the last piece of pie. When we became too big for physical discipline, she was reduced to verbal threats sometimes going so far as to say that if we didn't behave she was going to "jump off the roof." Whenever she said that we'd quickly remind her, often in unison, that the roof was on the sixth floor. In contrast, Dad rarely disciplined us.

My siblings and I had become accustomed to conflict at home that usually occurred at dinner. If Dad had a few drinks, she would let him know in front of us that she disapproved. And, if he came right home, albeit a rare occurrence, then, she would query him about why he wasn't bending his elbow with his cronies. As a result, my sisters and I ate quickly and excused ourselves, leaving them at the kitchen table to air their differences alone. We ate food fast before fast food became popular. We

---

[14] *Mommie Dearest*, Christina Crawford, William Morrow & Co., 1978

found dinner to be an unnerving experience. We ate in silence, speaking only when spoken to before making our way to the living room to listen to the radio or to our bedrooms to catch up on our homework.

If both of them were in the apartment at the same time we found it best to stay out of their way.

Dad did things his own way, and was used to getting his way. His father was one of the organizers of the Operating Engineers Union in New York City and was a confidant of the powerful Charles Francis "Silent Charlie" Murphy, who ruled Tammany Hall for 22 years. Dad started working with his father in construction at age 14, and at night, unbeknownst to his father, he was actively engaged as an amateur boxer in Catholic Youth Organization and Police Athletic League club fights in Manhattan and the Bronx. By the time he hung up his gloves in 1931 at the age of 22, he was a highly ranked professional with 110 amateur and professional fights to his credit, losing only four of those fights with two draws.

Dad was as independent as a man could be, but Mother decided that she too had the right to some independence. Her mother died in the influenza epidemic when she was five years old. She and her older sister, Anne, left Manhattan and went to live with their maternal aunt, Lillian, and her family in Jackson Heights in Queens. Aunt Lilly was a wonderful person – caring, proud, dedicated, capable of handling multiple tasks, clear thinking, and refreshingly opinionated. Life was different without the nurturing of her own mother, but Aunt Lily loved and cared for her and Anne and her own two young daughters, Julia and Elizabeth (Babe), as well as she could while working as a waitress in Manhattan and maintaining her household.

Mother's father, James, my Grandpa Jim, was a delightful person, but too much of a free spirit to raise two young girls. Even if he wanted to act in that role, the New York City welfare agencies would have objected, as the customs and traditions of that era dictated that children be raised by a female relative. Though Grandpa Jim lived a separate life, he managed to spend time with his daughters through the efforts of Aunt Lilly. She often had to search for him in saloons to wheedle money for their needs.

"Aunt Lilly would track me down," he told me, "and hit me up for money for new clothes and shoes for Anne and Rose."

When I asked Aunt Lilly about it she said children walked everywhere in those days. "By the time Jim came around, the girls had gone through their shoes. I had to go out and find him. They were young and attractive girls, and the styles were constantly changing. They always needed shoes."

Once on her own, Mother never lacked for shoes. When she died, my sister Carol discovered 18 pairs of shoes, barely, if ever, worn in a closet in Mother's apartment. At her funeral we joked that Carol had found the missing shoes from the Imelda Marcos collection. I also called for a moment of silence in her memory on the Home Shopping Network.

Mother was always coming and going, calling home late in the afternoon telling whoever was there, "to put on the potatoes," meaning peel six or seven potatoes and boil them in a large pot of water. Did we ever eat potatoes - we sure got our starch. They were purchased in 10-pound bags at the local Pick-Wick Market, and every apartment in the Gardens had enough in storage to weather another famine. We ate them every night –boiled, mashed, fried, baked, scalloped, in potato salad, and in other ways.

During the second phase of Mother's life, following her stint at Lexington Hospital, she worked for five years as a bookkeeper at the Forest Hills General Hospital. She uncovered financial finagling on the part of the administrator. Her discovery led to a grand jury investigation, and ultimately the closing of the hospital until sometime later when it opened under new management. When it shut its doors, she moved on to the newly opened Astoria General Hospital, where she worked for 32 years, and was instrumental in organizing its union, District 37, for which she served as a union delegate.

After working hours, she immersed herself in the activities of the Boulevard Gardens, her home for 62 years. Determined that there would be suitable activities for my sisters and me, she organized Brownie Troop 207, assisted in the formation of Cub Scout Pack 127, and served as the Leader of Girl Scout Troop 4-504.

There was also the Rosarians on Tuesday night and bingo on Wednesday night at Corpus Christi Church.

In the summer of 1948, Carol and Rose were stricken with polio. Their conditions were serious, but fortunately not crippling, and required that they be confined to our apartment. They were banned from school and special teachers visited on the days they were not at the hospital for physical therapy. Mother immersed herself in the effort to find a cure for the dreaded disease. She became the Queens County campaign chairwoman for the March of Dimes and led the effort to readmit recovering polio victims into public and parochial schools.

In spite of her dedication to causes on our behalf, Mother and Dad did little to supervise us. Given Dad's two jobs and his free life style and Mother's job, her involvement in Scouts and fundraising for the March of Dimes, there wasn't time for parenting. Her Girl Scouts involvement made our apartment a cookie warehouse for many months each year. Young girls and their parents were constantly coming to our apartment to pick up their orders of Thin Mints, Samoas, and the other cookie varieties. The long entry hallway of our apartment was jam-packed with cartons of cookies stacked from floor to ceiling. We had to enter sideways with our backs pressed to the wall to negotiate our way into the apartment. To this day, I cannot buy or eat a Girl Scout cookie.

Prior to, and during World War II, our telephone was a lifeline to many families in our 'I' building apartment, and our number, Ravenswood 8-9585, was well known in the Gardens. Despite the constant traffic of neighbors using our phone, I can't recall anyone abusing this neighborly privilege. My sisters and I enjoyed the company, and I welcomed the opportunity to dash up the stairs to a neighbor's apartment and announce that someone was waiting to speak to them. Many an emergency call was made and received in our kitchen. During the early days of World War II, most people used the phone to pass on military related news – a loved one had enlisted or was drafted, was coming home, was wounded, or was killed or missing in action. A number of Gardens' residents were killed or wounded in the war, including a sailor who lived upstairs from us whose ship was sunk in the Pacific. Towards the end of the war, more calls were associated with the arrival of babies. Within a year of the war's end many of the government restrictions were lifted and virtually everyone had a telephone.

Our number changed with Mother's March of Dimes involvement. By that time, we had moved to a larger apartment in the adjacent 'J' building. She was given a business number, Astoria 4-6400, which, on a daily basis, generated countless wrong number calls. With today's technology, we could have ignored the incessant ringing and simply listened to the messages.

Since we would not acquire a television until 1953, I spent my evenings at P.S. 151 playing basketball, or in one of the basement storage rooms in the Gardens engaged in a game of Black Jack. On warm evenings, after pick-up basketball or softball, we played cards under a lamp-post on 50th Street, next to P.S. 151, while we waited for the early editions of the

New York Daily News and the *New York Daily Mirror* to be delivered to the local candy stores.

It was an interesting period in my life, but it was no picnic growing up amidst constant conflict while trying to understand my father's unfulfilled potential and what he could have accomplished if only he had had my mother's focus and determination. Unfortunately, her potential was limited in that era by my father and the paternalistic society in which she struggled. There was no nurturing in that environment of two parents frustrated with the hand they had been dealt and taking it out on each other. Catholics never thought about divorce – it was forbidden – they were bound to each by a religious dictate. Everyone had to suffer together.

I had to find encouragement and nurturing elsewhere. I often visited my mother's sister Anne and their Aunt Rose on 46th Street, where there was always a hug, a smile, and a cup of tea. I had to forge friendships that would help me deal with the chaos of our apartment. I wasn't alone in this regard since a number of my friends were in the same boat – we sought solace from each other. For a spell, I had fallen in with the wrong people, others like me who had little parental supervision. We were easily bored and were always looking for something to stir things up. Sometimes we were fueled by half-pints of cheap liquor or wine. A few of us considered running away to Florida. I had saved $100 for the trip, but the other two guys chickened out at the last minute.

Working It Out

I had to correct my personal situation – to start thinking for myself, while at the same time escape from the frustrations of my parents' arrested potential. Work was one way to do that. I found the jobs interesting and sometimes exciting.

In the summer of 1953, I worked as a Western Union boy in an office on Sixth Avenue, between 36th and 37th streets, in the midst of the Garment Center and the Hat District. On weekends and some weeknights, I was an independent vendor, a "hustler" at the Polo Grounds and Yankee Stadium for the Harry M. Stevens Corporation. I sold hot dogs, peanuts, soda, and ice cream at Giants and Yankee games. It was a fun job with excellent pay – an 11 percent commission on sales. Even when I was tasked with selling the low cost items, peanuts or the watered-down orange drink, I could still clear $10 to $12 a game, a princely sum for a young teenager. When I sold the higher-priced items, hot dogs and ice cream sandwiches, it resulted in a larger payday. The older guys, who sold scorecards before, and beer during the game, made a very good living. I turned over all my money to Mother, who would give me $10 a week and with the remainder either buy me a $25 War Bond or deposit the money in my savings account.

In my three seasons at the Polo Grounds and Yankee Stadium, 1951-1953, I was paid to attend more than 100 major league baseball games, and saw every team in the National and the American League play. I worked three World Series – all won by my favorite New York Yankees – and met many of the ball players of that era including reuniting with Whitey Ford. I was there for Joe DiMaggio's retirement, the debuts of Mickey Mantle and Willy Mays, and the Yankee's World Series victories over the Giants in '51 and the Dodgers in '52 and '53. In 1953, when the Yankees won their fifth consecutive American League pennant, they bested the Dodgers again in an exciting Series. While it was my third consecutive World Series, it was the Yankees fifth consecutive Series victory, a record yet to be broken.

Working in Yankee Stadium and the Polo Grounds taught me early on that you had to hustle your butt off if you wanted to maximize your sales opportunities and commissions. You also had to use your voice, yelling at the top of your young lungs to sell your item. "Hey, get your peanuts here –

fresh hot peanuts only 10 cents," or "Ice cream – ice cream – get your cold ice cream only 15 cents." Selling peanuts and ice cream was not as taxing on my body as lugging a metal box full of steaming water with hot dogs swimming on the surface or a tank of cold orange drink strapped to my back up the steep stadium stairs. I would be exhausted and my uniform soaked after multiple trips up and down the stairs with those loads on my back. The commission I received amounted to about $1 a tank, and my goal was to sell at least 10 tanks. But once I had some experience under my belt I was moved from soda to hot dogs – a big step up and a lighter load to carry, but still a load for a skinny kid.

In the 1952 World Series, I averaged $60 a day for the three games against the Brooklyn Dodgers that were played at Yankee Stadium. I was rewarded for arriving early at the Stadium. The first game was on Friday. I took a chance and skipped school. When I arrived at 7:30 each of those mornings the temperature was hovering in the 40s, creating a market for hot chocolate and coffee, either of which I dispensed from a soda tank to those waiting in line to get into the bleachers. I sold hot drinks until about 10 o'clock each morning, when the gates opened. Once it warmed up I was selling hot dogs and ice cream sandwiches in the bleachers until we sold out. The crowds of over 70,000 were always hungry and thirsty. I sold nonstop and was fully rewarded money-wise, but Brooklyn took two of the three games at the stadium from my Yankees to go ahead in the Series three games to two. Fortunately, thanks to the heroics of Billy Martin, the Yankees won the final two games at Ebbets Field.

Hustling around the ballpark I quickly learned that I had to move to the flow of the game. I would stop to watch the action from time to time. Though my back was often to the field, the reaction of the fans was always a signal to become quiet when there were men on base for either team. You knew that if the Yankees or Giants scored a run that people were prone to buy – that's when you hollered out your product. I learned to speak up. Later in life, I never would have difficulty as a public speaker having practiced so often in front of indifferent fans at crowded ball parks.

Most importantly, I learned that honesty is the best policy. When we started off the day we would be issued metal discs valued in various denominations as high as $20 that we used to purchase the product we would sell in a section of the ball park that day. When we sold out we would return to the kitchen we had been assigned to and turn in the cash to buy more products. At the end of the day we turned in the remaining cash, our totals sales were tallied and we would be paid our commissions. One Saturday afternoon at Yankee Stadium the clerk gave me $10 more in commissions than I had actually earned. There was a line of guys behind me waiting to cash out, change out of their uniforms, and take the subway home. I hesitated as I counted the money. "Something wrong kid?" the clerk asked.

"I think you gave me too much money."

He smirked and waved me off. "No way, kid. Come on; the other guys are waiting to cash out."

I made the mistake of not waiting around to approach the clerk again. I kept the money and walked to the subway, but I was smart enough to tell Dad about it when I got home. "Jesus, don't ever do that again." The next morning I was the earliest person in the shape-up line for that Sunday afternoon double-header. When the hiring boss came out I immediately went up to him and told him what had happened. "Yeah, I know," he said. "Good thing you pointed it out to him." Smiling, he pulled a piece of paper from his shirt pocket and handed it to me. I looked down. It said, "Gillen. Get the $10." I gladly handed him the money.

"Thanks," he said, taking the $10 bill. "Don't worry, you'll work today, but if you hadn't shown up with the money you'd never have worked again."

The Western Union job took me into the fashion world and the offices of the leading dress manufacturers. The offices on 7th Avenue and in 1400 and 1410 Broadway were teeming with activity and attractive people. It was difficult to negotiate the streets with people coming and going or kibitzing in the middle of the sidewalks with large cases at their side. Young black men and new Puerto Rican immigrants were the mules in the Garment Center. They were either jostling push-boy clothing racks of coats and dresses manufactured in the factories on the side streets to the showrooms on 7th Avenue or Broadway or loading them onto the endless lines of double-parked trucks. They were also unloading trucks packed with bolts of cotton, wool and silk fabrics, liners, buttons and decorative accessories. Among those pushing racks of dresses and coats through the crowded streets at that time were Charles Rangel, the long-time U.S. Representative from Harlem, Red Foxx, the great comedian, and Malcolm Little, recently paroled from prison in Massachusetts and beginning his new life as Malcolm "X," the visionary Black Muslim. The Garment Center was a mass of confusion to the untrained eye, but to the experienced eye this was commerce moving at a world class pace.

The opportunity to visit these offices and linger and observe the fast pace of the business was exciting, though in the 1960s, I viewed the garment business from a different perspective. I was a political advance man accompanying President Lyndon B. Johnson, and later Vice President Hubert H. Humphrey to the show rooms and the factory of the legendary Abe Schrader, the dean of 7th Avenue.[15]

---

[15] Mr. Schrader was an extraordinary man who became a close friend if not my surrogate father and advisor for 36 years until he died in 2001 at the age of 100. Abe and I dined

The cigar makers were ubiquitous, they could be found on every street and in virtually every available nook and cranny in the Garment Center. They were fascinating to watch. They sat in the windows of narrow street level shops, for hours on end, patiently cutting and rolling tobacco into cigars, and placing them in wooden presses. I could have watched them endlessly, but was driven to return to the Western Union office for my next pickup or delivery.

The Hat District, just east of 6th Avenue, was another story. It lacked the pace and pizzazz of the garment district. The offices were dingy and quiet, and occupied by people with far less energy than their neighbors a few blocks away. At the edge of the Hat District, in a building on the east side of 6th Avenue between 39th and 40th streets, was the "Save the Rosenberg's Committee" office. Julius and Ethel Rosenberg were convicted of spying for Russia and scheduled to die in Sing Sing Prison's electric chair on June 19, 1953. As the execution date drew near, our office delivered thousands of copies of telegrams to the Rosenberg Committee office. The original messages were sent to President Eisenhower, urging him to commute the sentence to life in prison.

The tremendous surge in telegram traffic impelled the office to change its procedures. Normally the messengers were given five minutes to deliver or pick-up a telegram and return to the office. For multiple telegrams or pickups, three minutes were added for each additional message. I usually left the office with five or six messages to deliver, many of which were in the same or adjacent buildings, requiring that I be back to the office in 20 minutes. The Rosenberg traffic was so heavy that extra people were

---

whenever I was in New York and talked regularly on the phone about politics, economics, foreign policy, trade, and the demise of the garment business in the United States. At his 100th birthday dinner at the Plaza Hotel, I was honored to be among the handful of speakers paying tribute to his wonderful life. Former New York City Mayor Ed Koch was another speaker, as was Pauline Trigere, the legendary dress and coat designer.

brought in to help. The delivery time rules were also changed – a five-minute limit was imposed for multiple deliveries to the same location. I carried up to 50 telegrams a trip, including one from Pope Pius XII, and others from heads of state from across the world. Had the normal rules been in effect I could have stayed away from the office for up to two and half hours for such a delivery.

Had the truth been known at that time, Ethel Rosenberg may have been found innocent. She was sold out by the actual spy, her brother David Greenglass, a former employee of the Atomic Energy Laboratory in Los Alamos, New Mexico. Greenglass later admitted that to save his own neck he squealed on his brother-in-law, Julius Rosenberg. Lacking this knowledge, I had little sympathy for the Rosenbergs' cause and approached the second-floor walk-up office with a sense of dread. I felt this way because the newspapers and the television covered this event heavily. The coverage left little doubt about their guilt. I also would hear the neighborhood elders talking about the matter outside Sam's Candy Store while they were waiting for the evening papers to be delivered.

The Rosenberg volunteers were elated whenever a delivery arrived. The cry would go out, "The Western Union Boy is here." They would rush me, grabbing for the envelopes.

One young woman excitedly stated, "Look this one is from the Pope. Maybe Eisenhower will listen to him."

The campaign did not succeed. Eisenhower was convinced they were guilty, and the Rosenbergs went to their death maintaining their innocence. The people in our neighborhood supported Eisenhower's position, especially those in the Garden Grill. At the precise hour of the execution the bartender flicked the light switch on and off simulating the execution and stimulating his regular customers.

Late in the summer I was temporarily assigned to an office on 9th Avenue, delivering telegrams to a number of motion picture distribution offices. The most memorable pick-ups and deliveries, however, involved the 11th Avenue slaughterhouse. I could hear the bellowing of the cattle from blocks away as they were herded up ramps from the containing yard to their death. The cows knew where they were going and they were not the least bit happy about it. As I walked closer to the huge building the haunting noise increased in volume creating a chilling effect that made the hair on my neck stand up. Inside the abattoir's office the incessant noise was somewhat muffled - the men and women working there ignored it. For some time, I couldn't look at a steak without recalling the anguished cries of the cows soon to be the dinner of many New Yorkers.

At summer's end, I began my final semester of high school. I didn't have any plans, not a clue. More importantly, no one was advising me about my future. I was just putting in time. Deep thought and introspection about what I was doing and where I was going were sorely lacking as I continued working part-time after school for Harnick Florist, a few doors up from the Western Union Office.

Well-dressed executives often purchased a dozen long-stemmed roses for delivery to a young model in one of the dress houses on 7th Avenue or Broadway. My boss, Bill Harnick, was a "Draft Dodger," who bragged about avoiding military service in World War II by virtue of a special exemption for his work on an upstate dairy farm.

This less than admirable person gave me strict instructions as I set out on my first delivery. "Be nice. Do you understand?" When I hesitated he took my arm and walked me out of the store onto 6th Avenue, where he explained the importance of returning with a message for the sender that his flowers made a good impression on the recipient.

I was a quick study. If the recipient of the flowers said something like, "Who the Christ is trying to get into my pants this time," when I returned to the shop, I would tell Mr. "G" or Mr. "B" that the young woman was touched, she smiled when she read the card. It was a life-long lesson in diplomacy, and, better yet, it was highly rewarding. The ardent suitors winked, smiled, and reached into their pockets for a dollar and sometimes more. In my numerous deliveries, not once did any of the young women seem to appreciate being hustled by these garment center characters. Since the models never tipped, I was motivated to seek my gratification from the originator of the transaction. I took great pride and extensive creative license in describing the joy and receptivity expressed by the young female to whom I had delivered the floral tribute. As the deliveries increased in number, my stories became more elaborate. Pinocchio would have been proud.

The experience of working in the Garment Center connected me with the fascinating supply chain of that business. Telegram orders for dresses and coats resulted in corresponding telegrams ordering bolts of cloth and rolls of ribbon, lace, thread, pads, and linings and boxes of buttons. These materials were soon delivered and loaded from trucks and carried into buildings where they were cut and sewn, soon re-emerging on the street as dresses and coats, which were then hauled off to showrooms a few blocks away or loaded onto trucks for shipment to a retailer. I also got to see the buyers going in and out of the famous showrooms of the day, where they would look over the merchandise modeled by the young women who in turn generated orders of roses from their ardent suitors. I got to see close up all sides of the garment business including the steamier side. It also was my initial contact with Jewish people, as the garment and millinery businesses were a Jewish trade in New York. I had too often heard my father label someone as a "good Jew," which to him was a term of endearment. The ethnic prejudices in New York were visible on the surface, particularly against the Jews. What I found in the garment district was a cross section of people no different from the Irish. Some were tough, some were meek, some were funny, some were happy and others sullen. Some were cunning, most worked hard, while some were slackers, and they all stood together probably more so than the Irish. I didn't feel out of place working in this environment; if anything, I thoroughly enjoyed it.

In the fall of 1953, Freddie Siegel, a neighborhood friend and my only Jewish friend, posed an ecumenical challenge in the form of an invitation to me and a few of his other goy'im friends to a dance at the Rego Park Jewish Center. By then, I had developed an avid interest in girls, but my experience was still limited. I did have a few interesting experiences, but I'd never really had a girlfriend up to that point. I'd gone on a few movie dates and walked girls home after dances at Corpus Christi Church. Determined to improve my game, I decided to attend the dance at the Jewish Center.

My motivation came from Freddie's revelation that a large number of girls and very few guys attended the weekly dances at the Jewish Center, a spacious and inviting building on Queens Boulevard. I couldn't believe my eyes when I walked into the Center. The girls outnumbered the guys by large numbers. And, they were gorgeous and well-dressed, unlike the dowdy girls we were used to seeing at the Friday night Corpus Christi dances. I say dowdy because Catholic girls were discouraged from wearing provocative clothes or makeup. They were also brainwashed about not getting too close to boys while dancing.

Freddie worked in Pat Abrams' Pharmacy, and so was our supplier of condoms. Virtually every guy in the neighborhood carried one in his wallet, but few were ever used for the purpose for which they were manufactured. They usually atrophied leaving a telltale circular impression in the wallet slot.

Through Freddie's advance work at the Jewish Center, I met Myrna Goodzeit, a stunningly attractive young woman with a dynamite zaftig figure. She had shoulder length brown hair that complemented her large hazel eyes, a straight nose and a wide mouth, all of which lined up in perfect symmetry on her Ingrid Bergman-like face. Her skin was creamy white and her smile enticing, coming more from her eyes than the lower part of her face. Her eyes reflected a sensuous nature. She was serious minded, reflective, sexy, and fun to be with.

Myrna lived in Middle Village, near Juniper Valley Park, just around the corner from my cousin, Joe Dooley. Myrna's parents, while polite, were not exactly pleased about my interest in their daughter. The last person they expected her to bring home from a dance at the Jewish Center was a Roman Catholic.

My conversational skills helped to overcome their initial skepticism, as did the fact that her accountant father was familiar with the garment trade. Conversation about my summer experience provided the opportunity to ask him about the garment business. Myrna's mother watched intently as he answered in the measured responses one would expect from an accountant. He seemed pleased to impart his knowledge. As he began to relax in our discussion, it had the same effect on Mrs. Goodzeit – her body language taking its keys from her husband's posture and tone – when he smiled, she smiled. They were a quiet couple with a reserved, but warm manner. In time, they were accepting and made me feel welcome. Myrna's older sister never had a problem with my religion, was supportive, and made me feel comfortable in their household. Myrna and I liked each other, but a long-term relationship was not in the cards, and after a few months of dating, including some highly stimulating moments, we drifted apart. As I noted earlier in this story, I would soon see her again, but under different circumstances.

3

A Driving Lesson

Taking cars was easy. Many people left their car doors open, and some even hid the keys under the seat or in the visor above the windshield. If a car was locked, you could open it in five to ten seconds with a metal coat hanger. All you had to do was unfold the coat hanger, straighten it, curl a small loop at the bottom of the wire, force the hanger through the rubber seal on the side of the window, drop the loop over the door lock latch on the top of the door, pull it up, and you were in the car. The lack of keys was not a problem. The solution was simple. Just remove the tin foil lining from a pack of cigarettes, crumple it slightly, and then wedge the foil under the dashboard directly below the key insert where contact was made with the exposed ends of the connecting wires to the ignition switch that were wound around three small screws. Most of the cars were late 1940 and early 1950 models, which had starter buttons. Once contact was made, you simply pressed the starter button, and you had ignition. Within 30-seconds of approaching the car you were driving away.

My first driving experience occurred in Washington County, Rhode Island during the early days of World War II. Uncle Pete's car was parked on the lawn adjacent to the lakeshore house our family was renting. Sitting behind the wheel of this 1932 Chevrolet, pretending to drive my numerous cousins, crowded into the front and back seats, I was encouraged by my older cousin, Pat Healey, to press the starter button. To my surprise and delight, and that of my fellow passengers, the car jumped forward. I continued this maneuver until the car had moved about 10 feet across the lawn and down a slight incline. The car picked up speed and headed into Lake Tiogue. All hell broke loose – panic prevailed as my sisters and cousins, yelling and screaming, attempted to extricate themselves from the vehicle. Oblivious to the obvious danger, I was giddy and beaming with pride for having moved this mammoth vehicle with my newly learned driving skills. My feeling of levity quickly subsided as adults poured out of the house to rescue the children. Fortunately, the water barely reached the running board of the car, allowing the men to push it back onto the lawn. Needless to say, I had a sore ass for a few days.

I had boundless energy that wasn't reduced by going to school in Jamaica, working at a Florist in Manhattan after school, and then going out after dinner to play basketball. I read my homework assignments on the long subway ride into Manhattan and in the down time between flower deliveries. Aimless and still bored like my friends when we finished playing basketball we sought out other pleasures. That's when I got lured into taking cars. Once I took my first turn at the wheel I was hooked, and I stayed hooked for most of the fall. Throwing caution to the wind, a group of us would take cars three or four times a week. Usually we would take cars after 9 p.m. that were parked outside of apartment buildings. After about an hour, when everyone had had 10 minutes behind the wheel, we would return the cars.

Since most of our families did not own cars, we were able to introduce many of our friends to their first driving experience. It was a truly foolish way to get our kicks, but we never gave it a second thought. The excitement that resulted is hard to describe. We all visualized ourselves as tough guys speeding through the busy city streets in search of thrills, probably motivated by all the gangster movies we had watched.

The risks we encountered on these driving excursions were many and varied. One night it started to rain, and the windshield wiper on the car we borrowed was inoperative. Unfortunately, I was at the wheel. Believe me; driving a car with your head sticking out the window in the rain is not a recommended method of driving. More importantly, on two consecutive nights, we couldn't locate a parking spot close to where the car was originally parked. The first night we waited a few hours for a spot to open. On the second night, after a long wait and frustrated in our efforts to go unnoticed, we panicked and decided to double-park the car next to its original spot. Not a smart move. One can presume this piqued the interest of the owner, if not the police. If the truth were known, most of the people probably thought they were confused about where they parked their car and never reported anything to the police. Obviously, the guy who found his car double parked was more angered than confused. I cannot imagine what he told the owner of the car he was blocking. Whatever he might have said would not have been believed.

Following a few months of the thrill seeking driving activity, most of us involved decided to call it quits. Things had gotten out of hand with almost 10 to 15 kids participating, some of them racing the cars on Astoria Boulevard near the Grand Central Parkway. The increasing risks we were taking convinced me to change my ways. None of us thought of ourselves as thieves, but to the owners of those cars and to the police, we were. More importantly, we had no clue that we had become the core of a sudden crime wave.

Still hooked on driving, three of us, Bobby Collins, Kevin O'Sullivan and I decided to get our own car. We pooled our money from our after-school jobs and Bobby Collins purchased a black 1934 Ford sedan at a used car lot on Northern Boulevard for $50 – no doubt too high a price for a car that had seen better days. We parked it in an alley behind Bobby Collins' grandmother's house on 54th Street. Since we owned the car, albeit unregistered, the three of us, each lacking a driver's license, enhanced our driving skills with a stick shift by daringly speeding about the neighborhood in broad daylight.

Little did I realize that I was about to reach bottom in a few short weeks. My joy riding life would finally catch up with me and a friend in early December. Thereafter, I was confined to quarters and kept on a tight leash by my parents for the remaining days of 1953 and the early part of 1954. Being confined in a jail cell and a tense apartment is a lesson in life that I have long remembered.

The car we were charged with stealing was registered in the State of Maryland. I didn't remember the make or color of the car[16] that we were accused of taking, but I will never forget being called down to Astoria's 114th Precinct late in November, an appointment that unbeknownst to me had been arranged by my father through some of his high ranking police buddies from the Elks Club. Dad had raised the subject of stolen cars after dinner one night. It was just the two of us sitting at the kitchen table. He told me about the call he had from a detective who had named me as a primary suspect for the rash of cars that had been stolen from ours and surrounding neighborhoods. "Is this true? Are you involved?" I lied, and told him that I knew about the cars but had nothing to do with them. He was skeptical. "You better not be lying to me. You see, they want to talk to you. Do I have to get you a lawyer?" I stood my ground determined to talk my way out of it.

Dad, not convinced of my veracity, had invited my cousin, Pat Dooley, to dinner the next night. Pat was like an older brother to me. His being invited to dinner didn't arouse any suspicion on my part. My parents knew that I looked up to him. I figured it was their way of welcoming him home from the service.

Pat was the oldest son of Mother's older sister Annie. They lived close by on 46th Street just off 30th Avenue in Astoria. Pat was in the Army and

---

[16] The arrest record identifies the vehicle as a black 1950 Ford, Maryland License FF9230, registered to Vincent Dugan of 4509 Burlington Road, Hyattsville, Maryland.

had recently returned from a tour in Germany. When we finished dinner, Pat nodded at my parents and said to me sternly, "Neal, you and I have some talking to do." He stood up and said, "Come on. Let's go to your room."

Surprised, I reluctantly followed him down the hall, dragging my feet all the way into my room. They know about the car, I thought. I was scared shitless. I guess the word was out in the neighborhood about me driving around. That's how they found out about it. How can I get out of this? I have to win Pat over – convince him that I bought the car with my own money. He'll stand up for me. Pat had always watched out for me. He had looked after me and took me on exciting trips as a young boy, taking me along with his friends. We would dive off the pier at the end of Steinway Street and swim in the East River. He also took me on visits to the numerous Army anti-aircraft encampments surrounding La Guardia Airport during World War II, where we would run errands for the soldiers in exchange for insignias and gear for which they had no use for.

Fearful, I skirted by Pat in the narrow room and sat on the bed as he closed the door. He knew how adventurous I was and used to say that with all the daring things I'd do that I'd be lucky if I lived to be 30.

"Neal. Tell me what's going on?"

"I don't know."

"Don't give me that shit. You're lying – it's all over your face."

"Honest, Pat."

"I think your lying, Neal."

"Ok, but I bought the car with my own money."

"What car is this?"

"The one that me and my friends bought."

As he looked at me his eyes narrowed as he shook his head. "I'm talking about all the cars you and your friends stole."

There was no way to fool Pat. He had me dead to rights. I began to massage the truth. "It wasn't me. I was only riding in the cars," which was not exactly true. Once I learned how to do it, I was the instigator on a few occasions, though I always had someone with me.

He stood there, shaking his head. "I think you're trying to sugar coat this thing. Riding – stealing, it's the same thing, pal. Look, this shit is all over the neighborhood. Everyone is talking about you and your friends. The cops know all about it."

I remained silent, hoping he would think of something to resolve my increasing concerns about my pending rendezvous with New York's Finest.

"Neal, I think you're up to your neck in this."

"Honest, Pat."

He looked at me sternly. "Cut the shit. I don't believe it. Now listen to what I've got to say. Someone's obviously squealed on you, probably someone underage. They're looking for a non-juvenile to charge. Be careful what you say. If you tell them anything, they've got you."

I heeded Pat's warning, when questioned by Detectives Horan and Allmendinger, by minimizing my responses and denying involvement. It was apparent, however, that they knew just about everything. Given the number of people involved, that a friend and I were singled out still puzzled me. It took four years for me to learn that Steve Meyer, a 15-year-old from 45th Street, had been caught in the act the previous week and told all.

Though we only borrowed the cars for an hour or so before we returned them to their original parking spots or close to it, early in 1953 the legislature, the New York State Assembly, mindful that my contemporaries throughout the state were engaged in similar reckless activity, amended the law by upgrading joy riding from a misdemeanor to a felony.

The legendary Washington lawyer, Jacob A. Stein, discussed this issue in his essay on the "No Fault" automobile damage and/or injury doctrine in his 1981 compilation of essays, *Legal Spectator*. Stein observed that the No Fault doctrine could be expanded from the automobile to other activities where a vehicle was utilized, including "no-fault paternity claims, no-fault divorces, and no-fault automobile larceny." Arguing my case, Stein, though with tongue in cheek, raised the dispositive question, "How can the law hold criminally liable one who involuntarily responds to the overwhelming stimulation which the automobile offers?" Stein nailed it dead on. In my situation, it was really a case of "overwhelming stimulation" combined with a lack of maturity, direction, poor parental supervision and the opportunity to make use of someone else's property, albeit on a temporary basis. In recent years, neurological studies have confirmed that the frontal lobe brain function for impulse control is not fully developed until the early 20s. And more recently this was acknowledged in arguments before the U.S. Supreme Court.[17] There you have it, my conduct resulted from a combination of "overwhelming stimulation" and "undeveloped impulse control."

All of my crazy impulsive behavior raced through my mind as I tried to focus on the questioning of Detectives Horan and Allmenindinger. The large, high-ceilinged, squad room on the second floor of the 114th Precinct House was eerily quiet. It was just the three of us. Only a few of the overhead lights were turned on. The surrounding cabinets and desks were mere shadows lurking in the background. I was seated next to an old wooden desk. Detective Allmenindinger, a man of considerable girth, was seated behind the desk and leaning towards me. His face was no more than a foot from mine. Detective Horan was a handsome man - trim and well dressed. In a way, he reminded me of Richard Widmark, the actor.

---

[17] *Miller v. Alabama* and *Jackson v. Hobbs*, No. 10–9646, decided June 25, 2012 567, U.S. ___ (2012), wherein Justice Elena Kagan writing for the majority of the court ruled that in sentencing consideration must be given to "chronological age and its hallmark features – among them, immaturity, impetuosity, and failure to appreciate risks and consequences."

I didn't know it at the time, but a few months prior to my questioning, Horan's detective work had exonerated Christopher Balestero, a Stork Club musician lingering in jail falsely accused of robbing a Queens' insurance office. The case inspired the Alfred Hitchcok movie, *The Wrong Man*.[18] Ironically, my father, who was well known in political, union, and sports circles in New York, particularly in Queens, would call in his political chits, and retain as my attorney, our State Senator, Frank D. O'Connor,[19] who had represented Balestero.

Horan[20] was the more impatient or energetic of the two, pacing up and down while tossing out questions in staccato fashion. I knew he was trying to confuse me and trip me up. I tried not to panic, no less shit in my pants. Occasionally, he stopped and sat on the side of the desk and leaned down into my face asking questions implicit with accusations. "You see, we know all about you and who you were with," he kept saying while waving a stack of what I presumed to be stolen car reports in my face. "So make it easier on yourself and your friends and admit it." Jesus, what exactly do they know? I visualized myself in a detective movie as I kept thinking about

---

[18] *The Wrong Man*, starring Henry Fonda as Balestrero and Vera Miles as his wife.

[19] Twelve years later, in 1966, O'Connor was the Democratic Nominee for Governor of New York. O'Connor was defeated by the popular incumbent, Nelson D. Rockefeller, who also served as Vice President of the U.S. from 1974-77.

[20] When Horan retired nine years later, he was the most decorated detective in the NYPD. Upon his death, the story in *The New York Daily News*, by Owen Moritz on January 23, 2003, said that:

"Horan was promoted to detective in 1946 at age 28 after he tracked down three hoodlums who had killed an Air Force veteran and raped his girlfriend in Central Park.

"Horan worked undercover for a week patronizing bars before nailing the suspects in what was known as the Central Park Murder Case. All three went to the electric chair.

"He was promoted to detective by then-Mayor William O'Dwyer, who called the arrests 'one of the greatest this city has seen in my time.'

"But three days later, Daily News columnist Ed Sullivan wrote that Horan was not given a raise - prompting such an outcry that Horan was called back to City Hall, this time to get his raise."

"After retirement, he opened a private detective agency and supervised security at Sotheby's."

what Pat Dooley had said. I thought about the "Dead End Kids" movies where no one ever squealed. That was the last thing I would do. It was something that I could never live down. I held my ground, revealing nothing. Following an hour of questioning, and what I thought were consistent answers fully laced with denials, they told me I could go as soon as my father arrived.

They must've believed me. I'm going home, I thought. It was a long wait. It turned out that Dad was in a nearby tavern meeting with a high ranking police official, Chief Inspector Jeremiah "Jerry" Brennan, a long-time friend going back to their amateur boxing days. The Precinct Captain, Jim "Bud" Lancaster,[21] was also meeting with them. Following a brief lecture from Captain Lancaster about behaving myself, Inspector Brennan drove my Dad and me home.

The following Sunday evening, December 7th, the 12th anniversary of the Japanese attack on Pearl Harbor, Detectives Horan and Allmendinger surprised me by arriving at our apartment about an hour after dinner. I was sitting in the living room with my sisters and brother watching our new television. Dad poked his head into the room and nodded for me to follow him. Horan and Allmendinger were standing in the kitchen with stern looks on their faces.

"Neal, get your coat. You're going to be arrested," Dad announced.

I was totally surprised – dumbfounded. Mother was standing in the hall outside the kitchen. I looked at my parents for support, but none was forthcoming. What's going on? They let me go last week. How could this be?

---

[21] Lancaster, a former NYU basketball All-American, was the older brother of Burt Lancaster, the well-known actor who won an Oscar for his role in the movie, "Elmer Gantry."

"You'll be all right son. Just do what you're told," Dad said. Mother had her hand to her mouth and was shaking. She turned and ran to the back of the apartment.

That explained why Dad was home all day and not in the bars. That explained all of the phone calls to and from the house. It suddenly became clear, they knew this was coming and never said a word.

The detectives led me to their unmarked car and then set out to pick up one of my accomplices while he was visiting with friends in front of the Hobart Theatre.

How'd they know where he'd be? I was puzzled and confused. Why us? Why today? Everything appeared to be perfect that day – the weather, the friendly atmosphere at home, and a nice roast beef dinner. Mother and I were talking about the attack on Pearl Harbor during and after dinner. She related how she was preparing an early supper that afternoon when word came over the radio about the Japanese attack.

"I grabbed you and the girls and we sat under the kitchen table listening to the radio reports. I thought that New York was under attack."

I had no idea what would happen to me as I was taken from my apartment that night. I was scared, ashamed, and regretful of everything I had done.

It was not until 1964, upon the occasion of my graduation from Georgetown University Law School, that Dad informed me in great detail how he had conspired with Inspector Brennan and Captain Lancaster with the concurrence of Detective Horan to put me away for a few days to teach me a lesson. Dad expressed his pride that I had overcome the problems of an errant youth, noting, "I'd do it again, son."

I told him that the initial interrogation at the 114th Precinct was lesson enough for me – "Dad, I'd never put a child of mine through that experience." My statement didn't register with him.

It served no purpose to argue with Pat Gillen. In his protective, old-school mind-set, he was attempting to teach me a lesson, and hoping that it would be absorbed by my adolescent brain. He was betting on his visceral instincts that fear, rather than reason, would alter my lifestyle. In his mind, he was convinced that his actions positioned me to make the right choices in the years to come. Though his actions may have had the desired effect, I didn't concede this fact for many years. While I never resented this act of tough love, I regretted his decision, especially whenever the question appeared on employment applications, military and federal security clearance screenings, and during the Bar Association character interview process – "Have you ever been arrested? If so, please explain the circumstances?"

There always seemed to be a double standard when it came to his decisions. A few years after graduating from law school, the opportunity arose for me to question his self-righteousness, when he called seeking legal advice.

"Son, how are you?"

"Fine, Dad, just fine. Where are you?"

"I'm in Florida. I've been down here a few months staying with a friend, Captain Bradley. He's a retired tug boat captain."

"I think Mom mentioned something about it when I last talked to her."

"Let me tell you why I called."

"Sure, Dad. Is everything all right?" Keep in mind that Dad was not one to call just to talk about the weather.

"I need some advice. Can you help me?"

"Of course, I'll help you. What's the problem?"

"What would happen if you were living as a guest in someone's mobile home and they died?"

I asked an elemental question to confirm my suspicions. "When did Captain Bradley die?"

"About five minutes ago."

"That figures. Where did it happen?"

"Right here. He was alive and well, one minute, and the next thing I know he's dead as a mackerel."

I inquired as to how it happened, and he informed me that it was an apparent heart attack. Dad explained that he had just come back from his morning walk on the beach. The Captain had been sitting under the mobile home's awning reading the paper. He got up from his chair and said he was going inside to get a fresh cup of coffee. Dad said he heard a thump and thought that the Captain had knocked over a chair. In fact he had, with his body on its way to the floor. A few minutes later, thirsting for a drink of water, Dad entered the trailer and discovered the Captain's body. Upon examining the Captain, Dad found no heartbeat, pulse rate, or evidence of breathing. "So I figured, I better call you and find out how long I can stay here."

I seized the opportunity and launched into a lecture about seeking medical assistance, calling a priest, a funeral home, or the Captain's relatives. He listened impassively and responded, "How long do you think they'll let me stay?" I asked him if there were any relatives and he informed me there was a daughter somewhere in the Midwest. I instructed him to look through the Captain's personal belongings and find her telephone number.

"When you find the number, call her and explain the situation. Then, take the opportunity and volunteer to make the initial funeral arrangements, offer to watch the mobile home pending her decision as to what to do with it, and offer to assist in the sale of the property. If she accepts your offer, she will have to send you a notarized letter authorizing you to act as the Florida representative of the Captain's estate."

A half-hour later, Dad called back. "That was great advice son. The money we spent on Georgetown Law School was worth every penny." Then, he informed me how he found the Captain's address book and called his daughter.

"She went for the whole deal."

It took some time to sell the property, allowing Dad to enjoy a full year of the Florida sunshine – rent free.

4

The Trial & Error Method of Education

High school was sandwiched into three years and three schools, though one, William Cullen Bryant, was only a one-day sojourn. Placed in grammar school ahead of my time at the age of 5, I graduated from St. Joseph's Elementary School in January 1951 at the age of 13. Though too young and immature for high school, I immediately entered a rigorous course of study with the Society of Jesus, the Jesuits, at the Brooklyn Preparatory School in Crown Heights, Brooklyn.

The trip to school each day was an adventure in itself – 13 stops on the 'GG' train and a half-hour ride across Brooklyn on the Nostrand Avenue Trolley to Carroll Street. As a member of the last January Freshman class that Brooklyn Prep accepted, I had to accelerate and attend summer school for the second semester. I began my sophomore year a few months after I had reached the ripe young age of 14. The class cut-up, I was constantly in trouble and frequently admonished for habitual smoking in the locker room and numerous distracting classroom infractions that resulted in being sentenced to the Jesuit version of a road gang, known as Judgment Under God (JUG), where I stayed after school and walked the perimeters of the outside yard in the back of the buildings in what was sometimes a long line of offenders.

Early in my third semester, I had two days of JUG. On the second day, Gregory Weglien, a friend and classmate, encouraged me to join him at his aunt's nearby apartment where she treated him to tea and homemade cake each afternoon.

"I'd love to, but I've got JUG."

"Jesus, Gillen. You've always got JUG. Listen, the line goes right by the front of my aunt's apartment on Rogers Avenue."

"So, big deal. What are you going to do, throw me a piece of cake?"

He shook his head laughing as his eyes rolled upward. "No, stupid, I'll signal you to cross the street when the coast is clear."

"You mean you want me to skip the JUG line and join you for tea and cake?"

"I'll have a clear view of the schoolyard from her front window. When the line snakes around in front of the chapel all you have to do is run across Rogers Avenue and into her building."

"You don't think I'll get caught?

"Nah, I did it a couple of weeks ago, when I had JUG."

That afternoon, as the JUG line circled the school perimeter I pondered Gregory's offer. Each time the line walked around St. Ignatius of Loyola Chapel he was waving frantically from the window for me to make my break. Finally, I mustered up my courage and dashed across Rogers Avenue into the apartment house entrance and up the stairs to Gregory's aunt's place. It was a real high, sipping tea and eating freshly baked German apple cake, all the while observing the line from the dining room window and waving at the guys when they passed by.

At the right moment, I darted back across Rogers Avenue, and rejoined the group as it filed by the Chapel. Phew, I made it. I'm home free, I said to myself. Just as we climbed the steps at the rear of the Chapel a black cassock appeared, mushrooming out at the bottom like a bolero skirt as Father Frederick Engle, the assistant headmaster, rushed at me, his face flushed with anger. He spun me around and pulled me by my ear to his office where I sat, head down, trembling in an uncomfortable, straight-backed, wooden chair awaiting my fate. At the sound of his deep voice I looked up. The glare of the late afternoon sun streaming through the window behind him distorted his image. All I could see was a vague outline of his large form and the God-like gesturing of his arms. It was judgment day.[22]

"Gillen, you just might be finished at Brooklyn Prep." Then Father Engel sentenced me to indefinite JUG, and dictated a letter to his secretary summoning my parents to a counseling session. The new sentence required me to be present every day after school and on Saturday mornings when the marching was replaced with a four-hour study hall.

At the subsequent meeting with my parents, I was given a second chance and the opportunity to do something constructive in an attempt to channel my mischievous energy for the school's benefit. Father Engel came to the conclusion that it was senseless to have me walking the JUG line each day, and in his role as athletic director, put my talent and enthusiasm to better use as the assistant varsity football manager. It was a fun job and elevated my status with my classmates. As the season progressed, the co-head coaches, the Currello brothers, recently of Brooklyn Tech, noticed that I knew the number of every player and promoted me to the position of "Spotter." This was big time. During the games, I sat next to the announcer calling out the names of the Brooklyn Prep players who carried the ball, punted, received, made the tackle, caught or dropped the pass, or made the interception. It was a special thrill to sit in the press boxes at Ebbet's Field, Brooklyn College, and Randall's Island Stadium. As tough as the Currello

---

[22] Earlier this year, upon the death of Joe Paterno, the legendary Penn State football coach, *The New York Times* published an article (For Paterno, a Prep School Was the Foundation for Discipline and Bravado, page A-23, January 25, 2012) by Joseph Berger about his days at Brooklyn Prep, noting, "If they were late or forgot a notebook, students might find themselves detained after school for what the Jesuits called 'jug': an hour in the courtyard, walking in circles." The article accurately described Father Engel as a "tall priest with the fists of a trained boxer who could instantly silence an auditorium filled with 300 shouting boys," with one former student noting, "It wasn't hell you were afraid of, it was Father Engel."

brothers were, they still had the class to compliment players for their efforts even after a drubbing. They were also nice to me, encouraged me, and praised me for all my efforts. That meant a lot, but that would be the only praise I would receive at Brooklyn Prep. But unbeknownst to me at the time, what I did receive there was a sound academic foundation that would serve me well in the coming years.

At the end of the semester, my parents met with Father Engel and the Headmaster, Father Thomas Harvey. They reviewed my grades, which were marginal, my immaturity, record of constantly cutting up in class, and my failure to live up to my academic potential. Today, such traits might give rise to a diagnosis of borderline Attention Deficit Disorder, but I didn't have that problem in elementary school probably because the threating demeanor of the Dominican nuns suppressed such symptoms. It is accurate to say that I exceeded all bounds once I had escaped the eight years of strict supervision by the Dominicans and the five years of harsh discipline metered out at Camp Leo to daring and mischievous boys like me.

It was the view of Fathers Harvey and Engel that I should repeat my second year, which meant that I would have to leave school then and return in the fall as a sophomore. In the interim, they would place me in a private school that specialized in students such as me. The last thing that I wanted to do was start over. While it might have been better for me, I didn't see it that way. It would have been embarrassing. I told my parents in a private confab that I didn't want to repeat my sophomore year. I was torn. I badly wanted to stay at Prep, but I had blown it. I wanted to try Bryant, but that was a non-starter. It would have to be Delehanty's – the school my Jesuit inquisitors had recommended. Mother and Dad agreed with me and a decision was made for me to attend Delehanty High School.

Having made great friends at Brooklyn Prep, I had mixed emotions, but it was time to move on. Things might have been different had I behaved myself and spent less time reading Jack London, Charles Dickens, Samuel Clemens, and Nathaniel Hawthorne novels, Ray Bradbury's science fiction, and some great trash by Mickey Spillane and Irving Shulman and more time reading my Latin and math text books. Reading for my own pleasure and neglecting the pursuit of hard knowledge had taken its toll.

There were no options about public school – the Catholic beliefs of my parents would not allow it, though they would later relent when one of my sisters had similar problems at a prominent Catholic institution for girls.

Delehanty's was a new educational institution on Supthin Boulevard, in the Jamaica section of Queens, between the Court House and the Jamaica Avenue elevated train. The student body was eclectic, composed of World War II and Korean War Veterans rehabilitating at the nearby Saint Alban's Naval Hospital and disciplinary problems, like me, from many of New York's Catholic High Schools. The faculty was excellent and the small classes pressured me into studying since I was likely to be called on each day. As there were no sports at Delehanty's, I devoted my extracurricular time to organizing the school paper, *The Del-Hi Shield*, and serving as the Inquiring Reporter, my seminal beginning as a writer.

In January 1953, following the mid-winter examinations, after a pushing and shoving incident that escalated into a fight on the stairway, I received a disciplinary suspension. Unbeknownst to my parents, I enrolled at the local public school, William Cullen Bryant High School, where I was assigned to a home-room with the tougher guys from the surrounding neighborhoods. A friend, Dale Edwards,[23] consulted with the clique who controlled the room, and they decided, over my strenuous objection, that I was their nominee for home-room president. The other class members, fearful of voting for the wrong candidate, elected me unanimously.

---

[23] Dale Edwards retired as the Vice President for Human Resources of the Allied-Signal Corporation now a component of Honeywell.

Thereafter, the word spread quickly throughout Bryant and the neighborhood.

That night, Dad learned about my political success during a visit to Murphy's. He congratulated me with a smack to the side of the head when he got home. I returned to Delehanty's later that week. For the remainder of the semester, the teacher presiding over the Bryant home-room class was puzzled about the whereabouts of the skinny kid who the class had elected president.

I continued on a fast track at Delehanty's with a full load of course work in each semester and in the summer of 1952, while fitting in work on weekends and night games at the Polo Grounds and Yankee Stadium. Admittedly, I had the wrong attitude about high school. I was just biding my time. To do what, was something I had never bothered to think about. To me it was all about fun and socializing. Though my grades were great in some classes, they were mediocre in others. To me, school work was something that had to be done, not necessarily well – just done. Despite my modest grades, I was able to finish in January 1954, four months before my 17th birthday. With an academic diploma in hand, I still needed two more courses to be awarded a New York State Regents diploma.

Looking back on my high school years, it was more a life experience of trials and errors than an educational tour de force. Considering that I worked during the summers and part-time after school, it was too much too soon for an immature boy on an unguided track failing to focus on both his potential and purpose in life. Now, I had to find useful employment, attend night school to complete my remaining studies to earn a Regents diploma, reform my ways, and find the right direction for my future. Still immature, I was unaware how difficult it would be or how long it would take. I had lingering self-doubts, but I understood that a new direction was required. I had to avoid certain friends who were prone to trouble – albeit easier said than done – but I vowed to try.

I would soon begin to spend more time with Jack Healy, a classmate from Delehanty's, and his friends from the other side of Woodside and Sunnyside. They were a year or two older, fun guys, not into stealing cars, but they did drink a lot.

A Good Lecture

I was still under house arrest a month after my run in with the police. It wasn't fun being cooped up every night, but if there was a bright side to my restricted living conditions, it was the new attention I was getting from my father. Things were still tense, but he was coming home earlier and engaging me more in conversation. His sharp edge was beginning to dull. He was smiling more around me, which allowed me to relax, but I was extra careful not to provide a reason to anger him. I also appreciated the fact that he didn't lecture me about what I had done. He left that to two of his friends, Inspector Jerry Brennan and retired Fire Chief Jack Hertin. I received the lecture in a card room at the Elks Club after a swim and steam bath with my father. The Inspector and the Chief were blunt in expressing themselves. They told me about the promising kids that they had grown up with in the Bronx and Manhattan who had thrown away their lives and were either dead or served prison sentences. One mistake is all it takes. You decide to tag along with some guys you shouldn't be hanging around with in the first place and the next thing you know you're in serious trouble. They cited instances of how close they had come to finding themselves in such a situation, and how other friends went along only to have their lives ruined. It was a sobering recount and moving to each of them as they told me how good friends had made such mistakes. It affected me as I listened and hopefully learned. I would have to give up some of my trouble-prone and adventurous friends. That would be easier than I had envisioned since, lucky for me, the leader of our joy riding ventures knocked up his girlfriend and soon dropped out of the picture. After that, the core members of our trouble-prone group went our separate ways.

Being alone and isolated from the influence of others allowed me to fully reflect on where all the joy riding had led me. As Aunt Lilly used to say, "If you are careless or maybe dumb enough to place your hand on a hot stove, you'll get burned." I'd been burned. It was fully obvious that change was in store. I had to cast away the remaining doubts I had that I was capable of making those necessary changes. These were my recurring thoughts in the weeks since my arrest.

The Rabbit Returns Home

It was during that time, on January 5th, that I was jarred again. Mother, Dad, and I had lingered late after dinner at the kitchen table talking about my situation. Mother was lamenting that things might have been different had I gone to Cheshire Academy, a boarding school in Connecticut instead of Brooklyn Prep. Due to a connection with Camp Leo, the summer camp that I had attended for five years, I had been offered a partial scholarship to Cheshire, but I had no desire to attend a boarding school.

It had been snowing all day and we were having second and third cups of tea while Mother and Dad were discussing what kind of job I should apply for when the doorbell interrupted the conversation.

"I'll get it," Mother said. She walked to the end of the hallway and opened the door. "Mrs. Maranville. Is anything wrong?"

"It's Walter. He collapsed."

"Jesus," Dad said pushing back his chair. He rushed down the hall. "Where is he?"

"Downstairs, Pat. I think he may have had a heart attack," Mrs. Maranville said in a tremulous voice.

"Did you call an ambulance?"

"It just happened. He just slumped over on the couch."

I ran downstairs with Dad while Mom called Boulevard Hospital for an ambulance.

We found the Rabbit slouched on the couch, his face a grayish color. Dad slapped him, trying to get a response, and then he tried to find a pulse. "Walter, wake up. It's me, Pat. Wake up, Walter." Dad turned to me, speaking over his shoulder, "See if there's a bottle of ammonia in the kitchen, and bring it in here." His professional boxing instincts were in play, as many unconscious fighters were revived with ammoniated smelling salts.

I found the bottle of ammonia under the sink and took it to Dad. He opened it and held it under Rabbit's nose. While both of us were jarred by the scent, there was no reaction from the Rabbit. His years of hard living had taken their toll on his once tough little body.

Dad turned to me. "Son, I think he's gone."

I started to cry. Dad bit his lower lip and tried to hold back his own tears. Then, he called the *New York Journal American*, where the Rabbit was employed as director of youth programs, to alert the sports' desk. He also called Jack Schneider,[24] another close friend of the Rabbit. Mr. Schneider was the director of the Small Business Administration office in Manhattan. His brother was the agent in charge of the FBI's New York Field Office. The Schneiders were well-connected politically.

---

[24] Jack Schneider's skills and knowledge of financial transactions were passed on to his oldest son Jack, a life-long friend, who would accumulate substantial wealth and important friends in corporate America given his gift of bringing people together, along with the financing to consummate a deal. Jack became the managing director of Allen & Company and a major player in the investment world.

For a few moments it was eerily quiet. Dad sat in a chair staring at the Rabbit's body trying to control his emotions. I stood by the window looking out at the falling snow filtered by the venetian blinds and my tears. I remembered how the Rabbit had taught me how to properly hold my glove when catching a baseball, block a ball with my body, and lay down a bunt. I thought about his puckish nature and impish grin, his legendary career, baseball games together, the major league players I met through him, and what he meant to the kids in the neighborhood.

I didn't hear Mrs. Maranville come into the living room with Mother and Bella Clark, my friend Pete's mother, who lived in the building.

"Pat, is he?"

Dad's face answered her question. He went over to her and grasped both of her hands. "There's no pulse."

She slumped forward and he held her as she cried. "God help me," she said. "What will I do?"

Jack Schneider arrived and a few minutes later the ambulance attendants found their way into the apartment and asked everyone to step outside while they examined the Rabbit. They quickly confirmed his death and informed Mrs. Maranville, who began to cry uncontrollably. Mother and Mrs. Clark took her upstairs to our apartment to console her and help her contact family members. Mrs. Clark returned in a few minutes to tell Jack Schneider that Mrs. Maranville wanted to take the body home to Springfield, Massachusetts. Jack nodded. "Consider it done." He then began to work the phone to arrange the funeral.

The owner of the funeral home was reluctant to come out in the snow to pick up the body. Schneider reminded him that he never hesitated to apply for a low-interest government loan from time-to-time. Hearing that,

Dad reached another of the Rabbit's good pals, Frank "Sea Lion" Dwyer,[25] the local Democrat Leader, and explained the situation.

"Pat, I'll call that ingrate, right now. If he doesn't show up in a half-hour, we'll close down the son-of-a-bitch. We'll send our people to Farley's."

The funeral home attendants arrived about 45-minutes later, just past midnight. After Mrs. Maranville spent a few minutes alone with the Rabbit, they slipped his five foot four inch, 150 pound, body into a narrow, black, canvas bag and carried it away.

It continued to snow into the next day hampering the transportation system in the North East. Dad and Jack Schneider made sure that when the storm abated and train service resumed two days later that the Rabbit got home to Springfield. Dad and Jack Schneider rode in the hearse to Grand Central Station and accompanied the casket on the train to Springfield for the funeral and his burial at St. Michael's Cemetery. I wanted to go to the funeral as did my friend, Billy O'Donoghue, who idolized the Rabbit probably more than I did. I was saddened by what had happened and somewhat shaken as I'd never dealt with death that close up before. I would miss the Rabbit given his vibrant and mischievous personality and my wonderful experiences with this unforgettable character.

Getting To Skogel Hat

When Dad returned from Rabbit's funeral, we discussed when and where I would be employed. Mother called her cousin, Grace McPartland,[26]

---

[25] Frank Dwyer was a huge, good-natured, white-haired, florid-faced man about six foot three and 300 pounds. While he resembled a walrus, he made it clear to his friends that if they were to use a nickname he preferred that it be "Sea Lion."

[26] Grace was the daughter of Hugh McPartland, Grandfather Jim's brother. Her mother died when she was young, and she was raised by Rose McPartland Ford, Grandfather's sister who lived on 46th Street off 28th Avenue in Astoria. I spent a minimum of two weeks each year with Aunt Rose, her husband Frank, their son Joe, and cousin Grace and visited her many

who arranged an interview at the Equitable Life Assurance Society of the United States, where she worked as a secretary in the office of the president. I put on a suit and took the subway into Manhattan with Grace and was impressed with the Equitable Building at 393 7th Avenue. The lobby was massive, with a high-vaulted ceiling engraved with the gilded renderings of Equitable's protective goddess symbol.

I filled out an employment application and was interviewed by a pleasant middle-aged woman who told me there were no openings, but that she expected they'd be hiring in a few months. This is where I wanted to work. I was taken with everything about the building, how well I was treated, and the surrounding neighborhood dominated by the architectural grandeur of Penn Station. It was an inviting office, bustling with activity and numerous young people. The goddess symbol rang true as in my brief visit I noticed a significant number of real life young goddesses walking about the building, not just renderings on the lobby ceiling.

Grace repeated to Mother what her friend in the Personnel Department had told me, that Equitable would not have any openings for another month. So, rather than wait for a call that might never come, my father took me to the New York State Unemployment Office in Queens Plaza, where an acquaintance of his ran the office. Dad's friend had a selection of available, albeit dreadful, positions. Dad was determined that I would not work in the building trades, though it could have been arranged since he and his brother Pete were on the executive committee of Local 15 of the International Union of Operating Engineers. He used the excuse that I didn't have a chauffeur's license. The minimum age requirement for such a license was 18, so I had over a year to wait if I expected a high paying job

---

days on the way home from St. Joseph's School. Aunt Rose treated me to gifts of toy lead soldiers, cakes, tea with brown sugar and never sent me on my way without a warm hug and a shiny quarter.

in construction. Though unlicensed, my driving qualifications were unquestioned.

In short order, Dad and his friend decided that my initial career would be in millinery. I was destined to be a hat man. The call was made to Mr. Skogel of the Skogel Hat Corporation informing him that I was available to fill his 85 cents/hour challenge. It was a generous 12 percent premium above the 75 cents/hour minimum wage I had earned the previous summer as a Western Union messenger and floral delivery boy. This is just awful, I thought. Two weeks out of high school and now I was heading to a dead end job. But what did I expect? Dad said I had essentially finished high school and was really too young to do anything else. Mother advised me to be patient. "Try it out – you'll learn something. It'll be good experience."

After what I had put them through in the past month, I was not about to ignore their advice. As Dad said, "It's a job – make the most of it. Who knows? You might like it."

Making Ladies' Hats

This has to be the coldest place on the face of the earth, I thought as my body struggled to cope with the bone-chilling wind surging up 44th Road from the East River that January morning. The blast of Arctic air funneling down into the 23rd and Ely Street subway station hit me as I stepped off the train and made my way to the street. Dad had given me his warm jacket that January morning. Warm jacket my ass. I was ill prepared to face the elements.

I had ridden the subway with Bella Clark's oldest son, Pete, who worked at the Board of Education warehouse across the street from my new job.

"I never heard of Skogel Hat Corporation," Pete said as we neared the top of the stairs. "And I've been working here for almost a year." He adjusted his collar and put on a pair of wool mittens. "It's freezing. Don't you have any gloves?"

"Yeah, but I couldn't find them this morning." I stuffed my hands into my pants' pockets and rubbed them against my thighs to keep warm.

"Hey Neal, how about 'Jolting Joe' Di Maggio marrying Marilyn Monroe?"

"Bet he's jolting her right now," I said.

"Jeez, it's cold. I'd love to trade places with him."

"Who wouldn't?"

Pete agreed that Di Maggio was in a much better spot that morning. As we struggled in the quarter-mile walk from the subway entrance to Vernon Boulevard, we had to walk backwards to protect our faces from the stinging wind. The temperature was 15 degrees, with the wind gusts upwards of 25 miles per hour. Our ears were numb and our faces felt like they were going to crack open. As we slowly made our way to the river, I wondered what this job would be like.

Pete's place of employment, a huge white concrete building, loomed ahead as we trudged towards Vernon Boulevard. The City of New York, Department of Purchasing & Bureau of Stores fronted Vernon Boulevard and backed up to the river's edge. Just across the street from Pete's building, at the corner of 44th Road and Vernon Boulevard, was a dingy four-story red brick building that housed the Skogel Hat Corporation.[27]

I said goodbye to Pete, entered the building, climbed the linoleum-covered stairs to the second floor, and found myself in a turn-of-the-century sweatshop. A neatly dressed, gray haired man introduced himself as Mr. Skogel. He assisted me with my coat before he took me to meet my fellow employees. In contrast to the weather outside, the office was dark and dismal, but warm and accompanied by a symphony of sounds –

---

[27] More than a half century later, the building is now restored for upscale apartments.

radiators hissing steam and clanking from air blockages, sewing machines humming, a stapling machine thumping as it shot steel clips into hat forms, adding machines clicking away, and lead keys sharply hitting the paper in an ancient Underwood typewriter. The sounds combined with the low murmurings of the workers gave Skogel Hat a voice of its own.

Taking in the depressing surroundings – bare brick walls, exposed ceiling joists and rafters dimly lit by light bulbs hanging on loose ceiling wires – I wondered how I could extricate myself from this place gracefully without setting off my father, who had arranged for this less-than-prestigious position?

Mr. Skogel made hats for the so called "Five & Dime" stores, particularly Woolworth's and Kresge's, now the slightly more upscale K-Mart, which is part of Sears. Hat forms of various colors, liners, artificial flowers, and netting were delivered daily from some of the companies located in the Hat District that I had delivered telegram orders to. I unloaded the trucks, loaded and operated the freight elevator and moved the boxes of hat materials to their appropriate location on the plant floor.

In the rear of the darkened factory, eight men and women sat at ancient Singer Sewing Machines inserting liners into the hat forms. I noticed tattoos on the underside of their left forearms. They were Nazi death camp survivors. The images from *Life Magazine* and the Movietone newsreels picturing emaciated prisoners displaying similar tattoos flashed across my brain. An uninformed 16-year-old brought up in an intolerant neighborhood, I didn't comprehend their situation and was puzzled by them, failing to understand why they kept to themselves, stuck together at lunch, and didn't encourage conversation. Yet, they hummed in unison to classical music from a nearby radio. It was obvious that they wanted to be left alone. Their actions only encouraged indifference from their co-workers. It never occurred to me that they stuck together out of fear.

Silence and suspicion or distrust of others had kept them alive during their internment in the death camps. For them, it was a life-saving tactic. Now safe in New York, they still clung to their old habits that were not fully understood by a 16-year-old boy.

I couldn't begin to appreciate what they had experienced – how they had survived or continued to live with the realities of the past. They had endured years of stress, starvation, the loss of families and friends, near death experiences in the camps, and guilt-ridden survival followed by more aimless years as Displaced Persons (DP's) being shuttled from one European DP camp to another before finding a sponsor in America. Here, they were working away for a pittance. "Arbeit macht frei," work brings freedom, read the signs over the entrances to the concentration camps. Now in America, they were beholden to a new master – the sign over the entrance where they were now concentrated read, the Skogel Hat Corporation.

At that time, neither the U.S. Government nor the Catholic Church had fully acknowledged their failure to assist the Jews at critical points in Hitler's rise to power, or even to publicize what actually happened. Though we had seen newsreel clips of the liberation of the concentration camps at our local theatres, it would be years before the full story began to unfold. The tattoos indelibly marked their experiences as survivors of horror and inhumanity, a constant reminder of their debasement and dehumanization by the terror and insanity of man. At first, being around them gave me the chills.

Eventually, I tried to reach out to them, always smiling as I delivered materials and picked up their finished work. I greeted them warmly every morning and said good-bye when we closed at the end of each day before they made their way home together to their tenement apartments in Williamsburg.

1954 Adventures In New York

One day, I thought I recognized the classical music they were humming and began to whistle along as I approached their work area. They stopped humming and looked up as if insulted. What's with them? I thought. Can't I enjoy the music, too? I was soon told by Mr. Skogel that they were not humming, but reciting prayers. From that time on I respected the sanctity of their working area. For me, it became a sacred zone of silence.

At Skogel Hat they worked away with little time to reflect on the recent past. Given their suffering, they may have overlooked their low wages and working conditions, but they didn't complain about a warm place to work, even for a marginal wage.

Long after I left Skogel Hat, I received a complaint form from the Wage & Hour & Public Contracts Division of the U.S. Department of Labor. Apparently, someone was cognizant of their plight because the form posed questions about the working conditions there, including my operation of the elevator[28] and the loading and unloading of trucks. I was serving in the Navy when the letter arrived and was unable to respond in a timely manner.

One morning on the way to work I nodded off soon after Pete Clark and I had boarded the train. He nudged me awake when we approached our stop.

"Wake up, Neal. We're almost there."

"Thanks, I'm bushed. I watched the Late-Late Show last night."

"You see the paper yet?" He pointed to the sports page headline of *The New York Daily News* he was holding.

"No. Did you find anything interesting?"

"Some guy in South Carolina scored 100 points last night."

---

[28] The labor laws then in effect prohibited anyone under the age of 18 from operating dangerous equipment such as a freight elevator.

"Let me see that."

He handed me the paper and tapped the article about Frank Selvy's record game. "He plays for Furman University in Greenville, South Carolina. He hit the century mark against Newberry College."

"I've heard of Furman. Where the hell is Newberry?"

"It says that it's a small Lutheran College in Newberry, South Carolina – probably named after the guy who has all those stores – J.J. Newberry."

"I've heard of the stores, but not the school."

"Think of that Neal, 50 baskets. His Goddamn arms must've hurt after all that shooting."

I smiled at the thought. In the season that just ended I had a few 16-point games. It seemed like I was scoring every time I touched the ball. I couldn't imagine scoring 100 points.[29]

Making hats became second nature to me, like netting baskets was for Frank Selvy. Once the hats were lined, I sorted them by color and moved the boxes to the stapling machines. This is where Mr. Skogel's creativity determined how the hats would be most attractive to his five-and-dime clientele. He'd gather a selection of artificial flowers, hats and veils, and seek out a clean window with a northern exposure – somewhat of a feat in that dingy place. Utilizing the purity of the light, he would conjure up the right mix of colors for the veil, hat, and flowers. In a few minutes he'd return with the flowers and veils pinned to the hats. Then it was my task, using a foot-operated stapling machine, to carefully and expeditiously attach the

---

[29] Little did I realize that five years later, in my freshman season at New York University, I'd be shooting with Frank Selvy. He was then a star of the New York Knicks, who were visiting our gym to scrimmage the varsity. I was Captain of the freshman team, and just as our practice concluded, Selvy showed up in the gym well ahead of his teammates and ready to warm up. Freshman coach Jack Rohan suggested that I observe Selvy's shooting technique. Since I needed all the help I could get, I fed Selvy the ball and shot with him. It was a thrill to be on the same court and also a lesson in humility. Selvy didn't have much to say. All he did was hit shot after shot with amazing ease.

nets and flowers to the hats. And, it was critical to the operation that the staples not be visible.

Once my tasks as an apprentice hat maker were completed, I assumed my shipping department responsibilities by wrapping the finished hats in tissue paper, packing them into boxes, sealing and addressing the boxes, and stacking them on the freight elevator. Later in the day, I would cart the boxes almost a half mile to the Post Office near Jackson Avenue. The whole process of sorting and emptying boxes, distributing hat shells and liners to the workers, stapling, wrapping and packing, soon became a boring routine. I hated this job. It was mind numbing. There had to be something better that I should be doing.

The only break came at noon when I walked to the local diner on 45th Road to pick up Mr. Skogel's standing lunch order – an American cheese sandwich on white bread with mustard and a cardboard container of tea. A gourmand he was not.

In my young mind I was convinced that I had mastered the hat business, since I could predict with precision Mr. Skogel's color selections of hats, flowers and nets. Empowered with this new ability, I made the mistake of anticipating his choice and started to assemble a box of hats before he returned from his moment of inspiration at the north-facing window.

He quickly expressed his disapproval. "What customer wants those hats?"

"Does it make a difference? All the shipments seem to be the same."

"The orders may be the same, but the colors of the hats, the flowers, and the veils could vary. That's why I always look at the colors in the true light."

Yeah, sure I thought. Like it makes a difference to an old woman buying a cheap hat that was designed by a guy who eats American cheese on white bread every day, and was made by a skinny 16-year-old kid in a Long Island City sweat shop.

I nodded my acceptance and carefully unfastened my fashion mistakes and applied the veils and flowers pursuant to Mr. Skogel's prescribed color schemes.

After almost two months of this daily tedium, my life changed for the better unlike that of Vic Raschi, the great New York Yankee pitcher.

On the subway that morning, Pete Clark startled me awake. "Look at this," Pete said, jabbing at the article in the sports section. "The Yankees sold Vic Rashi to the St. Louis Cardinals for $85,000."

"You're shitting me," I said. I couldn't believe the Yankees would give up their stalwart pitcher for any sum.

"Honest, look at this."

I grabbed the paper from him and read the article with incredulity, shaking my head in disbelief. "Jesus, Pete. The guy averages 15 wins a season and they want him to take a pay cut because of one off year."

"Don't forget. He won 21 games three years in a row."

"What do the Yankees want, blood?"

The Yankees' General Manager, George Weiss, wanted Raschi to accept a 25 percent pay cut after he posted a 13 and 6 record in 1953, and Raschi refused. By today's standards, this off-year for Raschi would be considered a solid record for modern-day pitchers and command an annual salary of some $4 million. Given that Raschi posted a 120 and 50 pitching record and never missed a start in his eight-year career in New York, the city was soon in an uproar.

That night, Mother handed me a letter from the Equitable Life Assurance Society offering me a position at a weekly salary of $42.50 plus overtime – a 25 percent increase from my Skogel Hat pay. Though it was only 56 percent of the national average annual pay of $3,960, I felt like I had died and gone to heaven. My millinery life would soon be old hat. The following day, while picking up Mr. Skogel's lunch, I called the Equitable Personnel Office from the diner and accepted the position. My life began to change exponentially; little did I realize I was destined to have a better year than the Yankees and a far better year than JoeDi Maggio.

5

Equitable Life

The morning of March 1st, I alighted from the 'GG' train at Queens Plaza around 8:20 and boarded the 'E' train, waiting across the platform that would take me to Penn Station at 8th Avenue and 34th Street. The subway ride into Manhattan was filled with anticipation. I felt awkward wearing a suit, but Dad insisted that I do so. "This ain't no hat factory — you're going to business. It's your first day. Equitable's a respected insurance company. You want to make a good impression." Mom and Dad were happy that I was going to be working for such a respected company and thanked cousin Gracie for helping to arrange it.

Dad was right about first impressions, but I wasn't yet sure who I had to impress, no less what I was going to be doing at my new job, or even what I wanted to do in life. I knew one thing though; it certainly was going to be better than the Skogel Hat Corporation. I was pretty excited about going to work at Equitable – hopefully it would be interesting and perhaps adventurous. What really interested me were all the good looking girls I had seen in the building when I went for my first interview in January.

I was excited when the 'E' train stopped at 34th Street. I bounded through the exit gate and down the steps to the passageway leading me towards Penn Station. Once inside the expansive station, I paused to look up at the curving lines of the opaque arched glass ceiling framed by blackened steel supports and broke into a smile. Revved-up, I jostled through the crowds pouring out of the stairways leading up from the Long Island Railroad platforms and past the long ticket lines in the grand hall eager to begin my post-millinery career in the insurance industry. I was unaware that in that crowded ticket line were Puerto Rican Nationalists

Lolita Lebron,[30] an attractive woman, and her traveling companions,[31] who were fresh off the downtown 'A' train from the barrio in upper Manhattan. They would purchase one-way tickets for the 9 a.m. train to Washington, D.C., where they would lead an assault on the U.S. House of Representatives, wounding five.

Just before the escalator leading up to 7th Avenue, I paused to look up at the large Benrus clock indicating it was 8:40 and that I was early. Riding the escalator I looked back over my shoulder at the great expanse of this vast, cathedral-like public space. It was magical. What a way to begin a new day – a new job – a new life. I walked out to the street and gazed up at the impressive headquarters building of the Equitable Life Assurance Society. Off to its left was the Pennsylvania Hotel, the hotel and its phone number made famous by Glenn Miller's rendition of *Pennsylvania 6 – 5000*. Wow, I wondered what awaited me.

After reporting to the Personnel Department, a woman escorted me to the Lay Underwriting Department on the seventh floor where I began my position as an application chaser.

My new boss was the revered Andy Rosasco, a 45-year employee from Jersey City. My fellow application chasers – Joe Gianinni, John O'Rourke, Dick Pertrowski and Artie Wassen would turn out to be four of the greatest guys I have ever been associated with. As you will learn, we were engaged in an interesting line of work – though some would take issue as to whether it qualified as work. To me, it was an adventure in New York.

Mr. Rosasco, a short, square-shaped man with an engaging personality, took me in tow that morning, introducing me, albeit briefly, to the head of the underwriting department, Mr. Everett Lapp. "He's a good boss," Andy

---

[30] "A Terrorist in the House" by Manuel Roig-Franzia, *Washington Post Magazine,* February 22, 2004.
[31] Andres Figuero Cordero and Irving Flores Rodriguez.

said, "Now let's get you a locker out in the back hallway so you can take that jacket off." Then he introduced me to my fellow employees including a lovable, quirky and apparently wealthy woman named Grace Van Sicklan.

Grace was an avid tennis player, who left work each afternoon to play at the prestigious Westside Tennis Club in Forest Hills. She was responsible for the seventh floor's pneumatic tube station. When first installed in 1924, it was heralded as the most modern in use in the United States. It was considered state of the art in transporting documents from floor-to-floor within the 34-story building. It was still effectively functioning 30 years later, thanks to the extraordinary efforts of people like Grace. She was superbly coordinated though ungainly looking. Her long arms and legs resembled those of Olive Oyl, the girlfriend of the comic-strip character "Popeye." Working at a frenetic pace, she stuffed documents into large plastic tubes and loaded the tubes into the pneumatic delivery system. If she was not loading tubes, she was unloading them, and sorting the documents into the proper cubbyholes that served as mailboxes for the people in our department. Grace would be smiling, whistling, and in wonderful spirits while she worked. She could have run a battleship's 16-inch gun mount by herself. She reported to Andy Rosasco, who often said, "Grace is a study in perpetual motion. She never stops and doesn't require supervision like my application chasers." Her name suited her perfectly – she was graceful as she worked. She could have run the company, if she set her mind to it, and if women were provided equal opportunities in 1954.

At noon, as my fellow application chasers introduced me to the Equitable cafeteria, Lolita Lebron and her traveling companions had arrived at Washington's Union Station where they joined another conspirator, Cancel Miranda, for lunch. Following my lunch, I visited Gimbel's Department Store for a shopping spree accompanied by Mother's cousin Grace McPartland. I bought a few new shirts and a pair of slacks for work that came with a discount by virtue of Grace's part-time job in Gimbel's Men's Department. In contrast, the Puerto Ricans followed their lunch with a shooting spree. They entered the Visitors' Gallery in the U.S. House of Representatives, shouted out their support for independence for their island homeland, then pulled out their revolvers and fired down on the assembled members, wounding five congressmen. On the way home that afternoon, the evening newspapers, *The New York Journal American* and *The World Telegram & Sun*, described the shootings in bold headlines. People on the subway were muttering about the "crazy spics." I picked up a paper someone had left on a seat and read the story. Jesus, I was in Penn Station when they were buying their tickets this morning.

At dinner that night, Dad blamed a laundry list of politicians for the Puerto Ricans being in New York. "Who needs them? They're all on welfare, anyway. Let them have their goddamned independence. It'll save the country a lot of money," he ranted. Mom was silent, while my sisters and I just rolled our eyes.

Chasing Applications

Andy Rosasco controlled the flow of paper into and out of the underwriting department, where row upon row of underwriters toiled away on insurance applications. Some of the elders wore green celluloid visors to protect their eyes from the glare of the overhead lights and clear celluloid covers over their wrists to keep their cuffs and shirtsleeves clean allowing them to wear the shirt another day. At any given time, there were upwards of 100 underwriters working at adjoining desks in this open area half the size of a football field that ran the length and breadth of our sector of the seventh floor, on the 31st Street side of the building. The faster the paper moved through the underwriting approval process, the sooner the insurance agent received his commission. On a big policy, there was always pressure to expedite the application – that's where the applications chasers fit into the picture. I often wondered what in the world the underwriters were doing. I knew they were making decisions to approve or disapprove a policy, but I wasn't sure how they did it.

An insurance application in process of approval could be located in a number of different departments in this imposing 34-story structure, straddling 31st and 32nd Streets on 7th Avenue. Application chasers travelled throughout the building on the hunt for lost applications. We had license to visit the various departments to search through stacks of applications on anyone's desk and lay claim to an application by virtue of the fact it was on our list of cases to be found. Oftentimes, we extended this unlimited ability to roam throughout the building into a license to journey far and wide into the outer boroughs of New York.

The code of the application chaser was to dedicate one's self to his fellow workers, and not to the interest of Equitable Life and its policyholders. First of all, there was a daily quota. You were expected to find no more than 12 applications a day. On average we usually would find eight of them. Second, you never turned in all of your applications. You held a minimum of four to six in reserve in your locker each day. Third, you worked and stood together always protecting your associates' backs. One chaser, with a deep sense of guilt, had to be cautioned, from time to time, about the need to subordinate his personal goals to the common interest of his fellow workers. We were strict adherents to the primary principle of Jeremy Bentham's "Utilitarianism" – we pursued whatever measures created the greatest possible happiness for the greatest number.[32] Another

---

[32] Bentham's actual words were that the "greatest happiness of the greatest number is the only right and proper end of governments." *The Collected Works of Jeremy Bentham,* Bentham Project, Bentham Committee, University College London.

Bentham adage is that "The more strictly we are watched, the better we behave."[33] And, since we were not being watched, we behaved accordingly.

As young, entry-level employees, we weren't thinking promotion and advancement within the Underwriting Department. God forbid, if you did well you might become an underwriter and be stuck at a desk all day, depending on one of us young kids to find you work. We were still too young and immature, particularly me, to understand the advantages of getting ahead in life. But with no real responsibilities to worry about, a few dollars in our pockets made us happy campers.

The individual applications could be interesting. In addition to the requirements of a physical examination, those applying for policy coverage in the $50,000 and above category were subject to investigative reports on their personal behavior. Underwriters passed the juicier reports to each other and shared with us the peccadilloes of well-known people. Sexual activity, alcohol consumption, and gambling habits were factored into determining whether the insurance applicant was a suitable and prudential risk. Fortunately, today's office technology didn't exist, for if it did, these spicy reports would have circulated throughout the city and far beyond on the Internet.

In my initial travels throughout the building, I quickly realized that there were far more women than men working at Equitable Life. In fact, the ratio was rather large, about five to one. It was somewhat distracting in certain departments, especially on good hair days, when you walked into a large room and 50 young women suddenly looked up and gave you the once over. It soon became apparent there would be opportunities for misadventure developing in my immediate future.

---

[33] Bentham on the Panopticon, which is a type of institutional building that Bentham designed to allow an observer to see all the inmates of an institution without them being able to tell whether or not they were being watched.

"Who's the new guy?"

"How old is he?"

"Where's he from?"

"Does he have a girlfriend?"

These were the questions posed to my fellow workers when I first appeared on the scene. My tender age of 16 posed a problem. I added another year to avoid facing credibility problems when the expected opportunities developed, as they certainly would.

I soon got into the rhythm of the job, learned my way around the various departments, knew where I was likely to find cases and established the confidence and trust of my fellow workers.

On a typical day we started on the seventh floor and searched the files on the desks of the underwriters. Following that, we headed down the hall towards the Medical Department on the 7th Avenue front of the building. Medical was a rabbit warren of small offices occupied by doctors and medical technicians, who administered physical examinations to applicants for policies in the $50,000 to $100,000 category – sizeable policies in 1954 – equivalent to $400,000 to $800,000 policies today. We quickly reviewed the stacks of pending applications in each office, and then moved into the focal point in the center of the Department. It was a large room with four desks pushed together, on top of which sat a growing mountain of applications and related medical reports being sorted out for assignment for review by a doctor.

Presiding over this organized mess was an extraordinary man, Patrick "Pat" Shanahan – a friendly and inquiring person, who immediately stood up and introduced himself when I walked into the room. He was tall and thin with a ruddy complexion, fine white hair, friendly blue eyes, and a firm handshake.

"Well, a new one I see, and a fellow countryman, for sure. I'm Pat Shanahan. What's your name, son?"

"Neal Gillen, sir."

"What would be your middle name?"

"Patrick."

"And your confirmation name?"

"Daniel."

"Ah, a fearless one – good choice. Where's your father fit into all these names?

"In the middle, sir. His name is Patrick Aloysius Gillen."

"Tell me your birthday?"

"May 14th, sir."

"Enough with the sir, Neal. Call me Pat, like everyone else does."

"Let me guess where you're from. I'd say Brooklyn or Queens."

"It's Queens, but I attended Brooklyn Prep for three semesters."

"Only three. I guess there's a story there. What's the name of your parish?"

"Corpus Christi." Thank God he didn't go into my history at Prep.

"That would be Woodside and your Pastor is Father Charles Carey. Now the story of that church is quite interesting. Carey raised enough money for the foundation and the basement, but World War II delayed further construction because of the shortage of materials. He held Sunday services in a movie theatre, but he had to use St. Joseph's for baptisms, weddings, and funerals. As a result, he was losing parishioners to St. Joseph's so he took the bull by the horns, finished the basement as a church, had the Bishop consecrate it, and made it operational."[34]

How'd he know that? Better be careful with this old guy.

"Now, where in Ireland are your people from?"

---

[34] To this day, Corpus Christi is still a below-ground-level church.

"From right in the center of Tipperary."

"Find out the names of the villages and when they left."

I soon learned that Pat Shanahan, a volunteer for the Diocese of Brooklyn, possessed an encyclopedic knowledge of just about everything concerning the multitude of Catholic parishes in Brooklyn, Queens, Nassau, and Suffolk counties, and, of course, Equitable Life.

Pat was soon to be 65. He took note of my youth and informed me that he left high school at 15 in 1904 to work for Equitable. His knowledge was substantial. He was recognized as an institutional memory of the Diocese of Brooklyn and Equitable Life. He told me about the great fire of 1912 at the old Equitable Building at 120 Broadway that destroyed most of the records, describing in great detail the heroic efforts of the employees to keep the company going by working out of temporary offices until 1915, when a new building arose from the ashes at 120 Broadway. While Pat was too old for Army service when the U.S. declared war on Germany in 1917, he told me he was not anxious to help the British, especially after the brutal way its Army put down the Easter Rebellion in Dublin in 1916. He was particularly proud of the fact that he was one of the few employees still around who participated in the 1924 move to the new building on 7th Avenue.

Pat Shanahan was endearing to all he came in contact with and totally dedicated to his work.

"They didn't lay off a single person during the Great Depression," he proudly stated.

"There's security here, and a great future if you work hard," he added.

A few months later, there was a day-long open house in the Medical Department to celebrate Pat's 65th birthday and his retirement, where hundreds of people stopped by to wish him well. He knew everyone by name and their Catholic parish, the names of their wives and children, and many of them had received a birthday card from him the previous year.

There was one big problem – though it was company policy, Pat Shanahan had no intention of retiring. He was in total self-denial that his career at Equitable had drawn to a conclusion. His work was his life; it sustained him. In his mind, he was too valuable an employee. Pat truly believed that the rules would not apply in his special circumstances. It wasn't hubris, but his Irish pride and strong sense of self-worth that made Pat believe that the office could not function without him. He told everyone he had his health, loved his work, and that he would be there on Monday.

When Pat reported to work on Monday he found his desk occupied by a young man some 45 years his junior. Only then did the realization begin to set in that his career was over – his job had been filled. It was embarrassing for everyone, particularly the young man who replaced this icon. The word spread quickly throughout the Underwriting Department that Pat had showed up for work. A group of senior officials, who knew and respected Pat, were detailed to diplomatically inform him he couldn't continue to work. He broke down and cried. It was an appalling sight. Those requested to ease him out of the office had tears in their eyes. A number of people crowded around him, trembling, crying, and clearly stating their views:

"It isn't fair."

"He knows so much."

"Let him stay."

At Equitable, the rules were the rules. Pat was sequestered in an unoccupied doctor's office until two of his relatives arrived to lead this once proud, and now broken man, out the door. Pat was rarely seen or heard of again, and gradually people reported that his birthday cards stopped coming. The incident saddened me and everyone else who had to come to know this kindly and valued person. To me this was all about unfairness and a waste of a valuable asset. Pat was a father figure to me and many of the young Equitable employees. Just seeing him every day boosted our morale. I was hardened somewhat by his treatment and felt bad for Pat. While some people couldn't wait to retire, here was a guy who wanted to keep on going like Connie Mack who was still managing the Philadelphia Athletics well into his 80's and Stanley Bloom, the neighborhood bartender who was still going strong at 85.

Beating the System

After canvassing the Medical Department it was time for our coffee break, which took us east up 32nd Street to Markel's, a long narrow coffee shop with 20 stools and four or five small tables squeezed against the wall. Surrounding Markel's was a number of camera and television stores, and across the street was Gimbel's, New York's second largest department store – Macy's, its neighbor two blocks away being the largest.

Half a dozen men feverishly worked behind the counter at Markel's, cutting bagels and bialys, spreading cream cheese and butter over various kinds of toast, making bacon and egg sandwiches on kaiser rolls, and then wrapping and bagging them for delivery with containers of coffee. When the morning breakfast and coffee orders tailed off, the sandwich orders for lunch began to pour in.

Markel's telephone rang incessantly. There was virtually no let-up in activity until just after two o'clock, when the luncheon crowd thinned out. It was a highly efficient operation, albeit helter-skelter in appearance. The food was good and it was a pleasant place to visit because of our familiarity with the countermen.

Before we left the Equitable Building we would call the elevator starter in the lobby to determine the color of the meal tickets Markel's was using that day. In our office, we maintained a full assortment of colored meal tickets and a hand punch, purchased at a nearby office supply store. On days when our pocket change was limited we enjoyed a good breakfast below the actual costs by having on hand a meal ticket punched for a lesser amount. Since we always sat in the rear of the luncheonette, the mass of customers screened us from the cashier, who had no idea what we had ordered, and no reason to question our checks.

It crossed my mind that what we were doing was wrong, but this was a way of life in New York. Everyone had a hustle, and this was ours. While we considered our conduct risky, if not wrong, we rationalized our actions by a number of excuses: not many of us were doing it, we left a tip on the counter, they give free meals to the policemen who make more money than we do, and they do so much business that they wouldn't miss the small change we cheated out of them. We had inherited the crafty traits of New York's immigrant class – work the system, get an edge on the other guy and screw him before he screws you, an attitude or predisposition passed down to their descendants by immigrants who were taken advantage of when they first arrived in New York.

Another interesting facet of 32nd Street was the continual traffic of people heading in one direction for Penn Station, and in the other direction towards Gimbel's on the north side or to the many camera stores on the South side, and to the 6th Avenue and the Broadway subway lines. This made 32nd Street the ideal location for street vendors, who set up small stands and attracted sizeable crowds with a sales pitch about the magic vegetable slicer and dicer, a set of carving knives, or the novel toy they happened to be selling. They were polished operators who did a brisk business just before, during and after lunch, and at the onset of the evening rush hour. It's where I saw my first Slinky being demonstrated. I bought one for 50 cents for my younger brother Jimmy and promptly tested it on the back stairs of the Equitable Building.

Ace Corcoran

Following our break at Markel's, we returned to the building and headed for the eighth floor, which usually was a treasure trove of applications. It also was the domain of Thomas "Ace" Corcoran. Upon being introduced to a new guy at the office, Ace immediately tested his mettle by stating that he knew who he was, since he was fucking his sister. It's what he said to me. Joe Gianinni had warned me he would probably say this, so I was prepared. "Yeah, I heard you were hitting your own sister."

The Ace looked at Joe Gianinni and shook his head. "Where'd you find this fucking guy?"

"Queens," Joe said laughing. "He's all right."

The Ace looked me over carefully, smiled, and poked me in the chest. "Listen, skinny. I own this fucking floor. You'd better respect that."

This outrageous and unforgettable character was over six foot tall and weighed about 200 pounds. He had pasty white skin, piercing blue eyes, oily jet black hair combed in a duck's tail with a curl in front, a small potbelly, and discolored and protruding front teeth. His voice was raspy and a spray of spittle usually accompanied his words. His main contribution to the office place was encouraging the use of profanity.

In today's work environment, the Ace's language would be deemed to constitute sexual harassment, and his immediate work area, or wherever he happened to be in the building, would be considered a hostile work environment, in violation of Federal labor laws and regulations. According to current workplace standards, an employee who conducted himself like

Ace Corcoran would provide a law firm with extended billable hours and subject his employer to substantial monetary fines and punitive damages.

Ace's graphic and sexually explicit language was spoken loudly and clearly. He frequently discussed his "sweet shank," his preferred reference to the male organ, and "fuck," one of his milder words, was used like the word "the."

A native of East Harlem, he was cunning, insulting, incorrigible, and if anything tenacious. Despite these unfavorable attributes, he was highly intelligent, and possessed a likeable and devilish charm. His clothes were bizarre, pointed black shoes, tightly pegged pants with saddle stitching down the side of the pants legs in a lighter and contrasting color, long curved flaps on his back pockets known as "pistol pockets," a high rise on his pants fitted with narrow belt loops for his slim belts, and wrap-around, belted, gabardine jackets with patch pockets. He favored polka dotted shirts of various colors. If he wore a tie it was from his Tie City collection of Slim Jim ties that were no more than an inch wide.

Ace's gabardine, wrap-around jackets were a sight to behold. One was dark blue with powder blue shoulders and darts running down to the chest pockets. The other was powder blue with dark blue shoulders and darts. He would mix and match powder blue, dark blue, or black slacks with these garish jackets.

In the fourth-floor cafeteria he would ask women in their early 20's their favorite sexual position or if they "got any" over the weekend. The younger women were asked if they let guys feel them up on the first date or if they would handle his shank. To women in general, he would ask when they were going to "give me some." Surprisingly, most of them laughed and seemed to enjoy his banter – "Oh, that Ace, he says the craziest things." A few women had the courage and good sense to take offense at his rude and outrageous inquiries and summarily rebuffed him. Around female company the Ace made you appear to be a gentleman of absolute rectitude.

It was my fate to have daily contact with this unforgettable character. His typical office greeting, from a distance of 15 to 20 feet was, "How's your mudder?" or "Did you score with yourself last night?" I was usually on the defensive with the Ace. He often addressed Artie Wassen or me that way, given we were on the thin side, but he didn't take that tact with Dick Pertrowski, who was six foot four, or with Joe Gianinni who, though shorter than the Ace was muscular and quick to inform him that if he ever inquired about the status of his girlfriend or any of the female members of his family, "I will destroy you." I lacked Joe's strength and confidence to take on the Ace. It riled me that to many he was somewhat of a heroic figure. He was a character – a cad. I bided my time, waiting to get even with the Ace.

Macy's & Gimbel's

When we were out of the office, a portion of our time was spent roaming through the neighborhood's two massive department stores, Macy's and Gimbel's. It was long before the era of regional stores and, the first successful discount store, E.J. Korvettes, only seven-years old, was a few years away from being a serious competitor.

The two spacious stores stocked about everything used or worn in a household. Strolling through them in slacks, a shirt and tie, we were presumed to be fellow employees by the store personnel and supervisors, who were used to seeing us on a regular basis. As a result, on numerous occasions, they gave us employee discounts on our purchases. Also, many of the customers thought we worked there, and given our knowledge of the store we were able to point them in the right direction.

Late one morning, Artie Wassen and I, as assumed employees of Macy's, not only assisted in greeting Ava Gardner, the screen goddess, at the 34th Street entrance, but we accompanied her on the elevator to the floor where lingerie was sold. I was absolutely dazzled to be in her presence and surprised by her apparent shyness. I could barely speak, but I mustered up the courage to say, "Miss Gardner, you're my favorite actress."

"Why thank you," she said with a warm smile. Wow, I thought, this screen goddess actually spoke to me.

Artie and I watched her model what was then called "Intimate Apparel" for a large group of middle-aged women. Gardner was then starring in a popular film, *The Barefoot Contessa*. Her appearance at Macy's was a promotional tie-in for the film and the lingerie she wore in the movie. Ava was then in a shaky marriage with the singer and actor Frank Sinatra. Artie and I were thrilled with our encounter with this attractive film star. Our fellow employees were impressed when we reported back to them at lunch. Needless to say, Ace Corcoran was not.

"I would've grabbed her and humped her in that situation. You guys are useless, skinny bastards," he said to the amused cafeteria crowd.

Penn Station

Walking through Penn Station, coming and going to work, was memorable. It was a vast cathedral filled with people, in perpetual and well-coordinated movement, flowing to and from the arriving and departing trains of the Long Island and Pennsylvania Railroads and the subway's 'E', 'A', and 'AA' trains going downtown to Wall Street and uptown to Times Square, Columbus Circle, and 5th and Madison Avenues. People moved en masse toward 8th and 7th Avenues up into the Garment District and across 7th Avenue to Equitable Life, Macy's and Gimbel's and over to 6th Avenue and Broadway. The huge flow of humanity on the move, between eight and nine in the morning and 4:30 to 6:30 in the evening, was always orderly and efficient. In the hours in between, Penn Station was a temple to behold, admire, and explore, which we did at great length. Sometimes we acted as if we worked there, roaming about the track areas with clipboards in our hands, and through a guy in the Little Penn Tavern who worked for the Station Master we were introduced to other Penn Station employees, who granted our requests to show us how they routed baggage or mail, dispatched trains, kept track of them, and where the out-of-town crews rested between trips.

We examined the labyrinth of tunnels under Penn Station along with the interconnecting passageways from Penn Station at 34th Street and 8th Avenue all the way to 6th Avenue and 40th Street. The latter were open to the public, but only used in unusually cold or inclement weather, given that a walk on 34th Street was an enjoyable venture since there was so much to see and gather in as you moved along.

Until the wrecking ball decided the fate of this magnificent structure in October 1963, replacing it with the new Madison Square Garden and an ugly office complex, the large Benrus clock that hung from Penn Station's ceiling, above the foot of the grand staircase on the 7th Avenue side of the station, was a meeting place for me and millions of others about to embark upon a date or a journey.

There is a special feeling of importance when you visit or meet someone in a great structure. Penn Station's Beaux Arts architectural grandeur imbued you with a sense of belonging to something significant, of being a contributor to the everyday functioning of a great thriving city. It was a great escape from the boredom of the office and a fun place to roam about. In New York City, it was the finest landmark of its age, and its destruction was a travesty of enormous proportions, leading Ada Louise

Huxtable to exclaim, "We will be judged not by the monuments we build, but by the monuments we destroy."

For almost 10 years, passengers on the Pennsylvania Railroad trains coming into and going out of New York were sadly reminded of this urban-planning travesty when passing the massive columns and the huge eagles that once stood guard over the station's 7th Avenue entrance piled alongside the tracks in the swamplands of New Jersey. Sometime in the early 1970s, they were taken off to an unknown resting place.

Whenever I travel to New York City by train, I still mourn the original station's destruction. Penn Station no longer greets the traveler with the promise of grandeur one expects of such a great city. It's a harsh and unwelcoming place. Arriving passengers feel like they are sneaking into the city up through its garbage chute, much like its neighbor further up 8th Avenue, the Port Authority Bus Terminal, another dark passage littered with the dregs of life lurking in its hallways.

The destruction of Penn Station was a waste, if not an architectural crime committed in the name of progress. It is difficult to measure the value of exceptional architecture, but in this case it was a cultural, aesthetic, and historic loss for New York and its frequent visitors. Thank God, that in 1975, Jackie Kennedy elevated the public's consciousness of historic landmarks by giving stature to the successful public effort that saved Grand Central Station from suffering a similar fate.

Penn Station, Macy's, Gimbel's, and the surrounding area provided a grand setting for curious young men beginning the early stages of their adult lives. It was the center of my new universe, my starting point as I ventured out into the world. I found myself in perhaps the most exciting entry-level job available in New York City in 1954 – an Equitable Life application chaser. I was beginning to form a better sense of myself. I had developed a new level of confidence. Everything seemed so exciting and for me the job was literally an adventure in New York.

6

John McComb

Key to the narrative of the coming months is a lifetime friend, John McComb, who helped guide me in this formative year. John lived on 47th Street just off 31st Avenue between Bryant High School and Boulevard Hospital. His mother, Susan Rooney McComb, was a striking woman with long red hair, a beautiful Celtic face, and an engaging personality. She was born in Lochgelly, in Fife, Scotland. His father, John, whom I never met, was a seaman from Belfast, Ireland.

Mrs. McComb worked for many years in the Chateau Tavern, a popular restaurant in the financial district, across the street from Del Monico's, until she was 79. She would have worked well into her 80's were it not for the fact that the restaurant closed to make way for a new office tower. Though a successful investor, she never considered retirement. She had adequate income to live comfortably, but she loved her work. Susan McComb viewed each day as a new beginning, an opportunity to visit with old customers, and to meet new ones from near and far. Her perky personality and quick wit had a wonderful effect on people. One would quickly recognize her intelligence and be taken by her attractive physical appearance, particularly her beautiful hair.

John shared his mother's positive outlook on life and was personable and outgoing. A great conversationalist, since he was a good listener, John had the knack of turning an ordinary situation into a humorous event. He was also a good basketball player, an exceptional dancer, a sharp dresser, a great story teller and a perfect gentleman. Given these attributes, John was a popular guy. Girls were drawn to him and this provided his friends with the opportunity to hook up with the friend of the girl who had her eye on him.

John played on Bryant High School's great basketball team, which featured our childhood friend Wally Di Masi, who shared scoring honors with Lenny Wilkens, in the two years they played together at Providence College.[35] Another Bryant player was Richie Bennett, who had a tryout with the Knicks, though he never attended college. "Jumping" Jimmy Capers, the first black to referee in the NBA,[36] and Eddie Tertarian,[37] were also members of that team.

A few months after John graduated from Bryant in 1953, a neighbor in his apartment building asked him if he was interested in appearing in a movie. The man worked on the docks and was a technical advisor on the film. He told John that the production company was seeking to cast a few teenagers as members of a small gang in the story's locale. John, who had been active in the Bryant Drama Club, immediately agreed to audition for the part, and was accepted. He is now part of cinema history in the opening rooftop scenes of the Academy Award winning film, *On the Waterfront*.

---

[35] Wilkens, the National Basketball Association (NBA) Basketball Hall of Fame player and coach, and the coach with the most NBA victories, described Wally as one the best pure shooters who ever played the game.

[36] When Capers retired from the NBA he returned to his first love, music. Jimmy Capers is now an accomplished singer and piano player and can be seen in clubs in the New York area. He is also proud of the fact that his son James followed him to the NBA as a referee.

[37] Eddie Tetarian was a great baseball player. He signed with the New York Giants, but gave up baseball to pursue his education. He eventually became a successful high school coach. When I was discharged from the Navy in 1958, on Eddie's recommendation, Jim "The Wiedler" Toner, and a guy from the projects nicknamed "Otis," because of his jumping ability, and I worked out with Eddie and others at his alma mater, Long Island University. Following the workout, each of us was offered a scholarship. I declined the offer, since I was interested in attending New York University. The Weidler eventually found his way to Spring Hill College in Alabama for a brief sojourn, and Otis, lacking decent grades, went his own way.

John had the opportunity to associate with Marlon Brando, Eva Marie Saint, Karl Malden, Lee J. Cobb, and Rod Steiger – possibly one of the best movie casts ever assembled.

A week before I was arrested in early December, I accompanied John to the filming of the mob scene on the docks in Hoboken, New Jersey – the prelude to the great brawl between Brando and Cobb at the end of the film. Brando was real cool. He arrived on the scene in a maroon Cadillac convertible, with the top down, wearing a leather jacket over a t-shirt.

One of the bit-part actors in the movie was "Two-Ton Tony" Galento, a professional wrestler and former boxer who once fought Joe Louis for the heavyweight championship – losing badly, I might add, though he did jar Louis with a couple of lucky punches, one of which knocked Louis down for a mandatory eight-count. Galento also happened to be one of Dad's pals. To help the mob scene extras get into character, beer was liberally dispensed from two wooden kegs positioned in the back of a food concession truck. Most of the extras were longshoremen, who preferred beer, rather than coffee, as their morning drink. Two-Ton Tony drank a lion's share of the golden nectar that damp and chilly morning. When the director, Elia Kazan, called "action," the cast of well-lubricated bit-part actors and extras was transformed into a willing mob capable of destroying the entirety of Hoboken.

John also worked at Equitable Life as a claims chaser on the sixth floor, a location peopled mostly by male college students working part time to pay their way through school. He inherited his mother's work ethic, which made him the ideal person for just about any job, and he was well liked by his associates and supervisors. As a result, John was invited to numerous parties and usually asked to bring a friend or two. Tagging along with him helped me in many ways, particularly in learning how to better interact with people. Being John's friend validated you, even if people had their doubts about you. John would convince me to think positively about myself. "You know, Neal, you're not as bad as you might think you are," he would often say. And over time I began to overcome those doubts.

John was a great observer who paid close attention to what was being said and who interacted with whom. This skill required considerable patience, which I lacked at the time. Also, he was an optimistic person who managed to enjoy everyone in a given setting. John said everything you wished you could have said on just about any subject, and he did it better than anyone I have known and in fewer and even funnier words. These valuable social skills empowered John to move about a room and generate considerable good will, resulting in party invitations and dates with attractive women. Still immature, I approached life with all my senses blazing. I was outspoken and daring in manner. I was living life and not observing it. It would be a long time and a lot of prodding and observation before I acquired his social skills. John was my initial teacher. He helped me grow immensely, albeit gradually and imperceptibly to many other people who knew me in 1954.

St. Patrick's Day

I looked forward with great anticipation to St. Patrick's Day. For New York Irish Catholics, March 17th is the most important day of the year, especially for young men and women coming of age. To this day, I remain astounded by the extreme level of foolishness, drunkenness, and amoral conduct tolerated in the name of the good saint. Don't get me wrong, in 1954 and for some years thereafter, I was one of the leading scorers in all categories of outlandish conduct on this great Irish day of celebration. We empowered ourselves with a special dispensation – a free pass without consequences.

1954 Adventures In New York

My initial St. Patrick's Day experience[38] was in 1948 when I marched in the great parade up 5th Avenue as a member of St. Joseph's Brigade. Though the St. Patrick's Day parade is merely a backdrop for gaiety and mischief for many people, participating in the parade was a wonderful experience. The brigade members assembled in St. Joseph's schoolyard, about 9:30 in the morning, dressed in our baby blue gabardine uniforms with maroon piping, matching overseas caps, and white cotton gloves. Since it was usually a brisk day, I always wore a pair of wool long johns.

We marched up 30th Avenue to Steinway Street and down the long two blocks past the early shoppers to Broadway, where we boarded a special train at the Steinway Street subway station. The train carried us close to the parade assembly site on 5th Avenue and 44th Street, where marching bands from all over the city and the surrounding areas congregated for hours waiting for our call to march.

Standing idly in the chilly air was a minor problem compared to the logistical challenge presented by thousands of young men and women desperate to relieve themselves before their units entered the parade. This was an era long before portable toilets were invented. If sympathetic building and restaurant owners didn't make their toilet facilities available, there would have been piss riots before the great parade. Once we started our march, the cold was easier to endure, though putting my lips to a piston bugle's mouthpiece in cold weather was always a challenge.

In my first two years, I played the bugle in the Brigade's 'B' Section. In the big parades we participated as the marching unit that preceded the 'A' Section musicians. The 'B' Section did participate, however, in band competitions throughout New York. When my skills improved, I joined the 'A' Section, where I played the piston bugle alongside fife and xylophone players, cymbalists, and the snare and base drummers. We did well as a unit

---

[38] I marched in three parades from 1948 through 1950.

in band competitions, and overall it was a great experience during the last few years of my grammar school days. One of the highlights came late in the 1948 presidential campaign, when I got a brief glimpse of President Harry S. Truman as I stood shivering in a cold rain on Queens Boulevard, near Lost Battalion Hall. The brigade members were happy to endure our two-hour wait in a continuous downpour since we had been told that if the Republican candidate, New York Governor Thomas E. Dewey, won the election, school would be mandatory on Saturdays.

A prime example of my risky behavior came during the 1950 St. Patrick's Day Parade when Mayor William O'Dwyer was under intense public scrutiny. Telephone taps revealed that top O'Dwyer appointees were implicated with Harry Gross, a Brooklyn bookmaker, who was using police officials as enforcers for his collections. It was a difficult time for Mayor O'Dwyer. As we approached the reviewing stand on 61st Street, I was marching on the Central Park side of 5th Avenue. Just before the 'A' Section began to play, I yelled out "Oh-da-wires are tapped." While the Mayor's associates laughed at my remarks, the Mayor smiled at me in a Cheshire-cat manner. A parade official reported the incident, and at the following week's Brigade meeting, Father O'Rourke, our mentor, lectured us on appropriate conduct at public events. As I left the classroom, O'Rourke cuffed me solidly on the side of my face and told me to watch myself in the future.[39] Much to my surprise, someone had informed on me. When Father O'Rourke informed Dad of my transgression, Dad thought it was creative thinking on my part and told all his cronies. He had learned through other channels that all but one parade official had found it amusing, though

---

[39] Much to my horror and disappointment, over 50 years later, in 2002, it would be revealed in the *New York Times* that Father O'Rourke, among other priests in the Diocese of Brooklyn, was a pedophile. O'Rourke had betrayed the trust and naiveté of a number of young men he had sexually molested. Thank God, I didn't see that side of him. The other young priests at St. Joseph's, Fathers Murphy, Scanlon and Rausch were wonderful guys. The Pastor, a sickly man, Father Ulick Buckley, was rarely seen.

inappropriate, that a fresh kid from Queens would publicly mock the beloved Mayor of New York.

Aside from being a day of music and drinking, Saint Patrick's Day was an important political event to express concerns about the ignominy of what was termed to be "The Irish Situation" – the long festering and unresolved problems with the English in Northern Ireland. Hundreds of large banners declaring "England Get Out of Ireland" were strategically placed and carried by members of the Ancient Order of Hibernians, labor unions, and social clubs. Overall, it was a joyous day, but a day when tempers could readily flare, especially after a few drinks, when most of the participants would be itching for a fight.

After work on that 1954 afternoon, John McComb and I started at the terminus of the parade in Yorkville and worked our way from bar to bar, picking up a growing crowd of friends from work, school, and our neighborhood. Even without much to drink we were all in good spirits given the friends we were with and the camaraderie we all shared on this great day.

At the Jaeger House, on 85th Street, the crowd was four or five deep from the bar to the tables on the opposite wall. The laughter and crowd noise was most appealing. Suddenly there was a scream. The friendly banter was stilled for an instant, then, quickly followed by curses, shouting, the scrambling of feet, the screeching movement of chair legs on the wooden floor, the tinkling of broken glass, and the sudden lurch of people moving towards the epicenter of the mayhem. John leaned over to me and nodding towards the girls we had been kidding with said, "I think we could make it with these girls, but my instincts tell me it's time to leave." Good advice, I thought and we made our way to the next watering hole, as we limbered up for a genuine Irish party on the West Side featuring corned beef and cabbage and other bland Irish dishes.

We arrived at a party room in the rear of a bar in Chelsea, in John's words, "to find a room full of genuine Irish lasses dressed in taffeta dresses, buttressed by numerous crinolines, with their hair styled in Toni Home Permanents." They were a sight to behold. Unfortunately, they had little interest in or patience with "narrow-backs," the term given to first and second generation Irish Americans. We in turn, referred to them as "greenhorns." While I was proud of my Irish heritage, I did not dwell on it. My people had been in the U.S. for over 100 years. The whole Irish thing was never a big deal with me, but on St. Patrick's Day everyone celebrated being Irish, even the non-Irish.

While John was dancing the Savoy with an attractive redhead, I noticed another girl with red hair standing alone on the far side of the room. Tall and slender, her eyes averted mine. I knew that girl. Yes, it was Mary Foley from the Boulevard Gardens, the sister of John and Pat Foley. They lived two floors below me in an identical five and a half-room apartment. Unlike her brothers, Mary didn't socialize in the neighborhood. I often saw her coming into and out of 'J' building and was always puzzled by her aloof manner. For reasons I couldn't figure she was mortified when she saw me. Sensing her embarrassment, I approached her cautiously and attempted to strike up a conversation. It was useless. Mary let me know with terse words, "I'll have nothing to do with the likes of you." That said, I took my leave and had an enjoyable time dancing with May Sheridan, a recent Irish immigrant who worked in Equitable's third floor file room. May was pretty, funny, observant and wise beyond her years. We would become good friends, and in the months to come I would enjoy many an interesting conversation with her. I left the party having developed a friend in May[40] and, at best, an indifferent neighbor in Mary.

The Savoy

On the subway ride home that night, I asked John, "Who was the good looking redhead you were dancing with?"

John told me her name. From this point forward I will identify her with the initials TG, meaning that girl.

"Where's she from?"

"Washington Heights, but she works at Equitable."

"Where? What floor?"

"The eighth floor."

"I've never seen her there."

"That's because she works far back over on the 32nd Street side."

"I've been through there, but I never noticed her."

"That's because you weren't looking for her."

"Why didn't you take her home?"

"It's like 11:30 and we have to work tomorrow."

"Are you serious about her?"

John smiled. "You sound interested. I'll tell her you're a great Savoy."

---

[40] During part of my time playing basketball at NYU in 1958-59, I would sometimes see May on Burnside or Jerome Avenues in the Bronx pushing her baby carriage with presumably her first of many children. I was going to and from basketball practice at NYU's Bronx campus at the top of Burnside Avenue. It was May who recognized me as I came down the steps of the elevated train station. She called out my name, and despite a lack of contact for almost four years, she began the conversation as if we had remained in constant touch. She expressed her delight that I was trying to make something of myself, and offered assistance in finding a girl from Ireland to help me along. I declined her offer, noting that I had to see my way through college and law school before entering the Holy Sacrament of Matrimony.

The Savoy, a derivation of the Lindy-Hop, was a dance that originated in Harlem's Savoy Ballroom in the 1930s. It was refined into a dance with smoother and less frenetic flow by white kids from the Inwood, Washington Heights and the Chelsea sections of Manhattan, Parkchester in the Bronx and the Woodside, Sunnyside, Jackson Heights, and Elmhurst sections in Queens. The Park Slope, a similar version of the Savoy, was danced in the Park Slope, Brooklyn Heights and the Bay Ridge sections of Brooklyn.

You could dance the Savoy to music paced at a variety of tempos.[41] Done correctly, it looks effortless, though the girl does most of the work. A guy or girl who mastered the dance was referred to as a good or a great Savoy. Such a status increased your popularity and made it easier to obtain dances, which led to dates.

John Mc Comb taught Drew Doyle, Jack Schneider, Bob Perite, me, and other friends the basic steps in the P.S. 151 schoolyard at night, and over a period of weeks we mastered the dance. We traveled to Blondell's, a bar in the Parkchester section of the Bronx, to watch the master, Bobby Van Horn, dance the night away. If you could keep up with the Inwood or Parkchester girls, you were certified as a good Savoy.

In the summer months in Rockaway Beach, East Durham and the New Jersey Shore, and in the fall and winter at beer rackets or dances at the Jaeger House in Manhattan or Ascension Parish in Elmhurst, Queens, the guys and girls from the Savoy neighborhoods would come together, dance and drink until the function ended or the bar closed.

---

[41] The Savoy begins with a couple standing side-by-side, the guy on the left and the girl on the right, with their arms placed around each other's waist. They push off in a counter-clockwise motion for momentum before the girl is released and moves away from her partner, who maintains loose contact while holding her right hand in his left hand. When their arms are fully extended, she plants her back foot and springs back to him. He can either gather her in his arms and spin her out again, or improvise with deft movements featuring hand twirls, twisting and passing behind the other before returning to the original side-by-side circling movement where it would all begin again, until the dance number played out.

An Experienced Girl

As I came into the cafeteria, a few days after St. Patrick's Day, I spotted an attractive redhead on the food line. As I got closer to the line I realized it was TG. My heart began to pound. She was dressed in a green plaid skirt topped off with a cream colored sweater that highlighted her red hair. She looked perfect.

"Hi, I'm Neal Gillen – John McComb's friend. I saw you dancing with him at the party on the West Side the other night."

Pausing, she stared at me quizzically for what seemed like an eternity. "My name's TG. Are you new here?"

I nodded , "Yeah, sort of."

How long have you been working here?"

"I started a few weeks ago. I don't know if John told you, but I'm a good Savoy."

As soon as the words left my mouth I felt like a jerk. Looking at me like I was the Mad Hatter, she pulled her tray away from the cafeteria line and began to move towards the cashier. Just then, Ace Corcoran approached us and said, "Hey, TG, is Neal trying to get into your pants?"

Blushing from her embarrassment, TG bit her lower lip as she winced to hold back the tears resulting from Ace's insulting words.

"No, Ace. We're having a pleasant conversation about a mutual friend, and a great party," I responded.

At that, she took my arm, "Please sit with me. I hate that creep." We paid for our lunch and moved towards a table. "That guy's a loudmouth, always insulting people. The girls on my floor avoid him. He's an animal."

Seconds later, the Ace was hovering over our table.

"Hey, is she making a move on you, Neal?"

I cautiously raised my thin frame from my chair, and with my arms akimbo stood my ground as Ace tried to intimidate me. "Have some respect," I said. He gave off one of his throaty laughs, "heh - heh - heh," while he calculated how he would handle my insolence.

"So, we have some lovebirds who don't want to be disturbed." Pointing his finger at me he said, "I'll talk to you later about this," before he turned and walked away.

"Sure Ace, I'll see you later."

As I sat down and was wondering what his next move might be, TG smiled warmly. "Thanks. You put him in his place," she said, reaching across the table to touch my hand. I blushed and smiled meekly.

I was smitten. In my eyes she was perfect, about five feet seven with a terrific figure - long thin legs, a small waist, and large breasts. Her silky red hair, olive skin, and hazel green eyes were an exotic combination. On top of that, she had a pleasant personality and was a good conversationalist.

As I listened to her that day, I soon learned that she was raised in a strict Catholic environment, though she was reluctant to talk about her family or her upper Manhattan neighborhood. In the weeks ahead, we would see each other in the cafeteria and engage in friendly conversation. There were few, if any, applications to search for in her work area, so I had little reason to venture there. One afternoon, while passing through TG's department, I stopped to say hello as she was working away at her desk.

"Do you smoke?" she asked.

"Sure, Chesterfield's. Would you like one?"

She nodded her head and smiled. Then, she stood up and stretched her arms out and along the side of her body as she hunched her shoulders in. Her smile widened as she drew her arms back. In doing so her sweater pulled taut over her large breasts. Aroused, I felt myself blushing at this marvelous sight when she asked, "Would you like to take a break?"

Is the Pope Catholic? I followed her to the fire stairs in the back of her department. She walked up two flights of this rarely used stair well, before she stopped. She sat down and beckoned me to sit beside her. In short order, we were kissing, and soon we were groping and grabbing. This was far more exciting than joy riding – I couldn't believe what was happening. She was both affectionate and permissive leaving little to my sexual imagination though my brain was not in control of the situation.

Gay Talese, in his successful novel, *Thy Neighbor's Wife*,[42] discussed D.H. Lawrence's erotic writing in *Lady Chatterly's Lover*,[43] noting that this vital instrument of manhood "does indeed seem to have a will of its own, an ego beyond its size, and is frequently embarrassing because of its needs, infatuations, and unpredictable nature." This was certainly true for me that afternoon.

This unexpected session with TG took my breath away, arousing as much fear as it did lust – if we were discovered, it would be embarrassing, and probably cost us our jobs. Until that moment, it never occurred to me that there were more things to do on the back stairs of the Equitable building than smoking a cigarette or watching a Slinky make its way down the stairs.

This was an era of the good girl and bad girl standard. You couldn't get anywhere with good girls so you didn't try. You dated them for a long time, and gradually became familiar with their bodies, without going all the way. The solution to the ultimate mystery came on the wedding night. Bad girls were another story. The prevailing male ethic was you dated a good girl and did the things you wouldn't dare to do with your good girl with a bad girl. At the time, I didn't have a good girl, so, there were no concerns about a conflict of interest or being faithful. Nor, did I worry about the sinful

---

[42] Doubleday, 1981.
[43] Tipografia Giuntina, 1928.

nature of my conduct other than to think that I would be a happier and more devout Catholic if such conduct were encouraged. So, unconcerned about religious beliefs and having nothing to hide from another girl, I decided to get involved with TG in a big way.

If anything, she was possessive. As I partook of the forbidden fruit with increased frequency she expected more of my presence at her side during lunch. I had no problems with that since the pleasure she was providing was unlike anything I had ever experienced.

My only concern was that we had aroused the suspicions of the observant Ace Corcoran. This raised the possibility of a physical confrontation. The Ace's comments combined the cute and the obscene ranging from "How are the love birds today?" to "Are you using protective devices?" No one else had anything to say, except Artie Wassen, who knew TG from his Manhattan neighborhood. He confided to me that her older brother was probably the toughest guy in the neighborhood, if not all of Manhattan. Artie advised me to be careful in my relationship. Needless to say, I valued and followed Artie's advice.

TG and I began to date on an increasing basis, including more torrid and sexually fulfilling meetings on the stairs, and then Friday night sessions at the Little Penn Tavern, next to the alley entrance of St. Francis of Assisi Church on 32nd Street, where Franciscan Friars held confession around the clock. They were the most forgiving I have ever encountered. "Sin in the Little Penn or the Hotel Pennsylvania and confess next door," we used to say. Regardless of the severity of the sins you confessed, the maximum penance was usually three Our Father's and three Hail Mary's. We joked that the penance for murder was no more than 10 recitations of the aforementioned prayers, while a multiple murder would probably get you a rosary.

At the Little Penn, TG and I would snuggle in a back booth or dance before taking in a movie. It had a large selection of great songs on its jukebox, and we would clutch each other closely dancing to either the Sammy Davis or Rosemary Clooney renditions of *Hey There*.[44] As luck would have it, one night a new bartender carded me. I produced the draft card of a neighborhood friend who had recently been inducted into the Army. TG was aghast.

"How old are you?"

"I thought you knew, I'm 17," I lied.

TG was almost 19. If she realized she was dating a 16-year-old, she never would have spoken to me again. Worse yet, she was unaware that I was attending "Continuation School" every Wednesday morning until I was 17.

One Friday night, TG and I had drinks with a group at the Little Penn followed by a pizza, and then it was off to Radio City Music Hall to see the classic film, *Gone with the Wind*. The Margaret Mitchell Civil War saga was re-released after sitting dormant since its spectacular Atlanta debut in 1939. The huge and classic art deco theatre was crowded with couples equally enthralled with each other and this epic story. TG was particularly warm and inviting that night.

We were wrapped in each other's arms watching bits of the film between our own passionate kisses. Suddenly, her breath went rancid; her eyes rolled back, and out of her mouth gushed the remnants of a pizza with mushrooms and sausage and a few pitchers of beer. The good news was that I was sitting at the end of the row. The bad news was that each of us was drenched in her vomit. We made our way to our respective rest rooms, while those who were seated around us made their way to seats outside the range of the putrid smell. We cleaned up, left the theatre, and walked

---

[44] *"Hey There,"* from *"Pajama Game,"* written by George Abbott.

around to dry off, before I took her home on the subway to Washington Heights.

Following this incident, our mutual embarrassment cooled our ardor somewhat and we assiduously avoided each other – though I sorely missed the pleasure she provided in our staircase encounters.

7

The Strike Is Over

The end of the longest and costliest dock strike in New York history was good news for many families in the Gardens, including the Daggett's, Connelly's, Clark's, Ryan's, McGrade's, and the Murphy's. The wage issues that precipitated the March 3rd walkout were finally resolved on April 2nd, when many families were at their wits end given their limited resources. The settlement was hammered out just before the strike fund of the International Longshoreman's Association (ILA) was depleted.

Longshoremen were gritty, down to earth people – tough and enduring individuals with a surprisingly bright outlook on life. They worked cargo with their powerful hands and strong backs in a dangerous work environment because their fathers and grandfathers did so before them. The dockworkers who lived in our neighborhood were determined that their children would not follow them down to the piers. They were well paid, but if they were injured on the job, their families suffered since workers' compensation benefits were considerably lower than their wages. Most worked regularly, but it was always a struggle dealing with a corrupt shape-up system that required workers to pay tribute if they wanted to work. It was a work environment where looking the other way was part of the culture. Devoted to their families, they somehow managed to survive from paycheck-to-paycheck. They also were prone to the Irish disease, and when times were tough at home or on the docks, the weaker individuals would go on a bender.

After the first week of the strike, when it became apparent that no resolution was in sight, Dad lined up temporary jobs at construction sites in

Manhattan for Harold Daggett, Peter Clark, Red Connelly, and others through the Operating Engineers Union. Dad felt an obligation to help his friends since they had large families to support. This was the ethic of his generation – helping others during hard times. For years to come I could do no wrong in the eyes of these men because of the helping hand that Dad had extended.

In a few years, Daggett[45] and Clark would be part of the initial ILA crews working the new containerships in Port Newark, New Jersey.[46] Harold Daggett, Sr. was a large man with a heart of gold who grew up on the streets of "Hell's Kitchen" on Manhattan's West Side with Frank McGuire[47], the legendary basketball coach.

A few months later, Mr. Daggett, always appreciative of Dad's efforts to find work for him and others in trying times, was quick to return the favor when Dad's bragging led Daggett to inform his good friend McGuire that I was a good basketball prospect. Daggett innocently misinformed McGuire that I was the next Bob Cousy. Sure enough, Coach McGuire

---

[45] Today, Harold Daggett, Jr. is president of the ILA. In 2004, he was falsely accused and indicted at the urging of an overzealous federal prosecutor for an alleged attempt to steer union health and welfare benefit contracts to a company with ties to organized crime. At a well-publicized trial in November 2005, a federal jury in Brooklyn found Daggett and his co-defendants innocent of all charges. Testifying in his own behalf, Daggett defended himself in dramatic fashion, telling the jury of a threat on his life by a mafia capo resulting from his efforts to move a union office from Manhattan to New Jersey. The trauma of recalling the story had Daggett and a majority of the jury in tears. At one point in his cross-examination, Daggett parried with the Assistant U.S. Attorney only to be admonished by the judge to limit his answers. Daggett told the judge that since so many false things had been said about him, he wanted to get the truth out for the jury. After the unanimous verdicts were delivered, declaring him innocent, Daggett asked reporters outside the Federal Courthouse, "What doorway do I have to go through to get my reputation back?"

[46] Malcolm McClain, a North Carolina truck operator, developed this revolutionary concept by initially converting surplus World War II Liberty Ships from break bulk carriers into containerships that now carry the bulk of the world's ocean going cargo.

[47] McGuire led St. John's University to the NCAA Championship Game in 1952 only to lose a closely contested game to the University of Kansas. In 1957, McGuire turned the tables on Kansas, and its seven-foot star – Wilt "The Stilt" Chamberlin, when his North Carolina team beat Kansas for the championship in a thrilling triple overtime game. New Yorkers – Tommy Kearns, Pete Brennan, Lennie Rosenbluth, Joe Quigg, and Stan Groll dominated the North Carolina squad.

called and invited me to come and visit Chapel Hill. Flabbergasted and embarrassed, I made it clear to him that my skill levels in neighborhood play did not merit his attention.[48]

Indicative of how desperate the situation was for some Longshoremen was an incident during the 1954 strike that Dad reported to us at dinner one night. He heard the story from a friend who lived in the West Side neighborhood where the incident took place. As Dad related the story, a brooding man sat drinking in a West Side bar for a few hours, apparently working on his courage. Finally, when the crowd thinned, he called the bartender over and pointed to a brown paper bag he had placed on the bar. "Feel that," he asked the bartender, who in doing so touched the outline of a handgun. The patron withdrew the bag, stuck the gun into the inside pocket of his jacket, and handed the bag and a $5 bill to the bartender. He instructed the bartender to put two bottles of beer into the bag, and for his change to fill the bag with all the money from the cash register. The bartender reluctantly complied and handed him the bag. The man then asked the bartender for the contents of his tip glass. The bartender did as he was told and the hard up patron then walked back to the telephone booths near the men's room. Adjacent to the booths was a shelf holding the Manhattan telephone directory. Looking directly at the bartender, he

---

[48] During my Navy service, my basketball ability improved considerably - I was a consistent high scorer and rebounder in inter-service competition in the Far East and Europe. In 1958, following my discharge from the Navy, Mr. Daggett arranged for me to call Coach McGuire in North Carolina. McGuire was a persuasive individual and almost had me convinced that I was a better player than my skills indicated. I informed him that I had decided to attend New York University. It proved to be a great choice, despite my limited, but enjoyable experience in its basketball program. McGuire was gracious in our conversation and wished me well. Two years after our phone conversation I was working at the scorer's table in Madison Square Garden, during a New York Knick's game, when McGuire stopped by to say hello to a sports writer. I reintroduced myself and he recalled our earlier conversations. "How are you doing at NYU and how is Harold Daggett?" he asked. The man had a tremendous memory and was a born charmer. He made me feel like the most important person in the Garden that afternoon.

inserted the individual bills from the tip glass between different pages of the directory along with a few bills from the till. On his way out, he stopped, shook hands with the bartender and said, "I took care of you, now you take care of me. Don't make any calls for 10 minutes or you'll regret it."

When two uniformed police officers arrived, they questioned the bartender about the incident. Shortly thereafter, two detectives from the Robbery Squad arrived, one an old pro and the other a freshly minted Detective Third Grade. The veteran detective asked the uniformed patrolmen what they knew about the incident. The identification information was ambiguous and inconsistent. He motioned the patrolmen and his partner down to the end of the bar where another patron overheard the following discussion:

"Let's cut to the chase boys, the bartender probably knows the perp."

"How can that be?" One of the patrolmen asked.

"There's a fucking dock strike in progress, that's how it can be. These men have families to feed and rent to pay. These things happen when people are desperate," the veteran detective responded.

"The bartender will tell you it was a six foot four colored guy, the guy at the end of the bar will swear it was a five foot six Puerto Rican, and the guy in the middle of the bar will tell you it was Emmett Kelly, the clown from the Ringling Brothers' Circus. Let the insurance company figure it out, because we never will."

The BGTA Variety Show

A good portion of my spare time in March was devoted to rehearsals for the first ever Boulevard Gardens Tenants Association (BGTA) Variety Show. Bernie Duffy, the veritable spark plug of the Gardens and the father of a large outgoing family, produced the show. Bernie coached baseball and basketball, was an editor of the *Boulevard Gardens Beacon*, and an announcer at numerous events. Simply put, he was a likeable, outgoing, and well-organized person who continually contributed to the Gardens' community. In a month of rehearsals, he successfully organized 47 teenagers of limited talent into a competent, closely-knit, well-coordinated group of entertainers.

It was one of the most enjoyable experiences of my life up to that time, but more importantly it brought the Gardens' community together and demonstrated to young people what could be accomplished by working in concert. I was reluctant at first to get involved, but John McComb encouraged me to do it one night on the subway coming home from work. I signed up not knowing what to expect. Like the other guys my age, we were pretty much into sports, but some of us had still not fully accepted the team concept – we were still trying to get the critical hit, score the winning basket, or catch the touchdown pass for our own self-glorification and not necessarily that of the team. We rationalized our individual gratification and/or achievement as important to the team achieving victory.

I quickly found out that chorus and dance doesn't work that way. I knew a little about dance from the times I'd take my sisters to dancing school. I would wait outside for them in the adjoining alley. One day a sudden thunderstorm brought on a deluge of rain. The dance instructor invited me into the basement studio to dry off. The next thing I knew I was tap dancing to *Shuffle Off to Buffalo*. Though a pretty good dancer, I was tone deaf and couldn't sing for my life. Being in step was one thing, but for me, being in key was far more difficult. Everyone has to be in key and in step or the whole number bombs.

More importantly, for most of us, this was a social experiment on a grand scale, since this was our initial experience as young men and women working together outside our family units. It was Mars meeting Venus as part of a joint venture.

Despite having three sisters, I never realized how well girls worked together. They submerged their egos and made an honest effort to cooperate and get along. All the guys were puzzled at first until the realization set in that the girls were serious role players. We quickly got our egos in check, followed their example, and things began to jell after the first rehearsal. The girls set the pace and together we learned how to function successfully as a team.

As a result of participating in that activity, I began to realize that I grew up with a marvelous group of young men and women. Except for Joseph McGrath, who went on to be a professional singer, almost all the performers were either tone deaf or couldn't carry a tune. Betty Quinn, the first girl I found pleasing to the eye when the age of discovery arrived, though I never caught her eye, made a great effort and succeeded in singing a good rendition of *My Wonderful Alice Blue Gown* – a difficult song to carry off.

Despite our handicaps, we worked tirelessly in preparing ourselves for two sell-outs shows on April 9th and 10th.

The setting for the production was the home of Joe Carlton, a Broadway showman played by Bernie Duffy, who volunteered to help the mythical town's young people stage a review. As a member of the chorus, I got to sing the opening and closing numbers. My big moment came near the end of the show when eight of us[49] sang a popular song, of World War I vintage, called *Dearie*. The positive audience reaction made all the practice worth the effort.

The Variety Show was a positive experience and a turning point for me – a kid prone to do reckless things mainly to seek attention. It was a magical experience. When you are performing on the stage you are

---

[49] Rosaleen Harkin, Diane Schenkein, Terry Roughan, Carol Wright, Donald Stapelton, William Alexander, Drew Doyle and I.

something larger than yourself – it's a unique realization – a total high that provides one with a sense of self-esteem. The involvement pulled me towards others attempting to do something positive and constructive. I am forever grateful to Bernie Duffy for making that experience possible. Outside of sports, I had never worked in such an uplifting venture. The success of the Variety Show gave me new confidence and helped me in the process of changing my errant ways. It also grounded me to that place – the Boulevard Gardens. Further, my familiarity with one of the songs, *You Belong to Me*, would place me on stage a few months later.

Easter

Except for Ace Cochran, 1954 was the last year of the pegged pants and one-button roll suit jacket era. It was also the first time that my Easter suit wasn't fitted at the Boy's & Men's Shop on Steinway Street in Astoria, where many of my suits had been purchased over the years going back to my First Communion outfit – a blue suit with knickers. I wore a pair of blue corduroy knickers to school every day until I made my Confirmation, when I transitioned to long corduroy pants.

This time I made my wardrobe selection without the guidance of Mother. My fashion advisor was Joe Gianinni, a sharp dresser who I wanted to emulate. Joe guided me to a men's store on 6th Avenue and 31st Street, where $20 produced a suit with two pairs of pants.

Dad thought it was a prudent purchase while Mother, obviously resentful that I had broken the family's Boy's & Men's Shop tradition, commented, "You should think more about quality than some two pair of pants gimmick." In point of fact the, 31st Street suit was just as good, if not better, than an overpriced Steinway Street suit. The man who owned the Boy's & Men's Shop was into racehorses – there were racetrack photos lining the walls in all of the dressing rooms.

"It's time we stopped feeding that Jew son-of-bitch's goddamned horses," Dad declared.

"That's a terrible thing to say. He's a fine man. His religion has nothing to do with this," Mother responded.

"Well, every time I try something on in that place I feel like I'm feeding his goddamned horses."

"At least he doesn't spend his money in bars."

"What's that supposed to mean?"

"It's something about glass houses and stones – so be careful mister big-shot about being critical of others."

I buy a new suit and pretty soon I'm in a war zone.

It was a two-button, charcoal gray suit that I spiffed up with a pink shirt and a dark tie for the jazz-club look. Using a white shirt and a striped tie I affected the collegiate look. The extra pants gave me another item in my everyday wardrobe since we didn't wear suits to work. I completed my ensemble with an obvious fashion mistake, but the current fad – a new pair of $12, square-toed, Flagg Brothers' shoes.

The night before Easter, some in our crowd got the idea that we should wear our new suits and take the bus to the Palisades Amusement Park in New Jersey. It proved to be a bad idea. The hordes of girls we envisioned promenading in their Easter finery never materialized. They probably checked the weather, which we didn't. We arrived to an open but empty amusement venue in a chilly and brisk wind and light rain. There were about ten of us – Tom and Roger Kealey, Milton Russ, Dominic Pressamone, Kenny Ernst, Freddie Siegel, Frankie Brannigan, and Tom Kilty. We rode the roller coaster for almost an hour, and the grateful attendant treated us to a few free rides. We won teddy bears, stuffed dogs and other useless junk throwing baseballs and shooting baskets, ate junk food, and ruined our new suits in the rain. There would be hell to pay from our mothers when we got ready for Easter Sunday Mass the next morning.

By the time we left the amusement park a little after nine that night, another 20 or so people came on the scene. Not a single girl our age materialized, and the few women on the premises were escorted by their dates. On the bus ride back to Manhattan, an unsuccessful attempt was made to determine the identity of the originator of the dumb-ass idea to visit the Palisades. There were numerous recriminations about our poor choice and regrets that we didn't visit Harold Minsky's Burlesque Theatre in Union City to see Lili St. Cyr – the statuesque stripper. My preference was to visit one of my favorite haunts, Hubert's Theatre, on 42nd Street, which we did when we arrived back at the Port Authority Bus Terminal.

Then a hurly-burly thoroughfare of penny arcades, pawn shops, rowdy bars, cheap food joints, and theatres featuring lurid films, 42nd Street was peopled with pitch-men, con-men, pimps, prostitutes, pickpockets, voyeurs, drifters, servicemen, curious tourists, and hundreds of kids from all over the city seeking fun like us. Simply put, it was a place that someone of circumspection would avoid, but one that young New Yorkers loved to frequent for the sheer joy and the sense of adventure it provided.

Hubert's was the main attraction on 42nd Street. It featured the Ripley's Believe It-Or-Not Odditorium, Roy Heckler's Flea Circus, which used real but barely visible fleas, and the star of the show, Albert/Alberta, an alleged hermaphrodite. Billed as the half-man and half-woman, the barker claimed that Albert/Alberta possessed the sex organs of both a man and a woman, and "this would be revealed before your very eyes." This androgynous exhibitionist was undoubtedly the homeliest person in Manhattan.

Though we knew Albert/Alberta was a scam, we came time and again because of the skillful showmanship of the whole operation. What you actually saw was one male breast and what appeared to be a female breast. Though the police were concerned about partial nudity or a lascivious attraction designed to stimulate prurient interests, the Albert/Alberta show had clear sailing since it comported with the legal standard. One could say it was more about obesity than obscenity. It was strictly clinical and designed to arouse curiosity, rather than sexual interests. Hubert's Theatre was a successful operation that lasted for over 50 years, until change came to 42nd Street when Rudy Giuliani was elected Mayor in 1994.

McCarthy Spoils the Work Routine

In April, along with virtually everyone else, I got caught up in the Army-McCarthy hearings that dominated both the neighborhood's and the nation's attention. Joseph McCarthy, a Republican senator from Wisconsin, was a hero to every Irish American in our neighborhood and at Equitable Life.

In 1952, McCarthy began a campaign to root out communists reportedly employed in Federal Government agencies. In a speech in West Virginia, he claimed to possess a list of some 20 Communist Party members employed in the State Department. Though the main-line media generally ignored McCarthy's charges at that time, Russia's subsequent release of its KGB Venona Files in the early 1990s verified that U.S. civil servants, employed in the Treasury, Commerce, and State Departments during the late 1930s through the early 1950s were Soviet agents.

Fueled with information from Father Edmund Walsh, S.J., the founder of Georgetown University's School of Foreign Service, McCarthy went on an extended crusade, which culminated in hearings on alleged subversion in the Army Signal Corps. McCarthy charged that the Department of the Army, then headed by the textile magnate Robert Stevens of J.P. Stevens & Company, was hampering the Senate Permanent Investigations

Subcommittee's effort to uncover subversion. Secretary of the Army Stevens counter-charged that McCarthy and his counsel, Roy Cohn, had tried to pressure the Army into giving preferential treatment to a former Subcommittee staff member, G. David Shine. Shine, then serving in the Army, was rumored to be Cohn's lover.

Though I originally possessed an open mind on the issue, it was my maternal grandfather's influence that swung me against this bellowing bully. James McPartland was one of 11 children whose parents emigrated from County Leitrim, Ireland in the 1880s. He was patient, a good listener, and an exceptional judge of people. Further, though slight of frame, he wasn't afraid to take up the cause of the underdog. Taking sides against McCarthy in a neighborhood bar or in a street corner gathering could quickly provoke a fight. Most Catholics were behind McCarthy 100 percent, and many Americans were xenophobic about the communist, "commies," or the "commie pinko's."

My instincts told me that McCarthy was a wild man, but I kept my opinions to myself as the daily drama of the hearings played out. If you spoke out against him, you risked being branded a "commie sympathizer."

Dad was a McCarthy idolizer and a fan of Father Coughlin, a pro-Nazi anti-semite Catholic priest who influenced millions of hopeless Americans from his Detroit pulpit and radio show in the Depression years of the 1930s. Dad fit Damon Runyon's description of his own father "who was tolerant of the opinions of others only when he found those opinions coinciding with his own." [50] Dad's attitude on any number of subjects, particularly race, religion and politics, were not accepted by anyone else in the family, least of all me.

The arguments were heated. Dad's were reduced to "he's our kind, so he must be right," while Grandpa Jim was calm and unemotional in his

---

[50] *"The Tolerant Few"* from *"Short Takes"* at page 56, Whittlesey House, 1946.

approach, noting that the only things McCarthy seemed to be accomplishing "were raising hell and ruining people." After Grandpa Jim and I watched the CBS television special, *Edward R. Murrow Reports on Senator Joseph McCarthy*,[51] which exposed McCarthy as a faker – we were convinced that McCarthy and his henchman Roy Cohn were certifiably evil. Murrow effectively used excerpts from McCarthy's own speeches and proclamations to criticize the senator and to demonstrate where he had contradicted himself. Murrow provided McCarthy with the opportunity to respond two weeks later in an appearance on Murrow's popular show, *See It Now*. McCarthy came off poorly. His botched effort to defend himself added credence to Murrow's original report.

Given my own, and the general public's interest in the hearings, I often drifted from my fellow application chasers and planted myself in front of a television in an appliance store on 32nd Street, near Herald Square. The hearings would begin at 10 a.m., break for lunch at noon, and reconvene at 2 p.m. Almost all of the television stations broadcasting in the New York metropolitan area covered the event. Channels 5 and 7 covered the hearings live, and every night at 11:30, Channel 2 would run "Highlights" of the day's hearings. If this weren't enough, at midnight, Channel 4 would run a "Recap" of the day's hearing. Given the saturation coverage, virtually every New Yorker had an opinion about McCarthy. His charges were the number one issue of the day.

The hearings and the extensive media coverage went on for months until Joseph Welch, a kindly and wizened Boston trial lawyer representing the Department of the Army deflated McCarthy's balloon. The dramatic turnabout came when McCarthy attempted to impugn the integrity of Fred Fisher, a young attorney on Welch's staff for his membership in the ultra-liberal (some would say left-wing) Lawyer's Guild, while he was a student at

---

[51] The program aired on March 9, 1954.

Harvard Law School. Welsh couldn't countenance what he perceived to be an unfair attack. With consummate skill he found the perfect time to make his move when McCarthy paused during his slanderous meanderings. Welsh seized the moment with his famous plea, which soon became part of America's collective consciousness: "Until this moment, Senator, I think I have never really gauged your cruelty or your recklessness." When McCarthy tried to continue his attack, Welsh responded, "Have you no sense of decency, sir,? At long last, have you left no sense of decency?"[52]

The hushed audience burst into applause, drowning out the subcommittee chairman's call for order. At that dramatic moment, given the growing influence of television,[53] public sentiment made a seismic shift. Overnight, the public formed the opinion that McCarthy was a craven opportunist interested solely in destroying people's reputations for the sake of satisfying his insatiable desire for publicity. Welch became a national hero, and McCarthy's political career was destroyed. His witch hunting days were over. It would take some months, but eventually the Senate sanctioned McCarthy, who drank himself to death within three years.

The term "McCarthyism" was coined, and to this day it is used to describe false or reckless political charges. The late Richard H. Estabrook, the editorial page editor of *The Washington Post,* wrote on McCarthy's death, "his monument is a noun that has come to be a synonym for reckless slander. His memory cannot be divorced from a trail of shattered careers and groveling agencies, of cultivated suspicions that set Americans blindly against Americans, of a humiliating debasement of American's standing in the free world."

---

[52] June 9, 1954, U.S. Senate, Committee on Government Operations, Special Senate Investigation on Charges and Countercharges Involving Secretary of the Army Robert T. Stevens, John G. Adams, H. Struve Hensel and Senator Joe McCarthy, Roy M. Cohn, and Francis P. Carr, 83rd Cong., 2nd Sess., part 59 (Washington: U.S. Government Printing Office, 1954), pp 2429.

[53] On that day, an estimated 29 million American homes owned television sets.

Though politically finished and lacking credibility in the national media, McCarthy remained a hero for many years in the Irish Catholic neighborhoods of New York City. This in itself was a political anomaly, as these neighborhoods were then populated with rock-solid "New Deal Democrats." McCarthy's religion and his ancestry were the real reasons they strongly supported this conservative Midwest Republican. Certainly there was a fear of Communism, but it was McCarthy's ethnicity and religion that led them to believe in him. The Irish were with him on his way up, on his way out, and long after he died an ignominious and very Irish death from cirrhosis of the liver in 1957. Roy Cohn, his key advisor, died of AIDs in 1986.

The Irish are particularly good at holding grudges. This one lasted for over half a century. When McCarthy's name came up in a neighborhood tavern it was best to remain silent, as criticism usually provoked a heated argument or fist fight. To me, McCarthy was a troubled man who was reckless in his charges. I didn't fully understand the politics or the emotion of the time, but I had been taught at St. Joseph's that Communism, Godless Communism, was our mortal enemy and anyone involved in the movement was not to be trusted. That's what I was told and that's what I believed. It was all about Stalin and spies. Despite the uproar over the McCarthy hearings, I was listening carefully, observing what was happening around me, and enjoying every minute of it.

Interesting events were taking place everywhere, particularly in Washington, but for me New York, particularly Manhattan Island, was proving to be a veritable feast. John McComb, Joe Gianinni, and a girl from Washington Heights were my invitations to partake in this grand buffet of visible and sensual delights. Manhattan, for me, was right in sync with John O'Hara's description:[54] "working and living in New York suited his attitude of defenseless optimism. New York would take care of the newcomer." That was certainly true in my case.

---

[54] Draft introduction to the 1960 reprint of *"Butterfield 8,"* Vanity Fair, p. 56 August 2003.

8

Joe Gianinni

Joe Gianinni was a born leader. He was highly intelligent, funny, energetic, poised, well-dressed, and a total delight to be with. He had all the requisites for success and he carried himself as if he had arrived.

Joe lived in the Kingsbridge section of the Bronx near Manhattan College. Joe's father died of cancer in 1953 and his remaining family was closely knit. He had a great troupe of friends, including a guy by the name of Fred, an up-and-coming drummer schooling with the legendary Gene Krupa. Missing an eye, he went by the name "One-eye Freddie." I hate to think what would've happened if I called my father "One-Eye Patty."

Joe was a music aficionado who particularly enjoyed jazz and regularly followed the leading performers. I missed a great opportunity when I declined his invitation to attend Alan Freed's initial Rock & Roll Concert on May 1st at the National Guard Armory in Newark.

Ace Cochran told Joe, "Ain't nobody goin to Jersey to hear that jive-ass shit."

Was he ever wrong – 10,000 people showed up. Joe said it was a "blast." All you heard on the radio for the next few weeks was Rock and Roll. Alan Freed was onto something, and overnight he became the principal figure in contemporary music. From his perch at radio station *WINS*, he dominated the New York airwaves and heavily influenced our taste in music with his show, *The Rock 'n' Roll Party*.

Joe introduced me to a number of great jazz clubs in Manhattan. One Friday night, along with One-eye Freddie, we went to the Band Box to hear Louis "Satchmo" Armstrong. Upon our arrival, we met Joe Louis, the former heavy weight boxing champion. Waiting to be seated, we talked to him for almost 10 minutes. While the Champ was friendly, he was not particularly verbal. It didn't take long to realize that Joe Louis, a nice person, was far from being a rocket scientist. I immediately understood why he was easily cheated out of a large portion of the money he had won over the years.

Louis Armstrong was unforgettable. Freddie's budding celebrity status earned us front row seating to the right of the piano, where Armstrong was positioned. We watched and listened to him play and sing continuously in a set that began with his favorite song, *It's Sleepy Time Down South*. An hour later, he concluded with one of my favorites, *When the Saints Come Marching In*. Armstrong kept a stack of handkerchiefs on top of the piano and went through about 15 of them, wiping his sweaty brow and the spittle from his trumpet. On other occasions we visited Birdland to hear Dizzie Gillespie and some of the other great jazz joints on 52nd Street, including Jimmy Ryan's and Eddie Condon's.

Joe dated Mary Byre, an attractive girl with long blond hair. She was a fun person to be with, and she adored Joe. He was still seeing her six years later while I was in college. I have no idea if they ever married, but they were ideally suited for each other. During our time at Equitable, Joe may have looked at and joked about other girls, but his sole focus was Mary.

Joe drove a maroon 1953 Mercury convertible and on a few occasions during the workday he treated his co-workers to a drive. We took excursions to the Cloisters in upper Manhattan, the Bronx Zoo and other sites in the Bronx and Manhattan, including Ace Corcoran's neighborhood in East Harlem.

The visit to East Harlem served two purposes. Ace claimed it served the best pizza in New York and he bragged that gambling was such an integral part of the neighborhood's culture that anyone on the street could give you the winning "number" – the last three numbers of the total dollars bet at the New York track racing that day. It was published in the late afternoon newspapers.

We drove up to 116th Street and Second Avenue, and during our wait for the afternoon papers we enjoyed a delicious pizza, which we agreed qualified as New York's best. Then, we conducted the numbers test. Joe and Ace argued about who would ask the passers-by. We agreed it would be Joe. Coming up the street was a 10 or 11 year-old, dark-haired kid in a raggedy pair of pants, ratty-looking sneakers, and no shirt. Joe sized him up, stopped him and asked, "Hey kid, you know today's number?"

The kid looked up at Joe and shook his head. "Whatta you fucking dumb or something – the fucking number's 397." He kept walking up the street, looking back at us like we were hicks from upstate.

The Ace, beaming with pride that East Harlem had passed its second test, said, "I told you guys my neighborhood's tops." From that day forward, the Ace always reminded us how sophisticated things were in East Harlem.

Continuation School

I celebrated my 17th birthday on Friday, May 14th. Dad took the entire family and Grandpa Jim to the Elks Club on Queens Boulevard for dinner, a rare occasion. Better yet, no serious arguments developed during the meal.

That Wednesday was my last day of Continuation School at Queens Vocational High School. The concept of Continuation School still bothers me. It was designed for young men and women who quit school at 16 to join the work force. We were required to return to school for a half-day each week, in the hope that we would recommit ourselves to finishing our academic studies. Though I had completed the necessary high school academic requirements, and was taking two additional courses at night to obtain a New York State Regents Diploma, the employment regulations mandated that I attend. It was my first "Catch 22" experience in life.

What we did at Queens Vocational High School was academically meaningless. The students filed into the building at 8:45 in the morning and reported to the Continuation School classroom, where attendance was taken. We were presented with two choices, the woodworking or automotive shops. No discussions about completing high school – just make a choice, put in the time, and don't cause any trouble.

Initially, I choose the woodworking shop, where, unsupervised, we experimented with dangerous power saws and lathes. The better part of the morning was spent making lamp stands on the lathe or handles for zip guns on the jig saw. Wood-working proved not to be my thing, so I attempted to improve my expertise with cars. In subsequent classes, I opted for the auto shop, where a well-intentioned and capable instructor taught us the fundamentals of engine adjustments, troubleshooting for engine problems, and breaking down engines. This knowledge would serve me well over the years, until cars became computerized, making self-repairs or adjustments virtually impossible.

I was relieved to have the Continuation School requirement behind me. I was doing well in the two night courses I was taking at Delehanty High School. I felt confident and looked forward to taking my examinations in the coming weeks so I could earn a Regent's Diploma.

The Coming of Social Change

The week of my 17th birthday a significant event occurred. The U.S. Supreme Court, the now Warren Court, issued its landmark decision in *Brown v. Board of Education*,[55] requiring school desegregation and setting the

---

[55] 347 U.S. 483 (1954)

table for decades of unrest. The Supreme Court's decision, "In the field of public education … separate educational facilities are inherently unequal," set in motion forces that gradually changed every neighborhood, school, public facility, and work-place in the country.

In the 1948 election, Earl Warren was governor of California and the Republican nominee for vice president when President Harry S. Truman defeated New York Governor Thomas E. Dewey. In March of 1954, the Senate confirmed Warren as Chief Justice. This early decision in the Brown case was the most significant in his long service on the Court. Though President Dwight D. Eisenhower soon expressed dismay with Warren's rulings, it should not have come as a surprise. During his 10 years as governor of California, Warren worked to eliminate discrimination against Mexican schoolchildren, opposed loyalty oaths at state universities, and championed universal health insurance.

The Court's decision had little meaning to me at the time, nor was it of any significant interest to those I lived and worked with. Considered a Southern problem, the school segregation issue didn't stir things up in the neighborhood or at Equitable Life. There were really few black people in my life up until that time. The Robinsons, the great cooks at Camp Leo, a summer camp I attended in New Hampshire for five years, were wonderful people. There were only two black students at Brooklyn Prep and none at Delehanty's. The few blacks that lived in the neighborhood resided in the Woodside Housing Project. Their peers accepted them in school and in the playgrounds. One family, the Capers, was undoubtedly more capable than most of their white neighbors. The son, Jimmy, was quiet, intelligent, and athletically and artistically gifted. Friendly and well-liked, Jimmy was respected in the neighborhood. His older sister, Virginia, went on to a successful acting career. She was awarded a "Tony" in 1974 for her performance in *Raisin*, the musical version of Lorraine Hansberry's magnificent play, *A Raisin In The Sun*. I knew Jimmy from pick-up basketball games, but can't say he was a friend. I never got to know him as well as John McComb did.

Equitable Life also was devoid of blacks at the time, and few were seen in and around the vicinity of our office. New York was racially and economically segregated, but this reality was overlooked, since it was an accepted fact of life at that time. Blacks were ignored, not taken seriously, and unfortunately stereotyped by the Amos & Andy and the Beulah shows on the radio. Minstrel shows were standard fare for the theatre clubs and guilds of most New York Catholic boy's high schools. Young white boys delighted in being made up in black faces to sing, dance and carouse on the stage. Such derogatory shows could also be seen on television and in movie theatres. Prominently displayed on the bottom shelf behind the soda fountain, in Sam's Candy Store, was a large jar of Yeah Man Coffee Syrup, featuring the face of a black man with large pink lips. The Aunt Jemima pancake mix box featured the picture of a smiling, overweight black woman wearing a red bandana on her head. The association of black people with pancakes was further strengthened in the popular story, *Little Black Sambo*, by Helen Bannerman.[56] Regrettably, African Americans who excelled in music, literature, sports, and other endeavors in life were commonly referred to as "a credit to their race." They suffered countless indignities. Gradually, things would change, but it was slow in coming. In the 60s, people's awareness, sensitivity, and attitudes began to change in many areas of the country.

Isolated in our Irish Catholic neighborhoods, we didn't have a clue about the plight of African Americans, even those living in New York. America tolerated racial discrimination and segregation, and the national media, based in New York, turned a blind eye to this festering sore.

---

[56] Grant Richards, 1899.

Rye Beach

One of the New York City school rituals was the annual boat ride to either Bear Mountain State Park, just south of West Point near Newburgh, New York, or to Rye Beach in Westchester County, on Long Island Sound. I had visited Rye Beach on outings with the Corpus Christi Altar Boys, and I welcomed the opportunity to join neighborhood friends on the La Salle Academy boat ride.

The boat left from a pier on the lower West Side and traveled south on the Hudson River to the Battery, at the tip of Manhattan, where it steered north up the East River under the Brooklyn, Manhattan, Williamsburg, Queens Borough (59th Street), and Triboro Bridges, and up through the dangerous whirlpools beneath the great railroad bridge at Hell's Gate in Astoria, where the river turns east just before the Riker's Island Prison and LaGuardia Airport. When we passed under the Whitestone Bridge, the boat went north at Throggs Neck into Long Island Sound to Rye Beach, which is just below the border with Connecticut. The Rye Beach Amusement Park is owned, operated, and maintained by Westchester County and is still considered one of American's premier amusement parks.

The trip provides a view of New York at water level that allows you to fully appreciate the vitality and power of the architectural wonders dotting the majestic skyline. It's an overwhelming and unforgettable portrait. Ayn Rand[57] said she would "give the greatest sunset in the world for one sight of New York's skyline. Particularly when one can't see the details. Just the shapes. The shapes and the thought that made them. The sky over New York and the will of man made visible."

---

[57] Ayn Rand, *"The Fountainhead,"* Bobbs-Merrill, 1943.

1954 Adventures In New York

I took the day off from work and joined Howard Kelly and other La Salle students including Tony Zappola and Dan O'Brien at the 46th Street subway station. Dan and Tony lived on 50th Street near the P.S. 151 schoolyard. Dan took great advantage of his close proximity to the basketball court and developed into a great player at the University of Dayton. Another La Salle student who joined us was Walter Porr who lived on Broadway near 43rd Street. Walter with his Jimmy Cagney-like swagger was wearing his grandfather's black Derby hat, which drew a number of stares on the subway. When we arrived at the boat, one of the Christian Brothers ordered Walter to remove the Derby as we strode across the gangplank. Walter defiantly shook his head back and forth and smirked at the suggestion. The Brother rushed by Howie Kelly and me and lunged at Walter, who pushed him backwards towards the boat. He knocked him into Howie and me and pushed us into a stanchion. Walter kept his balance and moved quickly across the gangplank. The cleric struggled for his balance, grabbing and holding on to Walter as they swayed back and forth. Jesus, they're going in the river, I thought.

Fortunately, a major crisis was averted when Walter agreed to surrender his Derby. Lucky for Brother "Smart Ass" and for Walter, too, that Walter composed himself. I'm not sure what kind of disciplinary action Walter incurred for that incident. He was solid as a rock and skilled with his fists.[58] Aside from the Christian Brother's effort to provoke Walter, the boat ride was peaceful. The vigilant clerics were on constant patrol in an effort to curtail us from sneaking drinks from the half-pint whiskey bottles

---

[58] About six years later, Walter, in an acting role, was featured in a live television production of *"Body & Soul."* The main focus of this epic drama was a lengthy boxing match between Poor and the lead actor appearing in the role made famous by John Garfield, in the film version. Eventually, Walter became a New York City Fireman, and no doubt developed his cooking skills. He became involved in a catering business in Westchester County upon his retirement from the Fire Department.

carried on board by many of the students. Their presence also prevented any hanky-panky from taking place with the boys and the large number of Catholic high school girls in attendance – the girls being a key reason we were all on the boat ride.

When we arrived at the Rye Beach pier, I struck up a conversation with an attractive girl from the Bronx who had arrived on another boat. Both of us were separated from our friends in the swarm of people and the confusion as we disembarked from our respective boats, so we proceeded to the Amusement Park together. We stopped at a concession stand for hot dogs and sodas and enjoyed a number of rides. It wasn't long before we were holding hands.

The initial touch of her soft hand transformed me in an instant. I went from an emboldened young man to a nervous and hesitant suitor. Before I realized it, she had imprisoned my willing hand and led me about. The next thing I knew, we were in line at the Fun House. Once inside, she drew me towards her in a darkened corner where we kissed. It was a long, memorable, and sensuous kiss accompanied by the probing of caressing hands. Amidst the noises of steam hissing, girlish screams, doors opening and closing, and voices calling out to each other there was a mutual desire to linger, despite the apprehension of being discovered. I had found myself another TG, how lucky could one get?

We came out of the fun house joined at the hip with our arms encircling each other. There was no doubt where we were going next, and in the Tunnel of Love we aggressively moved at each other for a few minutes of furtive passion. Light proved to be an unwelcome antiseptic, for as it appeared at the end of the tunnel there was a frantic rearranging of clothes and hair as we made our way into the scrutiny of the daylight.

I was truly smitten and did my best to avoid my friends for the remainder of the day so that I could continue to enjoy these magic moments with my newfound love. The day sadly ended when her boat departed. When I called her the following week, her father answered the telephone.

"Who's this?"

Jesus Christ, I said to myself.

"Ah, Neal Gillen, sir."

"I don't recognize that name. Where's she know you from?"

"We met in Rye Beach, sir."

"When was that?"

"Ah, last week, sir."

"Oh, yeah. What school you go to?"

"I graduated from Delehanty High School in January, sir."

"Delehanty's. Where the hell is that?"

"Jamaica."

"In Queens?"

"Yes, sir."

"I never heard of it. Is that a Catholic school?"

I explained that the overwhelming majority of students had attended Catholic high schools at one time. I could hear him thinking that it must be a school for troublemakers.

"I think you're too old for my daughter!"

"Would it be all right to talk to her, sir?"

"Sure, let me go find her."

I knew then that this guy had a sixth sense.

A minute later, she came to the phone. She had been crying.

"I'm sorry. He's so strict."

"I understand. My Dad's strict too."

"I didn't tell you. I'm only a sophomore."

"So what? I still like you."

"I like you too, but I can't see you. He won't let me go out with anyone until I'm a senior."

"I can wait. We can talk on the phone or maybe we can meet in the City some Saturday or Sunday afternoon."

"That'd be nice, but I don't think he'd let me go alone."

"Get a friend to go with you. I'll get one of my friends. We can double."

"It's too risky. If he found out, he'd kill you."

I didn't want to take that risk, so I said goodbye and promised to call. I never did, however, for fear of her difficult father and the problems I would cause her, but I've never forgotten that wonderful day at Rye Beach.

On The Waterfront

John McComb was the most excited person in the world when he called.

"Neal, the picture is done. They're going to sneak preview *On the Waterfront* at the RKO theatre at 53rd Street and Lexington Avenue."

A few months later, just down the block from the theatre at 590 Lexington Avenue, Marilyn Monroe filmed her famous scene with Tom Ewell in *The Seven Year Itch*. With her possessive husband Joe DiMaggio looking on, she was filmed standing over a subway grate in front of Wright's Food, a restaurant that billed its food as "Always Right," when her white dress suddenly billowed up over her head as a train supposedly passed under the grate. Actually, it was a studio technician triggering a powerful fan from under the grate. Though the movie isn't memorable, the resulting photograph is iconic. Joe left in a huff, and when Marilyn returned to their suite at the St. Regis Hotel, she later claimed that he had slapped her around. They quietly slipped out of New York and flew to California.

Within weeks, Joe's marriage with Marilyn was over, but she would always remain part of his life.

John's mother Susan, Dorothy "Dottie" McQuade, and I joined John on that big night. The movie was an unmitigated success and was judged to be one of the best films of all time. Every actor exceeded his or her ability, including John and the numerous extras from the docks and the neighborhoods of Hoboken. While the sneak preview didn't have the flair of an official premier, it was glamorous to John's small entourage.

The preview was held to determine how the public and the critics viewed the film. They loved it. *On The Waterfront* would be nominated for an Academy Award in 12 categories and would win Best Motion Picture, Best Direction (Elia Kazan), Best Story and Screen Play (Bud Schulberg), Best Actor (Marlon Brando), Best Supporting Actress (Eva Marie Saint), along with the Oscars for Art and Set Direction, Cinematography, and Editing. Leonard Bernstein, who was nominated for an Oscar for his music, was at the preview along with most of the lesser members of the supporting cast. Also in the audience was the great actress Katharine Hepburn.

When the movie was released, John became a major celebrity at Equitable Life, and at the bars and dances we frequented. It was a heady time for John and his friends as his celebrity status reflected upon us. People would question me incessantly about John.

"Hey, I understand you know John McComb."

"What kind of a guy is he?"

"How'd he luck out and get in a movie?"

"Does he have a regular girlfriend?"

John had many female admirers. For a few weeks he couldn't go anywhere in the Equitable Building without people pointing at him. He enjoyed it. We all did for him, and we hoped it was the beginning of something big. John put his energy to work and helped organize a theatre group in the Woodside Housing Project. He also had fun with the girls in the coming months. I did, too, basking in his sunlight. In the years ahead he would appear in a number of movies and television shows filmed in New York, including three popular series, *The Naked City, The Defenders,* and *Hawk.* He eventually found his niche in television behind the camera, and was associated with Madison Square Garden Productions for 22 years until his death in 2008.[59]

Upon John's death, Stan Fischler, who worked with John on the coverage of the New York area NHL teams (Rangers, Devils, & Islanders) wrote in his tribute, "I wish you could have known John because he was one of the precious few who made folks around him happier than they had been a few minutes before he entered a room." Fischler noted, "Bar none, John was the best joke-teller I've ever met outside the realm of such classic stand-ups ... McComb not only knew virtually every gag ever written but owned the astonishing knack of being able to tell the jokes better than anyone I ever met." Fischler summed up John as "inimitable, irreplaceable."

---

[59] Following his death, the Madison Square Garden Sports Network ran a feature on John narrated by Baseball Hall of Fame member Tom Seaver. John had produced the New York Mets' games for which Seaver and Ralph Kiner provided the color coverage.

9

The Class of 1954

The advent of my formal high school graduation generated considerable pressure to find a date for the dinner dance that followed the graduation ceremony. I was in a quandary and asking someone from Equitable was out of the question. All of the girls presumed I had already graduated; I was not about to reveal myself.

I considered asking a girl from the Boulevard Gardens, but the downside risks discouraged me from doing so. If she declined my invitation, which was highly likely as my reputation was many years from being fully redeemed, everyone in the neighborhood would soon know. Worse yet, if she accepted, I'd be functioning in a fish bowl. Here again, the entire neighborhood would know. She would have to buy a dress, and the busybodies would be picking it out or providing advice. We called it "putting in their two cents." Worse yet, I'd have to buy flowers. As my wife of almost 50 years knows so well, spending money on flowers is something I have a strong aversion to.

I had never brought a girl home to meet my parents, and I was not about to introduce an innocent young girl to the tension of my family. I decided that subjecting anyone to such trauma, on a first and probably a last date, was asking too much from any person.

Today's young men and women face the same dilemma in finding a prom date. The social pressures are too strong and the chances of rejection are too high. Is it worth it? My conclusion was no. I had to figure out how to save face and have a good time.

Before deciding, I checked in with Howie Hallisey, a classmate from Jackson Heights, to see if it was likely that I'd be embarrassed to attend without a date, no less a car. Howie was a character – a funny and likeable guy. He inherited his sense of humor from his mother who was the proprietor of Flannigan's, a bar on 83rd Street and Northern Boulevard. He informed me that after the graduation ceremony and dinner the guys with dates intended to stay for the dinner dance and those flying solo planned to hit the bars in the City. I was relieved to learn that there were other guys in my situation.

Opting out of attending was never considered. Financial circumstances forced Mother and Dad into the job market before they had a chance to finish high school. It was a matter of pride for my parents. I had no choice. I had to attend, if only for them, although my overall academic record had not met their expectations. School for me was more like speed dating. I put my time in and did the minimum. It was live and learn, with more living than learning.

Since the graduation ceremony was at the Garden City Hotel in Nassau County, getting there was a logistical nightmare for a family without a car. But our transportation dilemma was solved when a friend of Dad's, a short, heavy-set guy named Charlie with a cheerful attitude and a bulbous whiskey nose, offered to drive us. He had a commodious 1940 Buick with enough room to transport Mother and Dad, my sister Carol, Grandpa Jim, and me to the graduation ceremony.

The Garden City Hotel was an exclusive establishment adjacent to the site where Charles Lindberg embarked on his famous trans-Atlantic flight to Paris in 1927, an event that H.L. Mencken described as "the greatest news event since the resurrection." My graduation followed Lindberg's accomplishment by 27 years, and while it was not a newsworthy event – although the names of the graduates were published in *The Long Island Star Journal* – to me it was my resurrection from the tedium of high school.

The 45 graduates were seated on a stage in one of the hotel's elegant reception rooms. The girls were outfitted in white gowns and the young men in white dinner jackets. As Carlos Berges, a classmate with classical voice training and a high opinion of himself, rose to sing *You'll Never Walk Alone*,[60] Howie Hallisey evoked a good laugh from our fellow graduates with his sotto-voce remark, "It doesn't figure, who'd walk with that guy?"

Later in the program, when Berges rose to sing a duet with the attractive Marie Sinatra (no relation to Frank), Howie flipped pennies towards him as he moved to the microphone. The majority of the class members had never encountered anyone with Berges' degree of sophistication, feigned or genuine. He seemed to strut while he was sitting. His suits were always tailored, and he looked more like a banker or department store floorwalker than a student. Suffice it to say, that we were put off by Berges and tended to poke fun at him. For all we knew, he probably was the genuine article, but lacking the sophistication that he obviously possessed, we were incapable of making such a determination.

One of our female classmates was Constance Ann Blow. Roll call in class often invoked giggles and smiles as the teacher made his or her way down the list. Anytime Connie's name preceded that of a male student it sounded as though she was being instructed to engage in an indecent act. One morning, our biology teacher, Dr. Henry Gilgannon, admonished us for our dirty minds when his calling of the roll resulted in a series of giggles from the back of the room. Poor Connie didn't know whether to cry or thank him for making an issue of the matter.

It was a great class that included Matt Donohue, a fellow exile from Brooklyn Prep, Bob Dineen, Jim Dudgeon, Marty Featherston, Edward

---

[60] *You'll Never Walk Alone* from *Carousel*, lyrics by Oscar Hammerstein. Music by Richard Rodgers.

Markey, Bob Philbin, John Denault and Howie Hallesey, to name a few. I had dated Ed Markey's sister, Elaine, the previous year.

The Markey's lived in a large house that straddled a small, odd-shaped block on 60th Street between Broadway and 34th Avenue just above the intersection of Northern Boulevard and Broadway, two of the busiest thoroughfares in the country. Our fathers were regular habituates of the bar at Connell's on Northern Boulevard across 56th Street from the Jackson Social & Field Club, where they also sampled their share of suds.

Following the graduation dinner, my grandfather slipped me $20 and four of us got a ride into the city to embark upon a celebratory night of revelry. We ended up drunk, sick, and with barely enough money for a taxi home. We stopped at P.J. Clarke's on Third Avenue and 55th Street, where the roar of the Third Avenue El enticed us to ride it down to the Bowery, where we visited Sammy's Bowery Follies on Third Street. Sammy's was a raucous and nostalgic place where over-the-hill vaudeville performers belted out show tunes and bawdy songs. We enjoyed our sojourn there before we closed out the night in Greenwich Village. I still have a souvenir photo from our stop at the famous Village Barn.

The New Crop

The June graduating class produced a number of new employees for Equitable Life, including my second cousin Bobby McPartland and my friends Bob Perite and Billy Giebler from Saint Ann's Academy, the school I had always wanted to attend. Since many of my other friends from the Boulevard Gardens – Donald Stapleton, Tom Reddy, Billy O'Donoghue, and Bob Dulaby Savage also went to St. Ann's, I attended its dances and basketball games.[61] It was after one of those games that Bob Perite and I were served our first beers in Driscoll's a bar near St. Ann's. A glass of draft beer was 10 cents and a pitcher of beer was 80 cents.

Bobby McPartland was Mother's first cousin. He was the youngest of 11 children of my maternal grandfather's younger brother John. The close-knit McPartland family lived in St. Mary's Parish in Winfield, located in the southeastern part of Woodside on the Maspeth border. Bobby and I played baseball against each other a number of times. An excellent shortstop, he played for the Win-Wood Incas and the St. Mary's team. Bobby's height and long arms gave him a wide range in playing this difficult position. He worked at Equitable until he was drafted into the Army.[62]

Billy Giebler, a terrific guy, was an excellent hockey player. He and John McComb played ice hockey together in the Sunday afternoon junior games at Madison Square Garden. His father, Walter Giebler, was the head usher at the Garden and at Forest Hills Stadium. Mr. Giebler was only too happy to seat one of Billy's friends close to the action whenever such seats were available.[63]

---

[61] In 1954, St. Ann's great basketball team, coached by Basketball Hall of Fame Member Louis "Louie" P. Carnescecca, who later had a successful career coaching St. John's University, won the Catholic High School Athletic Association (CHSAA) championship in an exciting victory over La Salle Academy at the 69th Regiment Armory. The two starting guards for St. Ann's, Tommy Kearns and Danny Lane, made the All-City Team and were All-Americans at North Carolina and Dayton in their college days. Kearns led North Carolina to the 1957 NCAA Championship and played briefly for the Philadelphia Warriors and the Syracuse Nationals before injuries ended his playing days. He went on to a brilliant career as an investment counselor.

[62] Following his Army service, he joined his father's trade and became a steamfitter. He recently retired as vice president of his steamfitter's local.

[63] After college, Billy followed his father to Madison Square Garden, where he worked in ticket sales. On a few occasions, he gave me much better seats than those I planned to purchase. He became a member of the Treasurer's Union and embarked upon a successful career in ticket sales for all the major shows, concerts, fights, and concerts held at the Garden. In 1988, Billy would suffer the loss of his 29-year-old son, William David Giebler. William was a passenger on Pan American Flight 103, the Boeing 747 blasted out of the sky above Lockerbie, Scotland by Libyan terrorists.

Bob Perite was a life-long friend and a great athlete. While he excelled in basketball and baseball, he never attempted to play in high school. His muscular body generated unusual power. I was catching for the opposing team when he hit a fastball within 10 feet of the 360-foot center field fence at Queens Park. The home-plate umpire was as shocked as my pitcher. "Holy shit," he said, "the ball may clear the fence." When Bob crossed home plate he was beaming from ear to ear.

"How old is that kid?" the umpire asked.

"He's 12," I said.

"No way he's 12 – he hit that ball a ton."

Bob's father, Nick, an accountant, was of Italian and French extraction. Mr. Perite was a serious and dedicated man who managed Charles Karen & Sons, a handbag frame company on 32nd Street and 6th Avenue. He was exceedingly devoted to his job of the bookkeeping, tax reporting and overall business management. The Karens forced him to retire after 50 years of devoted service and put him out on the street without a pension, health, or life insurance. It hit him hard and according to Bob, "It helped to kill him in the end."

Bob's mother, Claire, whose maiden name was O'Grady, was vivacious in contrast to his father. They grew up together in the same Ocean Hill neighborhood in Brooklyn with the actor and television star Jackie Gleason, attended P.S. 73 on Mc Dougal Street with Gleason and remained in contact with him throughout their lives. The Perites were wonderful people and would do anything for their children and friends. Bob and his older sister Pat inherited their mother's red hair and freckles – often subjecting them to kidding for being redheads with a French-Italian name.

Bob was conscientious in everything he undertook and was assigned to work with computers in a new department at Equitable. I visited him often in the Spartan-clean area where he worked sorting computer cards with a steel needle. He would push the needle through specific holes on the card which had the effect of culling out either the cards he wanted or didn't want. Elsewhere in his department a vast number of women, called key punch operators, typed information into keypunch machines that created the computer cards. I never determined how Bob's work figured into the grand scheme of things, but he was always busy and had all the overtime hours he could handle.[64]

Bob was intrigued by the daily exploits of the application chasers and because of his work constrictions was satisfied with vicariously enjoying our collective experiences. He got to meet and observe Ace Corcoran and agreed that he was certainly an unforgettable character.

---

[64] Bob talked frequently of his plans to work at Equitable until he put in his military service, and following that, to join the New York City Fire Department. He also would consider an offer from his uncle, Jimmy O'Grady, an official in Local 3 of the Electricians Union, to be sponsored as an apprentice. When he completed his Army enlistment Bob returned to Equitable and began to prepare for the Fire Department examination. He passed the test, achieving one of the top grades, and six months later he received his acceptance notice. On his last day at Equitable, the Friday before he would report for training at the Fire Academy, a Fire Department official called to inform him that in a second review of his medical examination his x-rays revealed problems with his back that would preclude him from performing his duties.
Bob was stunned. His hopes and dreams were dashed. Something was amiss as there was nothing wrong with his back. A subsequent examination by a prominent back specialist determined that Bob was one of the strongest people he ever examined. There were no spinal, structural, or muscultature problems with his back. Puzzled by this anomaly, Bob decided to stay at Equitable while he dug further into the situation at the Fire Department. It proved difficult to learn what had happened, but over time he discovered that a number of individuals scheduled to join his class received similar calls that fateful Friday. According to Bob, he learned from Fire Department sources some years later that they had been lied to in order to qualify a number of minority applicants. Though bitter with the Fire Department, Bob channeled his energies into his work and was later transferred from the computer division to Equitable's Group Life and Health Administration Department with responsibility for 60 employees and $150 million in premiums.
Bob thrived in this new environment and was promoted to division manager, and eventually vice president of the Central Administration Department, with responsibility for over 500 employees and a large area of the country. In 1990, the CIGNA Insurance Company acquired Equitable's Group Life and Health Division and Bob moved to CIGNA. In 1992, at the age of 55, he retired and never regretted that decision. He and his wife Lorraine, a retired registered nurse, originally settled in New Hampshire before moving to Fort Mill, South Carolina. Bob died earlier this year as a result of a ruptured aorta.

Bob's uncle owned The Idlewild Rest, an Italian Restaurant near Idlewild (JFK) Airport. The restaurant sponsored a baseball team so Bob convinced me to restart my baseball career. The team was loaded with talent. My best position was catcher. I possessed a strong arm and was fearless behind the plate. However, the other candidate for catcher had the same abilities, could hit the ball with power and outweighed me by 50 pounds. Clearly outclassed, I was relegated to the outfield for the week of tryouts, an insufficient period of time to elevate my fielding and hitting skills to the level of the competition. This was serious baseball. The tryouts included a few prospects capable of playing professionally, particularly Charlie "The Milkman" Chinelli, with whom I would share a beach house in West Hampton some eight years later. Bob made the team, along with Bob Dulaby Savage who had excelled at first base for St. Ann's Academy's baseball team. Though I didn't make the cut, adequate compensation for my efforts came in the form of the free pizza and beer every night after practice. The team had an extraordinary season and capped it off by winning the Queens Championship at the title game in Dexter Park.

My friendship with Bob had always been good. One year I was his primary catcher when he pitched for the Corpus Christi baseball team. Each of us knew how the other was thinking and we really got along well. During our time at Equitable we spent a lot of time together after work. Bob could be cautious even secretive at times, but he was always candid with me and often confided in me his feelings about other people. When Bob began talking about going to college at night that fall, I didn't encourage or discourage him. I didn't know how serious he was, but he kept talking about it on a regular basis. My focus was not on college, but on immediate satisfaction – having fun at the office and the beach.

10

Rockaway Beach

Rockaway Beach was Nirvana – freedom, fantasy and a playground for people of all ages. Located on the south shore of Long Island in the Borough of Queens not far from JFK Airport and the Aqueduct Race Track, it sits in the center of a narrow 10-mile sand peninsula that begins at Breezy Point across the Rockaway Inlet from Coney Island and ends on the Queens-Nassau County line in Far Rockaway near Atlantic Beach and Long Beach. In 1954, Rockaway was far different from New York journalist Jimmy Breslin's description of it as a place "where wood rots and people waste."[65]

Settled mostly by the Irish, it was a popular resort that drew throngs of people during the summer. For two summers in the later days of World War II, our family rented a bungalow near Saint Malachy's Orphanage on 112th Street. When visiting just for the day, the family would take the bus to the Long Island Railroad's Woodside station for a special train running directly to Rockaway's 116th Street station. If we missed the direct train we would have to change in Jamaica – a logistical nightmare for a large, fully provisioned family. When the train pulled into Woodside station, the children would climb through the open windows and save seats for the adults carrying the toddlers, collapsible strollers, shopping bags full of sandwiches and fresh fruit, and various beach paraphernalia.

Once we reached our destination and staked out a spot on the beach, I would accompany Mother back to 116th Street to rent an orange and black striped umbrella – the only color offered at the time. The beach was wide,

---

[65] The quote was attributed to Breslin by Richard George in the October 23, 2003, *New York Times* article "Last Stand for Bungalow Backwater" by William L. Hamilton.

clean, and welcoming. The boardwalk was a masterpiece of sturdy Ipe wood from the Brazilian rain forests installed under the supervision of the legendary Robert Moses, who gave New York its scenic parkways and beaches during the Great Depression. Like the beach, the boardwalk was wide and clean with art-deco concession stands every few hundred yards. Playland, an amusement park on 98th Street had a so-so roller coaster, a carousel, bumper cars and the usual rides and junk food stands one finds at such places.

The main traffic artery was Rockaway Boulevard. Though the word boulevard is usually associated with a wide and/or tree-lined thoroughfare, Rockaway Boulevard was an ordinary two-lane macadam street. On every block in the most-traveled stretch of the boulevard, from 96th Street, where the Cross Bay Bridge entered Rockaway, to 116th Street, there were two or three bars on each side of the street, including one in building that once housed a bank closed during the Depression. The buildings along the Boulevard were shabby weather-beaten two to four story wooden structures with retail establishments on the ground floor and seedy apartments and rooming houses on the upper floors. Spread out behind the structures on the Boulevard in each direction, north to Jamaica Bay and south to the Atlantic Ocean, were row upon row of single story two and three bedroom wooden bungalows inhabited by local residents or summer renters.

The bars on the Boulevard were not air-conditioned and the loud music from their jukeboxes would echo out through the open doors onto the street and like a pied piper lure passers-by in for a drink. The voice of Astoria's Tony Bennett (Antonio Dominic De Benedetto) singing *Rags To Riches* would resonate up and down Rockaway Boulevard. [66] The number one song in 1953, it remained one of the most frequently played tunes in the summer of 1954. It frequently played simultaneously on juke boxes in

---

[66] *Rags To Riches* – lyrics by Gerry Adler and music by Richard Ross.

bars on the same street creating a surreal disharmony for this classic melody. It was a hold-me-close slow dance, in contrast to the other hit tune that summer, *Sh Boom*,[67] sung by the Crew Cuts, that got everyone on their feet and dancing to a smooth-paced Savoy.

The street of joy, 103rd Street, no longer exists. It was replaced by high-rise apartments in the late 1960s. The Irish Circle, at 102nd Street and Rockaway Boulevard, is the only remaining bar in that area. The beach and the boardwalk are still the same, though our beloved basketball court at 108th Street is now a roller-skating/roller-hockey rink. More future college All-Americans and NBA All-Stars improved their skill levels on one end of that court in three-on-three games in the 1940s and '50s than on any other basketball court in America.

Except for the Greek restaurant and sandwich shop on the northeast corner of 103rd Street and Rockaway Boulevard, owned by the father of a former Delehanty classmate, every building was a bar from the beach to the bay. Above many of the bars were rooming houses and hotels that catered to the Irish. The bar closest to the beach, on the west side of 103rd Street, was the Lietrim Castle. It had a large enclosed front porch on the street, where you could sit and drink and watch the crowds stroll or stagger by. Inside was a long bar and a large dance floor. It was usually the first stop on 103rd Street and the best place to dance in the evenings. Next to the Lietrim Castle was the Sligo Hotel, a large three-story Victorian-era building where rooms could be rented for under $10 a night.

Across the street at the southeast corner of 103rd Street and Rockaway Boulevard was another large hotel and bar, The Dublin House-By the Sea. It was a four-story structure with a widow's walk perched atop a corner tower rising above the roof. A semi-enclosed and arched porch was located

---

[67] *Sh Boom* – lyrics and music by James Keyes, Claude & Carl Feaster, Floyd McRae and James Edwards.

on the second floor above the bar where an older crowd encamped, including Lawrence Tierney, a well-known movie actor. Tierney, a regular at the Dublin House, could be seen late in the afternoon or the early evening being carried or helped to a waiting car or taxi after having had his fill of drinks. Tierney always played a tough guy, appearing in films such as *Dillinger, Born to Kill, The Devil Thumbs a Ride, San Quentin* and *Kill or Be Killed*. His movie roles often resulted in his being goaded into fights, and on the Rockaway scene he was a frequent and willing brawler.

Across the boulevard and down the East side of 103rd street was a troublesome place called The Snake Pit. Unless you were adroit with your fists, it was a good place to avoid. The Snake Pit was the only bar in Rockaway with an honor roll. Patrons qualified for this distinction by consuming 50 beers during opening until closing time – some 12 to 14 hours. Tommy Murphy, a Boulevard Gardens resident, was a proud and loyal honor roll member, if not one of the more distinguished. Asterisks appeared next to his name for accomplishing this feat on many occasions. Close by on that side of the street was the Blarney Castle where either a banjo player or an Irish Brisker, who played multiple instruments assembled together on a washboard, provided lively entertainment.

The anchor establishment at the end of the street was Gildea's, which was housed in a large three-story, square-shaped wooden structure covered in gray asbestos shingles. The top two floors were a rooming house, while the bar and dance floor, the largest in Rockaway, occupied the entire first floor. Six bartenders worked the bar and as many as five waiters served pitchers of beer in the back room. Without question, it was the best place to meet friends and hook up with girls.

The complex was large and airy with the bar situated on the right side of the building in an enclosed porch area. You entered the bar through one of two large wooden doors that folded back along the wall to open a space about 20 feet wide. The adjacent dancing and so-called "dining area" was entered through three similar doors. The large entryways allowed for excellent airflow, providing relief to the customers three-deep at the bar or crowded together on the dance floor. The accumulated moisture in the wood floors and walls combined with the odor of stale beer gave Gildea's and the other bars at the beach a unique smell, which John McComb called Rockaway Musk. Adjacent to Gildea's and under the Long Island Railroad's elevated tracks, where the 'A' train now runs, was a vacant lot with a sufficient growth of flora that made it a Mecca for young lovers who could not afford the price of a room.

The proprietor, John Gildea, a huge man in both height and girth, and his brother of similar stature towered over people. They were polite, friendly, and, when necessary, quite adept at breaking up fights and ejecting trouble makers from the premises. John also ran a popular establishment of the same name on Queens Boulevard in Sunnyside.

In such a popular place, with beer and testosterone flowing in great abundance, fights often broke out among the young men vying for the favors of young women. The fights usually occurred in late afternoon on the dance floor area, which seated over 100 people. You knew a fight was starting by the noise of the screeching of chairs as they grated against the wooden floor when suddenly pushed back by the combatants springing into action. Chairs, glasses, beer pitchers, and people would fly through the air. Guys would run across the tops of tables and jump into the melee. John Gildea and his brother were quick to respond. Once they reached the epicenter of the action they would peel off the battlers like skin from a banana. When order was restored they would sweep up the fight area and the dancing and drinking would start anew. John Gildea had good relations with the Police, and if he thought the battlers were going to continue making trouble he would have them taken away.

In Gildea's, there was always safety in numbers; therefore, you assumed the risk of getting into a fight if you were foolish enough to venture there alone in the off hours, especially if members of the Corona Dukes were present since they were always looking for trouble. I made that mistake one Saturday afternoon. Mostly Italian, the Dukes dressed like retro Zoot Suitors. If they appeared today, you would mistake them for the cast of *Grease*. They wore t-shirts with the sleeves rolled up to show off their tattoos, along with pegged pants and pointed black shoes even though black shoes at the beach were never in fashion. They would congregate at the far end of the bar with cigarettes stuck defiantly along the side of their ears. Incessantly combing their long and well-lubricated hair, the Dukes were quick with their insults in the hope of provoking a fight.

One Saturday afternoon about 2 o'clock, while searching for the Woodside crowd, I wandered into an almost empty Gildea's. In short order, I found myself surrounded by a group of four or five of the Dukes.

"Where you from kid?"

If I said Woodside, they would associate me with the Woodside Rangers – rivals, if not enemies, of the Dukes. The Rangers and the Junior Rangers were Woodside/Sunnyside football teams. Though I never played for either team, I was friendly with many of the players, who, if provoked, would never hesitate to engage the Dukes. On a few occasions, they did battle at summer dances in the school yard at 77th Street and Northern Boulevard or at the beach. It was an Irish versus Italian thing, based on ignorance and prejudice. The Irish considered themselves a step or two above the Italians. That feeling still predominates the thinking in some neighborhoods. Irish dated Irish and Italians dated Italians. The resentment was deep seated. Fights were sparked at football and basketball games and at dances. Ethnic slurs were common. The Italians were called Guineas and Grease Balls while they referred to the Irish as Micks and Donkeys.

"Astoria - 46th Street," I lied, giving the street my cousins lived on.

"Where'd you go to school?"

"St. Joseph's."

"Hey, you know Jimmy Drago or Genie Malease?"

Scared and trying to carefully think my way through the situation, I nodded my head affirmatively. Drago and Malease were both great guys, who I wished were there with me. Jimmy's father owned a funeral home in Astoria and went to St. Ann's Academy. Malease went to Bryant and I knew him through Dale Edwards and other friends in the Boulevard Gardens.

"How do you know them?" one of them asked.

Just about then, I was lamenting that I didn't join Jack Dadian and Jack O' Grady, two very strong and capable people in a fight, who I had just seen up the street in the Snake Pit. Suddenly, and much to my relief, the Calvary arrived in the form of Tommy Kearns. He sauntered into Gildea's wearing a cut-off sweatshirt exposing his huge arms. Tommy approached the group smiling and shook hands with me.

"I didn't see you on the court this afternoon."

"I played this morning," I responded.

Tommy had no idea that he had just rescued me. Impressed with his bulging arms, the guys from Corona drifted off to the end of the bar. When I told him he saved me from a beating, he smiled, clasped his hand on my shoulder and said, "I guess you owe me a pitcher of beer." I paid up and he promptly drunk it down. Three years later, Tommy was a consensus All-American guard at the University of North Carolina.

A typical weekend in Rockaway began on Friday evening. A budget of $20, if used prudently, could carry you through Sunday evening. I usually left for the beach wearing a pair of jeans or chinos, and a short sleeve shirt over a t-shirt, loafers or sneakers, and a light windbreaker. In the pockets of the jacket I stuffed a bathing suit and a toothbrush. Since my beard was light I would shave before I left for the beach and that would last me through Sunday.

John McComb, Bob Perite, and sometimes Drew Doyle, and I would usually leave together. We would take the subway to Woodhaven Boulevard and hitchhike to the beach. It never took long to catch a ride since people were more than willing to give kids a lift. Upon our arrival in Rockaway we usually stopped at a pizza and clam bar between 102nd and 103rd Streets for a slice of square pizza and a half-dozen Little Neck clams. Fortified with these Rockaway delicacies, we would head for the bars where the primary agenda was beer and girls. Hopefully, as the night ensued, we would luck out and convince someone to let us crash in his or her room or in their car. If all else failed, we would seek out a cheap room or sleep under the boardwalk. One cool night, John McComb, Lester Anderson and I slept up against the narrow ledge of the jetty wall overlooking Jamaica Bay. It was one of most uncomfortable nights I have ever experienced. Lester, however, had no problem sleeping. When John and I woke up about 7:30 that morning, Lester was still in a sound sleep.

Saturday would begin with a late breakfast followed by pick-up basketball at the playground on 108th Street. If we weren't wearing sneakers we could always borrow a pair from someone on the beach. After an hour or two of play, we would take a swim to cool-off, visit the girls on the beach, arrange to meet later at Gildea's, and then venture off to the bars. Lunch usually was a Sabrett's hot dog at George's corner stand near the beach. Dinner was usually a step up - a hamburger and fries or more pizza. The previous night's social routine would be repeated, followed by more of the same on Sunday. On Sunday evening we would catch a ride back or take the bus into Woodside. Since no ticket was required to get on the bus, we frequently avoided paying by crawling under a seat just before the fares were collected at the first stop in Middle Village.

At 1954 prices, with well-applied frugality, $20 would go a long way. If I lucked out, I could get by with no transportation or rooming expense, and with minimal food expenses, I might have $10 to spend on beer. At 15 cents a beer and a free beer after every third drink, the weekend consumption potential approached 80 beers – more than enough for a fun weekend. While I never reached that level, I certainly approached the 50 mark a few times.

Bronx Irish Catholics

The girls we befriended and bonded with during the course of the summer were a similar type who came to be known as Bronx Irish Catholics (BICs). Rockaway was frequented by a large number of eligible young women from the borough of the Bronx, particularly the neighborhoods surrounding Parkchester, a large apartment complex in the South Central part of the Bronx. In short order, the type or reference of BIC was coined. The label was soon applied to all girls, provided they were Catholic, danced the Savoy, and dressed in a similar manner. BICs clearly fell into the category of good girls.

Their standard uniform was a pair of white or khaki shorts, a sleeveless blouse with a light wool sweater draped around the shoulders, and on their feet white socks and penny loafers or dirty white bucs. Their jewelry was a charm bracelet, a high school ring, and a gold circular pin attached to their blouse on their left side above the breast, allegedly signifying their purity in the eyes of God. To many, the pin was a challenge, it was tantamount to a neon sign reading, "Sex on the condition of marriage!"

BICs were a wonderful group of young women, who, like us, were exploring their limits, while trying to have a good time and meet new friends. Willie Nelson's lyrics come to mind when I wonder what became of many of these great young women – "To all the girls who shared my life.

Who now are someone else's wives."[68] Hopefully, they lived wonderful lives and from time-to-time think of the good times they enjoyed in Rockaway.

Playland

TG sat down next to me in the cafeteria one day. "Long time no see, Neal. Where've you been hiding?" she said in a coquettish way as she lightly stroked my wrist and the back of my hand. That's all it took. We met on the staircase a few hours later and we were off to the races. The next weekend we arranged to meet in Rockaway. Not sure if she would show up, I didn't share my plans with any of my friends, including John McComb. On Friday night, I suggested to John that we start out at the Lietrim Castle where TG and I had planned to meet. He argued for Gildea's.

"That's where I told the guys we'd meet them," he said. Reluctantly, I went along to Gildea's. Sure enough, that's where the crowd was. I said hello to everyone, headed for the bathroom, and slipped out the side door. When I walked up the street to the Lietrim Castle, I was relieved to find TG standing outside. She had just arrived. We secured a table near the dance floor, ordered a pitcher of beer, and enjoyed ourselves dancing the Savoy. During a slow dance she suggested that we walk to the beach. There, we kicked off our shoes and walked to a secluded spot under the boardwalk where we made out passionately. "Let's do this the right way," she said, and taking my hand she led me up the boardwalk. We walked to Playland and made our way past the various rides and shooting galleries to a point in the center of the Midway. She pointed to a faded hotel sign just above the neon lights of a bar on the other side of Rockaway Boulevard.

"That's where we're staying, Neal."

---

[68] *To All the Girls I've Loved Before,* words and music by Willie Nelson.

Her words caused me to pause as I grasped their impact. Staying – where we're staying. Be cool, I kept saying to myself. I didn't know exactly what to say. And, before I knew it I said something dumb. "Is it clean?" Like who cares if the place is clean? Why should that matter, I'm going to be sleeping with this girl. Besides, this is Rockaway, where all the rooms are miserable. She gave me a quizzical look, broke into a smile, and shook her head up and down assuring me that it was clean. We crossed Rockaway Boulevard hand-in-hand and entered a place shabbier than the Skogel Hat Corporation. I was apprehensive when we walked past a small darkened room lit only by a small television. From the shadows a woman asked in a whiskey voice, "You got your key, hon?"

"Yes," TG said assuredly.

"Let me know if you need anything," the landlady said as I nervously followed TG up the narrow staircase.

When we got into the room I asked TG if she knew the woman. "Sure," she said. "I stayed here a few times last year."

It was readily apparent that TG had done this before. I mean in a hotel room. Aside from my wonderful times with TG on the back stairs, my prior sexual experiences had been furtive efforts in apartment building hallways or in bungled attempts in the back of parked cars. Until that moment, I had never seen a fully unclothed, real, live, naked lady - ready, willing, and anxious to get it on with me. Well, almost, but that's another story.

The small room's only window overlooked Playland. The garish reflection of its colored lights and that of the bar's neon sign danced across the walls and ceiling of the darkened room. The noise from Playland and the street below had their own consistent rhythm that ebbed and flowed with the movement of the roller coaster. Accompanied by this mood lighting and the noise from the amusement park, I put myself in the hands of a polished expert as I began my sexual training.

She took my hand and pulled me down next to her as she sat naked on the side of the bed. We kissed and fondled each other as we progressed towards my first genuine, full-fledged act of fornication. We fell backwards onto the bed and enjoyed a series of long sensuous kisses as we groped each other. I was hesitant at first, and sensing my lack of experience, she adjusted to my novice approach by guiding me into her. As the night wore on, my learning curve accelerated before sleep came. I was awakened by the touch of her hand tracing down my chest towards my stomach. Playland had closed and there was little if any traffic. We had left the window open to cool the room. The only sounds were the buzz of the neon sign, the low roar of beach in the distance, and our heavy breathing. We kissed and whispered to each other. In the words of Joyce, "my body was like a harp and her words and gestures were like fingers running upon the wires."[69] It was a night I would remember forever.

By the end of the weekend, I was sated by the sexual activity. It was my basic introduction into many of the progressions of the Kama Sutra. If anything, she verified the conclusions of Dr. Kinsey's study of the sexual behavior of women. TG was intrepid pursuing her needs, acting with sexual abandon in that room. Her lack of inhibitions never concerned me – I had found paradise in a Rockaway hole in the wall.

Simply put, it was wonderful and instructive, if not an unforgettable experience. She was an accomplished lover, tender, imaginative, and considerate. When I was not on my back or in the missionary position, I was walking on air that weekend. And, having disappeared, I was the envy of my beach buddies, who quickly formed their own conclusions when I didn't show up at the beach on Saturday. When John McComb saw us that night he put his hand to his mouth and doubled up in laughter. TG didn't notice John in the crowd at Gildea's, but I did and also began to laugh. She

---

[69] Araby, Dubliners by James Joyce, Grant Richards, 1914.

was in such a good mood that it never occurred to her that I was laughing in response to John's discovery of our weekend tryst. "We had you missing in action Neal. Where've you been all weekend," John playfully asked when TG and I had finished dancing. I proudly explained that I'd been with TG, who beamed at my response. Later that evening, she was especially appreciative and overly generous with her favors for my display of pride for being with her.

A few weeks later, she slipped up to me in the cafeteria and whispered, "Meet me at three on the stairs." I smiled and nodded affirmatively. I was certainly ready for another exciting afternoon session.

At the appointed time and place she informed me that she had missed her period.

I was dumb struck and lost for words. Oh Jesus, I thought, this can't be happening to me. Feeling lightheaded and woozy, I grabbed hold of the stair rail and sat down.

"Are you sure?"

"Of course I'm sure."

"Jesus, what are we going to do?" I began to panic.

She was relatively calm. She obviously had thought through this scene carefully. Sitting down beside me, she hugged me and kissed me on the side of the face. "We'll get married," she whispered. My head dropped to my chest, I felt an asthma attack coming on.

I wasn't yet aware of Damon Runyon's advice to the youth of America - "fall in love with an heiress, if you must fall in love…"[70] I certainly wasn't in love. At best, I was obsessed with sex. Unfortunately, the ethic of the day was to marry the girl and bring the child into the world as part of a Catholic family. It was happening all the time in neighborhoods throughout New York. It was the honorable thing for the young man to do. In the words of

---

[70] *"Magnificent Mammon"* from *"Short Takes,"* Whittlesey House, 1946.

our elders, you "stepped up to the plate," "faced the music," or "took your medicine." Two lives ruined, the young woman disgraced by her conduct, and the young man committed to support a family despite his immaturity, inexperience, and economic instability. It was a given that two unprepared and hapless people would bring an innocent child into the world. Faced with the likelihood of a life sentence of misery, I visualized my life's options quickly fading into oblivion. I flashed back to my epiphany in jail and thought I was destined to fail in life.

I was confused and frightened, breathing rapidly and gasping for air. I pulled away from her and started to babble random statements as they came to mind. "I'm just out of high school. We're too young to get married. Who'll support our child?"

She drew back and looked at me, disappointed by my inability to handle the situation.

I was incapable of saying anything meaningful. My doubt and her absolutes raised the obviously insensitive question, "Is it mine?" I said as I grabbed the stair railing for support to stand up. Once those words passed my lips I couldn't take them back – the damage was done.

Enraged, she pushed me into the stairwell wall and lashed out at me for doubting my putative parenthood, "You fucking bastard. How can you say that?" She burst into tears and dashed down the stairs, and effectively out of my life. Too confused to follow her, I slumped down again and cried. If she was knocked up, I was knocked down.

I couldn't sleep that night. The air was a still. No breeze was coming through the window. I could hear the crickets on the lawns between 'I' and 'J' buildings doing their mating calls. The symbolism didn't escape me. Once mated, how does one get out of it? I had dealt myself a hand that was a certain loser however I played it. Why me? I kept asking myself as I tossed and turned looking into a dark abyss that looked back at me and seemed to be saying, "Go back. Don't come here." Go back where, to where I'd been? How do I get from this situation to where I want to go, wherever that is?

I was frightened and confused when morning came. That day I was brain dead as I drifted aimlessly about the Equitable building. I should have called in sick. My co-workers suspected something was amiss.

"What's wrong, Neal?"

"Are you ok?"

I just hunched my shoulders and shook my head. "I don't know. I don't feel well," I would say and walk away, ignoring their solicitude, instead thinking of my predicament and not looking blissfully at a potential marriage.

As my head began to clear in the next few days I realized that TG and I shared the same predicament. I was scared to say anything. Who do I talk to? How do I deal with it? Before I did anything I decided to talk to TG about what we should do. But my usually forward person lacked the courage to do it. A few days later, when I did work up the gumption to do so, she rebuffed me when I attempted to approach her in the cafeteria. As I waited for another opportunity to meet with her, I began to think. Was everything fine down there with her again? Thereafter, I avoided her. Our relationship was finished. I never found out if she was testing me or had actually missed her usual time. The warmth of her soft curves was alluring but would be mine no more. I would miss that, but my inner voice made it clear that I was playing with fire. Then and there, I resolved that I wouldn't experience the burn. In the months to come, we had a number of pleasant conversations, but the spark was gone. Still, given my teenage libido, if she had invited me to the back stairs I doubt that my resolve would have held fast.

While others may have suspected my involvement with TG, only John McComb knew the full story of our relationship. It has stayed that way until I decided to write this story. I have often thought about the potential consequences of that union. What if she was carrying my child and if she had had my child? What would have become of TG and me? Life takes strange turns. As my own fate would have it, for me it was a right turn.

Curly Monahan

Later that summer, TG took up with George "Curly" Monahan, a friend from Rockaway who lived in Chelsea. Curly was a character right out of James T. Farrell's, *Studs Lonigan*.[71] He was dashing and reckless in manner, a great dancer, and constantly involved in fights that he usually precipitated. Curly was tall and thin, but sinewy with curly blond hair, and always successful with the girls. He was in constant trouble throughout the summer, but it never seemed to faze him. Curly and TG made an interesting couple.

A few years later, our commonality of interests would link up again. I arrived on Okinawa in February 1956, a day before the Third Marine Division rotated in from Japan to replace the Army's First Cavalry. My billet the first night on the island was a Quonset hut in Naha, at the Naval Air Repair Facility. The next day, I was moved to a small radio direction finding station in Futenma, just up the hill from the Marine's huge base camp. Two buddies and I visited the bars in Futenma Village and then decided to drink with the Marines. Proceeding down the hill from Futenma, we walked under the huge red and gold Torii (arch) near the entrance and were cleared into the base, eventually making our way to a barracks building that had been hastily arranged into an Enlisted Men's Club. As we

---

[71] Penguin, 1932.

proceeded up the stairs to be admitted, two large Marines, wearing Master at Arms arm bands, rushed forward and literally tossed a squirming body in our direction. I instantly recognized the body in mid-flight. It was Curly. I rushed to help him to his feet, and despite his obvious intoxication and dust-up with the Masters at Arms, he immediately recognized me.

"Neal, it's just like Rockaway."

"Some things don't change, Curly – you're always in the thick of it."

"Vouch for me, Neal. Get me back in."

"I'll see what I can do."

I approached the sergeant in charge, explained that Curly was a friend from New York, and that I would make sure that he behaved himself. The sergeant looked at me suspiciously and smirked.

"That I seriously doubt, but if you're willing to vouch for him, you'll be responsible for him. You sure you want to risk your rank over Monahan?" he asked jabbing his finger on my three Seaman's stripes, only a rank below his. The sergeant reported that the Division had been cooped up on transport ships for a few days and he expected a degree of high spirits when the men were unleashed. He advised me that, if I was a friend of Curly, I was obviously aware of his propensity for mischief, and that I had best watch him closely, or, like him, I would be persona non grata. I left our table to dance with an Okinawan girl and the next thing I knew Curly was at it again. He tossed a glass onto the crowded dance floor before he was brought under control. He was quickly ushered out of the building by a phalanx of huge Marines. Rather than incur the wrath of the burly Sergeant, I made a quiet departure with my two buddies.

I didn't see Curly again until 1958, when we happened to be dating the same girl, Dorrit Riegert, a beautiful, willowy, intelligent, raven-haired German émigré who lived on Davidson Avenue in the Bronx. Dorrit was an avid and skillful dancer, and was obviously impressed with Curly's dancing acumen and his zest for life. Her attraction to Curly was short-lived. Though Dorrit was adventuresome and fun loving, she had a strong sense of propriety and was seeking stability given the difficult times she encountered growing up in war-torn Germany. Curly was a lovable character, but he drew the line when it came to propriety, and stability was certainly not his strong suit. Unfortunately, he didn't enjoy a long run.

He lived his life at a full and fast pace, but his fiery candle burnt out relatively early. Curly, who lived, loved, and fought like Farrell's Studs Lonigan, died a similar death at a young age in a dismal apartment near 32nd Avenue in Jackson Heights. I can't say that Curly ever tried to rise above his circumstances. All I know is that like Studs he succumbed to them much too soon. Nevertheless, he was a memorable and likeable person.

Jack Kehoe tells an interesting story about Curly involving the actor Douglas Fairbanks, Jr. For a time, Curly worked as a greeter at "21" the famous restaurant and New York institution, which was up the street from Toots Shor's, another classy watering hole on 52nd Street, where television personalities like Jackie Gleason, well known athletes such as Joe DiMaggio, Mickey Mantle, and Billy Martin, and a number of film stars would camp when in New York. Another Rockaway regular, from Curly's Chelsea neighborhood, Joe McConnon tended bar at Shor's.

As Fairbanks was leaving Shor's at closing time early one morning, Curly, McConnon, and Ronnie Riding were outside waiting for him. As Fairbanks approached they began to recite a number of scenes from the classic 1939 film, *Gunga Din,* in which Fairbanks starred in the role of Sergeant Ballantine. Curly, Joe, and Ronnie had seen the film countless times in Chelsea movie theatres and on the Late Show and the Late-Late Show. They had committed the entire dialogue to memory. Curly, playing Ballantine, McConnon in Victor McLaughlan's role of Sergeant McChesney, and Riding in Cary Grant's role of Sergeant Cutter impressed and amused Fairbanks and a growing crowd of revelers. Even Toots Shor was impressed, a feat in itself since he was forever needling people. Whenever Fairbanks returned to Shor's he would always ask Joe McConnon[72] about Curly and his friends.

The Spook

Rockaway drew characters from all over the city. One such person was Fred Fitz Stegman, otherwise known as the "Spook." Fred was from Jackson Heights. His main interest, when he was not freeloading, was scouting talented New York basketball players for obscure colleges. Gaunt and of medium height with blond hair and a slightly hunched back, he always wore a ratty London Fog raincoat, regardless of the weather. His beach attire was dirty white buc shoes, wrinkled khaki pants, and a t-shirt. He was just beginning his scouting endeavors after developing a direct line to schools such as Belmont Abbey and Elon in North Carolina, and Spring Hill, a Jesuit college in Alabama.

The Spook could be found wherever a large group of people congregated. He began his day watching basketball games at 108th Street, in the hope of spotting new talent, before walking across the street to Fitzgerald's or down the block to McGuire's. Both were popular bars in Rockaway. The mother of Dick and Al McGuire ran the latter establishment. Dick and Al are both members of the Basketball Hall of Fame, Dick[73] as a player and Al as a college coach.[74] Former basketball stars

---

[72] Unfortunately, Joe McConnon lost his long battle with cancer in 2003. John McComb tracked him down to the Irish Circle bar in Rockaway. I had a number of long and interesting telephone conversations with Joe in 2001 and 2002 about Curly, who he referred to as "Georgie," our Rockaway days, and his bartending experience at Toots Shor's and the Melody Lounge in Sunnyside.

[73] Dick attended LaSalle High School and St. John's University. As a 17-year-old freshman, he played in 16 games at St. John's, a team that won the 1944 NIT title. Due to wartime commitments, McGuire transferred to Dartmouth, where he played five games and led the Big Green to the 1944 NCAA Finals. He became the first freshman to win the Haggerty

at St. John's University, they played for the New York Knicks. Their older brother, John, was a detective with the NYPD, and a frequent attendee at sporting events where he usually had a betting interest. Al's playing days over, the Spook would help him recruit his first good team at Belmont Abbey. The Spook delivered Danny Doyle of Astoria, McGuire's original blue chip player who went on to play briefly for the Detroit Pistons. Al Maguire often told the story that he once invited the Spook to his mother's for dinner, and he didn't leave for a month.

When the bars filled up with people drifting in from the beach, it was common to start a pool of money or a pot. Individuals would contribute a dollar or two, and the pot would continue to be replenished as each new person joined the group. Since beer was 15-cents a glass, if you had staying power, you could consume a substantial amount of beer including the traditional free round the bartender delivered after your third round of drinks. Here is where the Spook was a master. He would slip into a group, pretend to put money into the pool, and drink free. As one would expect, sometimes the pools went dry for lack of money. Worse yet, there were

---

Award as the best player in New York City and was voted a Helms Foundation All-American. In 1950, McGuire, now one of eight people with a St. John's affiliation in the Hall of Fame, was voted the best player in school history. McGuire's brilliant college career blossomed as a professional, playing eleven years with both the New York Knicks and Detroit Pistons. As a rookie, McGuire led the NBA in assists (386). In seven of eight seasons, he led the Knicks in assists and ranks third on the all-time list with 2,950. McGuire's court savvy led the Knicks to three straight NBA Finals (1951-53).

[74] Al finished his coaching career at Marquette University in 1977 (1964-77) following seven seasons (1957-63) at Belmont Abby College. He lead Marquette to 11 consecutive post-season appearances beginning in 1967; won the NIT championship in 1970 and Marquette's only NCAA Championship in his final game as a coach in 1977. He won coach of the year honors in 1971 and 1974, and his .739 winning percentage is in the top-20 all-time among Division I coaches. He was elected to the basketball Hall of Fame in 1992, and spent 23 years as a broadcaster, first with NBC in 1977 and then with CBS from 1992 until March 2000. He died of a rare blood disorder at the age of 72.

many occasions when the participants lacked the financial resources to replenish the pool and sustain the drinking.

Berry Stainback of Sunnyside was the one exception in our Rockaway crowd. He was not a beer drinker and did not participate in the pools. He preferred mixed drinks. Berry, who went on to a career in journalism and public relations, always seemed to have money and did things in moderation. While he stayed with the crowd, he always comported himself well. Berry and I would spend time together after our military service, while both of us were attending NYU.[75]

When the money in the pot was depleted, the condition was known as being "tapped out" - out of beer. Al Maguire described it as "Tap City." Fertile minds flourished in such dire situations. By August, our collective thinking spewed forth a scam known as the Flower Pot.

Members of our crowd, lacking monetary resources, would identify a well-liked friend who didn't show up at the beach that weekend. Armed with a name and a sympathy card purchased at a nearby candy store, we would fan out along the boardwalk, beach, and bars and prey upon those foolish enough to listen to our come-on.

"Eddie Crowley's brother, sister, mother, or father died and everyone was chipping in to send flowers to the funeral home. Can you spare 50-cents or a dollar? We need at least $25?"

---

[75] Berry had a part time job running the School of Journalism Morgue, which was just across the street from the School of Commerce, where I was studying. The Journalism Morgue was located on the second floor of the building where the "Triangle Shirtwaist Company Fire" occurred in 1911, killing 146 sweat shop workers trapped on the building's upper floors. I visited Berry regularly and we discussed world and local events while he cut articles out of the New York Times and filed them away in folders. In addition to his career in public relations and journalism Berry authored three enjoyable sports biographies including, *"Snake," "Extra Innings,"* and *"Joe, You Coulda Made Us Proud,"* detailing the on and off-the-field lives respectively of the great Oakland Raiders Quarterback Ken Stabler, Cincinnati Reds and Baltimore Orioles outfielder Frank Robinson, and Joe Pepitone, the former New York Yankee first baseman, who had a brush with the law.

The girls were easy marks. They would usually pony up a dollar and were eager to sign the sympathy cards. When the target amount was reached, the collectors would regroup, count our newfound fortune and head for a bar off the beaten path to avoid coming in contact with our marks. On one occasion $25 was collected within an hour. Initially, the person who missed the beach that weekend was puzzled when approached the following week with expressions of sympathy. To assure continued success on future weekends, it was deemed essential to inform the absent person about the falsified story of their relative's demise and to seek his full cooperation in responding appropriately to the expected expressions of sympathy when he returned to the beach. A suitable response was suggested, such as, "The flowers were beautiful. I really appreciate your friendship and generosity." Not wanting to miss out on future Flower Pots, everyone fostered the continuation of this scam.

One Sunday morning about 10:30, John McComb and I had a relatively early breakfast and decided to check out the girls on the beach. We ran into the Spook on the boardwalk at 108th Street. He was perched on the railing, with his back to the beach, lamenting his hangover from the previous evening. On a good day, the Spook looked like death warmed over. He gave off a low moan and a grunting sound and complained that the concessions stands and the bars were closed, leaving him without a place to go to the bathroom.

"Fred, why don't you go under the board walk, like everyone else," John said.

"Christ, there're rats down there. I'll get sand in my shoes, and everyone will see what I'm doing."

"Well, Fred, since you're already in position on the railing, why don't you take your dump from there – nobody will notice," John dared him.

"Will you hold my rain coat?"

"Sure Fred, I wouldn't want you to spoil that fine coat."

At that, the Spook removed his dirty raincoat, adjusted his pants and while straining intensely managed to defecate in front of hundreds of stunned people sunning themselves on the beach and those passing by on the boardwalk.

"That was a noisy crap, Fred. We should've had a sound meter on that baby," John said.

"Don't be so funny. I'm sick."

"There's certainly no argument on that point, Fred."

"Stop being such a wise guy, John. You know you're a good enough player to get a scholarship."

"Just what I need, Fred – a recommendation from you. No thanks!"

"That took a lot of courage, Fred. You're now a legend," I told him.

"Your legend will be greater if you don't have any paper with you," John added.

"You don't expect me to wipe my ass in front of all these people, do you?"

"God forbid Fred, you'd never do anything that gross, or would you?" John asked.

Paper or pride was not a priority for the Spook. He was a person of the moment. He didn't give any thought to his actions. His focus was on surviving, and the day had just begun. It was his inalienable right to act as he pleased. It's July – its Rockaway – I'm the Spook – therefore, I think that I can crap wherever and whenever and the evidence could be seen clearly and distinctly in the sand beneath his perch on the rail. [76]

---

[76] Two years later while sitting in my barracks on Okinawa. paging through the latest issue of *Sports Illustrated,* I discovered a feature article on the Spook acclaiming him for his success in discovering talented basketball players in his scouting efforts, not only for small colleges, but for some of the better known and nationally ranked schools.

The Squirrel

While John and I were not in a league with the Spook, we were capable of gross behavior. One afternoon we left work early to watch friends on Equitable's softball team play a game in Central Park. As we were leaving the park after the game we came across a dead squirrel. The cute little thing had made his last stand next to a trash receptacle. I noticed a large brown envelope sitting on top of the pile of trash. An idea quickly formulated, and the deceased was inserted, albeit gingerly, into the envelope and sealed inside with the metal tab at its top.

"Neal, what in God are you doing with that squirrel?"

"Well, we can walk over to Bergdorf-Goodman on 5th Avenue and leave it on one of the first-floor display counters."

John jabbed my arm as we walked towards the 59th Street and Fifth Avenue exit of the Park. "Get real. They won't even let us in there. I've got a better idea."

As we walked by the Plaza Hotel he said, "Let's stop for a drink, and pretend that some guy, who just walked out of the bar, left it on his stool."

"You mean here?" I said. "If they won't let us in Bergdorf's, we're certainly not getting into the Plaza." [77]

"Don't worry, I know the perfect place."

We stopped at a bar on 57th Street near Madison Avenue, ordered our beers, and waited for the occupant of one of the stools on either side of us to finish his drink and leave. After a while, the guy standing beside the stool next to John's drank up, said good-bye to the bartender, and walked out the

---

[77] Ironically, 12 years later, John playing the role of a bellman in the movie, *Barefoot in the Park*, would pick up Robert Redford and Jane Fonda's luggage as they stepped out of a Hansom cab in front of the Plaza Hotel in the opening scene.

door. I slipped the large envelope out from under my shirt, passed it to John, and he called the bartender over.

"Excuse me. The man sitting here left this envelope on his stool."

"Thanks. I'll hold it for him. He comes in every day. If he doesn't remember it before he gets to Grand Central, he'll pick it up tomorrow."

The bartender took the envelope, and was initially startled by its weight and form. He placed it on a shelf just below the cash register and walked to the end of the bar to refill the drink of another customer and engage him in conversation.

"Did you see the look on his face when he picked up the envelope?" John asked.

"He's obviously curious about the contents," I responded.

"We have to wait this out. I just know he'll look inside that envelope."

"I hope he makes his move soon because I have to piss like a racehorse."

"Me too, I have to go, too," John said.

The wait seemed endless. John suggested that we turn away from the bar. Sure enough, the bartender had been waiting on us. When he thought we weren't looking, he made his move.

"Here he comes, Neal. If you start laughing, we're in big trouble."

The bartender nonchalantly walked past the cash register, grabbed the envelope in full stride, and moved to the deserted end of the bar adjacent to a darkened luncheon area where the lighting was poor. We had difficulty watching him through the mirror behind the bar. He was bent over holding the envelope near a decorative light that illuminated the liquor display on the bottom shelf behind the bar. "O' Jesus," he suddenly exclaimed. John and I used all of the self-restraint we could muster to avoid exploding into laughter. As we turned towards his voice he was moving in our direction.

"This envelope you found – that fucking guy is a sicko – a fucking sicko."

"What happened?" John asked in feigned wonderment.

"There's some kind of hairy thing in here," he said holding up the envelope.

"Is it a toy?" I asked.

"It's no fucking toy – it's some kind of animal."

"Is it alive?" John asked.

"Whatever it is, it's fucking dead."

"You have some strange clientele," John noted.

"Wait till I see that fucker again."

At that moment I headed for the bathroom as I was about to pee in my pants. John quickly joined me. We did all we could to hold in the laughter as we voided into the urinals. We returned to the bar and John left the bartender a dollar for his troubles.

"Well, we better get going or we'll be in trouble with our girlfriends," John said, as we gracefully made our exit. We walked around the corner and let the laughter pour out. We were laughing so hard that we ended up sitting on the sidewalk nodding our heads up and down as we tried to restrain the tears resulting from our convulsive laughter. People in the rush-hour crowd must have thought we had just escaped from the mental ward at Bellevue. Going home on the crowded subway, we would look at each other and suddenly burst into laughter. We had turned an otherwise routine day into a lasting memory, given our innovative use of an innocent squirrel.

11

July 4th

Since the Little Penn Tavern was overflowing with people starting out for the long weekend, Bob Perite, John McComb, and I walked over to a bar that someone had recommended on 31st Street on the south side of Penn Station. To our surprise, it was packed with young women from the nearby J.C. Penny's headquarters. Before we knew it, we were dancing with three of them. The hormones were raging and soon we were making out in a booth.

The only problem was that the girls we had teamed up with had an eight o'clock train to the Jersey Shore, and we were going to Rockaway the next morning. They begged us to join them, but we were unprepared to leave that night. After some stimulating goodbyes, we helped the girls board the train. As the train vanished down the tracks, I thought that with it went a promising weekend. I would wonder for weeks to come if not tagging along had been a mistake. Probably not, since all we had were a few bucks in our pockets and the clothes on our back. Besides, as John McComb reminded us, the drinking age in Jersey was 21. It was 18 in New York, so we probably couldn't get served in Jersey. We decided to play it safe.

We arrived in Rockaway early Saturday afternoon and hooked up with Lester Anderson, Billy "Doc" Doherty, Frank "Nipper" McPartland, John Power, Billy Thomas, Jack Healy, and a large gaggle of other characters, with whom we engaged in a long weekend of fun and debauchery. The Sugar Bowl[78] crowd from Astoria also joined us - Jack Kehoe, Brendan

---

[78] The Sugar Bowl crowd was Airborne bound; most of its crowd enlisted in the Army to become parachutists, including Kehoe, Malone, and Courtney.

Malone, Ed "Mo" Burns, Gene Carbine, John Courtney, Dick Oliver,[79] and many others. Jack Kehoe[80] was home on leave from his Airborne training at Fort Campbell, Kentucky. He regaled us with stories of his zany parachuting buddies. Jack joined Brendan,[81] John McComb, and me for a few games of basketball at the 108th Street playground where he displayed his effective two-handed shot from beyond the key. Some 25 years later, moviegoers witnessed Jack's shooting skills in his starring role as the character named Set Shot in *The Fish Who Saved Pittsburgh*.[82]

Billy Thomas startled people by making comical use of his large and hairy beer belly. Using lipstick, he'd paint a full-lipped face of a woman around his navel. He'd light a cigarette, insert it in his navel, and move his belly in and out to simulate the hairy-faced woman smoking. Nipper

---

[79] Dick Oliver became a prize-winning investigative reporter with the *Associated Press* and *The New York Daily News*. Eventually, he was named editor of *The News*, and then moved into the greener pastures of television reporting. He appeared regularly on Channel 5 in New York City until he retired in 2004.

[80] When Jack Kehoe was discharged, he pursued a career as an actor. His tremendous talent brought him numerous roles on stage in New York and on the large and small screens of Hollywood. He has appeared in some 35 feature films, including *Panic In Needle Park, The Gang That Couldn't Shoot Straight, Serpico, The Sting, Reds, Star Chamber, Melvin & Howard, Dick Tracy, Night Run, The Game, Car Wash, The Untouchables, Young Guns II* and *The Paper*.

[81] When Brendan Malone completed his Airborne service, he used the basketball skills he crafted at the P.S. 10-schoolyard, 108th Street in Rockaway, and Iona College as a coach at Power Memorial High School in Manhattan, before moving to Syracuse University as an assistant coach. He was head coach at the University of Rhode Island before joining the New York Knicks. He was an assistant with the Detroit Pistons during their championship years before being named the first head coach of the Toronto Raptors. He recently served as interim coach of the Cleveland Cavaliers, following another stint with the Knicks, a few seasons with the Indiana Pacers and finally the Orlando Magic.

[82] In another of Jack's movies, *The Pope of Greenwich Village*, Jack played the role of a NYPD Officer. At Jack's request Ed "Mo" Burns, then an NYPD sergeant, provided technical advice and assistance. Jack had his name changed in the movie script to Ed Burns. As fate would have it, Ed would marry Mollie McKenna and while residing in the Boulevard Gardens they produced two sons, Ed and Brian, talented screenwriters, actors, and producers. While they both wrote and acted in *The Brothers McMullen* and *The Fighting Fitzgeralds*, Ed also wrote and acted in *Sidewalks Of New York* and *Life Or Something Like It*. Ed was also one of the leading actors in *Saving Private Ryan* opposite Tom Hanks, co-stared with Robert DeNiro in *15 Minutes*, and played leading roles in *She's The One, No Looking Back, Any Given Sunday, Life or Something Like It, Confidence, Looking for Kitty, Purple Violets, Entourage, Will and Grace, The Breakup Artist, A Sound of Thunder, The River King, The Groomsman, The Holiday, One Missed Call, 27 Dresses, The Lynch Pin, Echelon Conspiracy, Nice Guy Johnny, Newlyweds, Vietnam in HD, Man on a Ledge* and *Friends with Kids*.

McPartland, who always had something funny to say, would act as a circus or sideshow barker introducing Billy Thomas to the crowds on the beach, boardwalk, or in the bars.

The daily litany of beach, bars, food, bars, sleep, eat, beach and bars with intermittent games of basketball, would continue through the long weekend. It was a ritual in which hundreds of young men and women participated at the time. There was the strengthening of old friendships, the making of new, loads of laughter, endless dancing and all the levity and foolishness that evolves from the chemistry of idle yet fertile minds.

Amidst the laughter, friendship, and loyalty of friends that weekend for reasons I cannot explain, other than the influence of alcohol, we focused on the political and sexual persuasions of His Imminence Francis Cardinal Spellman, Archbishop of the Diocese of New York and the Vicar General of the catholic members of the armed forces. Our discussion soon evolved into the crowd chanting:

"Cardinal Spellman is a communist – a communist – a communist ..."

The chants were repeated over and over. It startled many of our contemporaries who maintained an abiding respect for their Catholic faith. The older Irish Catholics in the bars and on the beach were enraged.

"Shame on you."

"You'll rot in hell."

The angry responses didn't resonate with the majority of us, who were more than happy to undo the years of brainwashing by the Sister Mary Josephs of our parochial school days. If our declarations of the Cardinal's political persuasion were considered sacrilegious to our growing audience, our introduction of the unspoken subject of his sexual preference really set them off.

We were summarily evicted from some establishments. Fueled by 15-cent beers and the knowledge we could push people's hot buttons, our anarchy was encouraged and our singing accumulated an endless tally of mortal sins. To attack the Cardinal was reckless and absurd, since New York Catholics idolized him, primarily for his pious manner and his rigid anti-communist posture. While we had no clue as to Spellman's sexual preferences, we were certainly on to something that in time developed into a significant problem for the Catholic Church.

Greenwood Lake

In mid-July, I joined John Mc Comb, Bob Houlihan, Dottie McQuade, Joan Dean, and Maureen Connaughton for a week's vacation in Greenwood Lake. The lake straddles the New York and New Jersey border about 50 miles northwest of downtown Manhattan.

We arrived by bus on Saturday afternoon and went to our separate lodgings. John, Bob, and I stayed in a converted garage. While commodious, it was dimly lit and damp. The girls stayed down the street in a cleaner and more comfortable rooming house. The location of our lodgings, a block from the beach at the New York end of the lake, could not have been better. A half-mile up the road that circled the lake was the famous Long Pond Inn, where the leading professional boxers trained. The center of town was just up the street to our left, where restaurants, a drug store, the movie theatre, other convenience stores and the Greyhound Bus stop were located. Though lacking a car, we enjoyed full flexibility of movement – everything was literally at our doorstep.

Joan and Maureen had planned the vacation. Dottie, who occasionally dated John, had invited him and he proposed the idea to Bob and me. We decided it would be fun and joined them for what turned out to be a memorable week. It was strictly a platonic venture. We were more like brothers and sisters on a vacation. Dottie McQuade and Joan Dean lived in the Boulevard Gardens and were six months ahead of me at St. Joseph's.

Dottie was an outgoing and fun loving person who could be counted on for her social staying power, good dancing, and great sense of humor. Joan was more attractive, introspective, and quick to tense up, but she too had social energy and was a good dancer. Maureen Connaughton was from 95th Street in Jackson Heights. She was tall, attractive, and elegant with a long neck, blonde hair and blue eyes. Her younger sister Eileen looked just like her and was an equally nice person. Maureen was a gifted dancer who moved smoothly across the floor, especially with a capable partner like Bob Houlihan. She possessed a marvelous sense of humor and a generous and kind nature. Dottie was the leader, Joan the serious one, and Maureen added a happy attitude to the group.

Bob Houlihan was from 88th Street in Jackson Heights. John and I met him at Ascension Parish dances in Elmhurst, Queens. Coincidentally, he was originally from Woodside and was born in Boulevard Hospital down the street from John's apartment house. Bob's grandparents emigrated from Ireland and settled in Hell's Kitchen. His maternal grandfather worked on the docks and with his savings purchased a two-family home in Jackson Heights. Bob's parents lived on the first floor and his grandparents lived on the second floor with their five remaining unmarried children. Bob's mother, the only one of her siblings to marry, was an absolute saint and the main bread winner of the family. His father, like many others in Queens, was a heavy drinker.

Bob was a serious person with a quick sense of humor and a resonating laugh. To John and me, he was very much an anomaly. He achieved exceptional grades at Power Memorial High School and was proficient in Latin, but for some reason was working nights as a shipping clerk for a photo-engraving company on 8th Avenue and 52nd Street. John and I were puzzled. We knew Bob was destined for something better.

Eventually, we learned that in Bob's senior year in high school there was no money in his household for college tuition. His father had major surgery about that time and was rehabilitating at a veteran's hospital in upstate New York, near the Canadian border. Like John and me, Bob's first job was at Equitable Life in the Group Claims Department on the sixth floor, and while his brief career at Equitable, in 1953-54, overlapped ours, neither of us knew him while he was there.

It seems that just about everyone worked at Equitable at some point in their life. Bob's wife, Pat Monaghan, an attractive young woman from Washington Heights, worked there from 1955 until they married in 1959.

Without question, Bob was the best dancer of the group, if not one of the best Savoy's in all of New York. Perhaps it was the influence of his high school classmate, Bobby Van Horn, the master of the Savoy. In the coming months, Bob, who had a keen ability to judge limits and knew when to quit, would have a positive influence on me.

In 1955, Bob joined the New York City Police Department and rose to the level of inspector while still in his early 40s. At one point in his distinguished career, he was head of the Police Academy. His record in the police department is unique. He was promoted from lieutenant to captain to deputy inspector in a little over two years. Bob was the gold standard for integrity during his career. He disdained the common practice of taking advantage of a feigned disability claim to bilk taxpayers out of generous life-long benefits. Bob is believed to be one of few individuals to retire as a full inspector without applying for such suspect compensation. Upon his retirement, he joined a major New York bank for a few years before being recruited by Master Card, where he served as vice president of the credit fraud department. As expected, he thrived in this position, which required him to travel throughout the U.S. and to many of the world's capital cities. Bob's success illustrates how some highly intelligent people often have rough starts or are sidetracked in their journey through life. He seized the available opportunities for success in the police department and distinguished himself during his tenure before moving on to a rewarding career in the private sector.

We began our days at Greenwood Lake, with a late breakfast in a small restaurant up the street before reading and relaxing on the beach or swimming in the chilly waters. Unlike Rockaway, where the Gulf Stream's current warmed the water, the cold lake water was initially shocking.

Each morning on the beach we scoured and discussed articles in *The New York Times*. One day we found ourselves discussing the obituary of Frida Kahlo, the radical Mexican surrealist painter who was twice married to Diego Rivera, the renowned muralist. The art section of the paper also discussed her interesting and tragic life, including her affair with Leon Trotsky and the controversy surrounding Rivera's famous mural in Rockefeller Center.

"What's surrealism?" I asked.

"It's an abstract form of art," John responded.

"That explains everything. Can you be more specific?"

"You remember when we met those girls at the Museum of Modern Art last year?"

"Yeah. That place was filled with girls."

"Ok. So you remember the building?"

"Sure, it was just off 6th Avenue in the 50s."

"Let's get back into the museum now. You remember those paintings of the clocks dissolving or dripping like candles?"

"Yeah. They were neat."

"They were painted by Salvador Dali - the Spanish surrealist. All his paintings are like that – like way out, man."

Weird people make weird paintings, I thought.

"Frida's surrealism was somewhat more primitive than Dali," Dottie opined.

"Her sex life was pretty primitive, if you ask me," John retorted. "Trotsky. What the hell did she see in Leon Trotsky? That old commie prune. Come to think of it, what'd she dig in that fat commie Rivera?"

I listened intently as John and Dottie discussed Frida's love life. Like TG, Frida slept around a lot.

"You clearly don't understand women," Dottie said.

"Would you sleep with those two creeps?"

"I haven't slept with anyone yet. That's not the issue. These men were important figures in her circles. That's what attracted her to them. They were interesting people. After all, Trotsky was a leader of the Russian Revolution and Rivera was one of the most famous people in Mexico."

After a short pause, John responded, "If that's the case, why don't you sleep with me – I was in a movie and I'm interesting."

"John, you never give up."

"Well, there's no harm in trying."

I laughed with them. I found the issue of female-male attraction mentally stimulating. I began to realize that it wasn't only physical attraction that drew people to each other. While that was the case with young people like us, to a larger degree it evolved around power, be it through fame, fortune or intellect. Admittedly, I had a lot to learn about the topic, but after TG, I had a better understanding of the power women had over men.

Dad had recommended that I visit the Long Pond Inn. At the first opportunity, I wandered off alone to find it. It is a fascinating, enormous rustic lodge built into the side of a hill above the west side of the lake. Its upper level housed a large bar and dining room with a view overlooking the water and the athletic training area was on the lower level where a boxing ring was centered. People milled around the ring to watch the sparring boxers.

Floyd Patterson, a young heavyweight from Brooklyn, who had won a Gold Medal at the 1952 Olympics in Helsinki, Finland, was having his hands taped when I first visited.[83] Patterson's coach in Helsinki was Pete Mello, a friend of Dad's who managed the Catholic Youth Organization boxing program in Manhattan. Dad often assisted Mello with his instructional program, and when I was 11, he enrolled me in the program for a few months. This background gave me an opportunity to introduce myself to the future Heavyweight Champion, a shy and well-mannered person, who was friendly and polite in conversation.

Walking down the road from the Long Pond Inn after that meeting, I stopped on the road to talk to Jake "The Bull" La Motta and Vickie,[84] his comely wife, who was pushing a baby stroller. La Motta, who had lost the middle weight championship to Sugar Ray Robinson in 1951, was a popular fighter who retired that April, following his loss of a 10-round decision to Billy Kilgore.

Having introduced myself as Pat Gillen's son, he remarked, "I know your father, but I never saw him fight. He's always at the Garden on Friday nights. Fast hands. He had fast hands; my manager told me. He came to my dressing room before and after my fights. Nice guy. Pat's a nice guy. Hey, what's your name again?"

---

[83] The previous month, he had suffered his first loss to Joey Maxim in an eight-round split decision. Patterson had already faced five opponents in 1954 and was training for another fight the following week. In the remaining months of the year, he engaged in a series of five fights against opponents the sports writers dubbed the "The Bum of the Month." He won 18 consecutive fights in the next two years cumulating in a fifth round knockout of Archie Moore for the Heavyweight title vacated by the retirement of Rocky Marciano, the undefeated champion.

[84] His stunning wife would pose nude for a *Playboy Magazine* centerfold when she was 51, and in 1980, Robert DeNiro won the Academy Award for Best Actor for his portrayal of La Motta in *Raging Bull*, the hit movie about La Motta's bizarre and violent life.

"Neal."

"Hey, Neal. This is my wife Vickie. We're going up to the Inn to watch that Patterson kid from Brooklyn."

"I just talked to him. They were taping his hands."

"Nice to meet you, kid." We shook hands and I nodded and smiled at Vickie. She returned the smile and they continued their walk towards the Inn. Lucky guy. What a beautiful woman, I thought as I watched them walk up the road.

We knew other people staying at Greenwood Lake that week, including Mary Timothy from Skillman Avenue in Woodside. A wonderful person, Mary also worked at Equitable. She was cute, intelligent and fun to be with. Her older brother Dan worked part time at Equitable while attending college. Her younger brother was a leading high school quarterback, who went on to play at Brown University. Unfortunately, the culture of the time precluded capable young women, like Mary, to attend college. The Catholic education system stressed a commercial orientation that discouraged girls from thinking that higher education was a realistic option. Otherwise, Mary, like Dottie, Joan and Maureen would have enjoyed many more options and opportunities in their lives.

Eddie Chester

Early in the week we had wandered into Eddie Chester's, a roadside bar on the other side of town. We wolfed down the inexpensive dinner special and made good use of the dance floor. In a lull between our dances, an affable, middle-aged man stopped by our table and engaged us in conversation. He commented that he thought we were great kids and hoped we were having a good time. We assured him that we were, especially after he treated us to a round of drinks. When he introduced himself as Eddie Chester, we invited him to join us. Eddie sat down and enlightened us about his years in Vaudeville as a song and dance man. Not sure if he was putting us on, we listened politely as he talked of the performers he appeared with who had gone on to great fame – Bob Hope, Jack Benny, Jimmy Durante, and many others.

Eddie invited us to an amateur night later that week. He encouraged us to enter the competition if we could sing or dance. Dottie McQuade immediately volunteered us to sing. We all did a double take.

"Dottie, are you out of your mind?" John said.

"Come on. It'll be fun," she responded.

"She's right, kids. Give it a try," Eddie urged. "You never know. That's how I got started."

Walking back to our lodgings, someone asked Dottie if she had any great ideas about who would sing and what we would sing.

"This will be fun; we'll all sing," Dottie exclaimed.

"Sing what?" Maureen asked.

"Well, in the BGTA Variety Show one of the songs was *You Belong to Me*,"[85] I said. Jo Stafford's recording of the 1952 hit song was still popular in 1954 and familiar to everyone who owned a radio or television set.

Since everyone knew the lyrics, Dottie suggested that the girls sing and the guys back them up with a *Boo Wop* sound.

It rained the next day, and after breakfast we assembled in our garage and rehearsed the number for a few hours. It proved to be an awkward rehearsal venue, since our ersatz garage-room didn't have an enclosed bathroom. It was off to the side and shielded by a tattered curtain. Whenever nature called, we would sing to drown out the noise and save the person using the toilet from embarrassment. At one point, Joan Dean leaned too hard on the sink and dislodged it from the wall. Miraculously,

---

[85] *You Belong To Me*. Lyrics and Music by Pee Wee King, Redd Stewart and Chilton Price.

the pipes held, and thanks to our understanding landlady, the tottering sink was quickly repaired by a local handyman.

It rained part of the next day, which let us work on perfecting our harmony. We finished around lunch time and concluded that we were ready. Whether we would perform credibly was another question. We did accomplish our other objective of not informing anyone we knew at the lake about what we were about to do. Secrecy was necessary to minimize our embarrassment in the event we bombed.

John Mc Comb, a good judge of talent, facetiously inquired, "What do you mean if we bomb? Is there any doubt about that?"

In our inquiries around town, we learned that Eddie Chester was the real thing. He enjoyed a successful career as an entertainer and was well thought of in the community. Eddie was the Vaudeville partner of the famous Ted Lewis, appearing as the dancing shadow in Ted Lewis' signature tune, *Me and My Shadow*.[86] In January 1958, Eddie would appear again with Ted Lewis on the Ed Sullivan Show.

On the night of our performance we debated whether we should eat or drink before we performed. We concluded that with our limited skills it didn't make much of a difference. We ate supper in the restaurant near our lodgings and then headed to Eddie's for the beginning and end of our budding singing careers. At the appointed hour, there was a drum roll and Eddie Chester announced that the Savoys would sing *You Belong to Me*.

We looked at each other with a collective thought: "Is another group singing our song?"

"Eddie needed a name for our group, so I made one up," Dottie said, as we gathered to approach the small stage.

---

[86] *Me And My Shadow*. Lyrics by Billy Rose; music by Al Jolson and Dave Dreyer, 1927.

1954 Adventures In New York

Eddie sensed we were nervous and helped us relax by asking where we were from. Six voices simultaneously said, "Woodside – Astoria – Jackson Heights."

"I don't know if these kids can sing, but they certainly can dance. Here they are ladies and gentlemen – The Savoys."

Without hesitation we began our act. The girls sang the lyrics, pausing after each line. John, Bob, and I filled in, cooing, *"Boo wop – boo wop."*

> *See the pyramids along the Nile*
> *Boo-wop, boo-wop*
> *Watch the sunlight on a tropic isle*
> *Boo-wop, boo-wop*
> *Just remember darling all the while*
> *Boo-wop, boo-wop*
> *You belong to me …*

We finished to polite applause and sheepishly rushed back to our seats. Aside from our poor voices and singing in the wrong key, the other major problem in the rendition was our inclusion of the *Boo-wop* fills. In Jo Stafford's recording, vibraphones were used for the fill.[87] Since there were only two other groups with the gall to appear that night, finishing third in the competition was far from being a significant achievement. In the remaining few days, we ran into people who amusingly commented about our appearance.

Dottie opined that secrecy was a mistake. "We should've packed the audience with friends. Then we would've won."

---

[87] Eight years later, in 1962, The Duprees – five Italian-American guys from New Jersey, (Tom Bialoglow, John Salvato, Joe Santollo, Mike Arnone, and Joey Canzano) kept the song alive and remade it a hit, replacing the vibraphones with the words *"shad rack"* as a fill between the lines.

"I don't think so," a skeptical John McComb noted.

Over the years, that experience proved to be a fond memory of a fun week with five great people. It was also a maturing experience for me. The relatively quiet surroundings and casual atmosphere had slowed down my usual frenetic pace and allowed me to engage people in serious conversation. It felt good to be accepted and to know that I was capable of holding my own in conversations. Though I felt more confident about myself, I realized that there was so much more to learn in life, particularly about art and current events. For the first time I had read *The New York Times* and *The New Yorker*, which Dotty McQuade had brought along. I had seen the latter in doctors' offices and loved the Barney Tobey cartoons, but I had never delved into its lengthy short stories and interesting topical articles.

Tommy Murphy

At the end of the week we ran into Tommy Murphy, the Snake Pit Honor Roll Member of Distinction, at the Long Pond Inn. Tommy recognized me from the Gardens. We often nodded hello when we came across each other in the neighborhood. I really didn't know him well, but I knew of his growing reputation as a character of sorts, particularly for being a night owl and brawler. He and his brother Kenny had recently been discharged from the Army where they had served in an Airborne Division. Tommy had a high-paying job as a checker on the West Side docks.

After a few drinks with Tommy that night it became clear that his reputation was well deserved. He was generous, funny, smart, and a great story teller, but his capacity for alcohol and trouble was prodigious. In the years to come I would get to know the Murphy family well.

Tommy and his brothers, Kenny, Donald, and Patrick lived with their spinster aunt, Grace Connolly in the Gardens. Grace was their late mother's sister. Her brother, their uncle Patrick J. "Packy" Connolly, was the de facto head of the powerful Manhattan Local 824 of the International Longshoremen's Association (ILA). It was commonly known as the Pistol Local. Packy, an ILA vice president, was respected, some say feared, and reportedly called the shots on the West Side piers.

Myles Ambrose, a former federal prosecutor and the executive director of the New York Waterfront Commission, observed, "If Packy gave the word, the Port of New York would cease to function." According to Ambrose, Packy would see the inside of the Grand Jury Room in New York's Federal Courthouse in Foley Square on many occasions over the years. Though some of his associates were indicted, convicted, and sent away, Packy avoided such a fate. The lengthy investigations could only produce income-tax evasion charges, which were quickly resolved with a civil fine.[88]

Grace Connolly and Mother were good friends and frequently dined and attended the theatre together, and in the coming years Don Murphy and I became close friends.

In 1960, I was the best man in his wedding to Barbara Frost, the most beautiful girl in Astoria. In 1964, he was my best man at my wedding when I married the attractive, brilliant, patient, supportive and understanding Mary-Margaret Donnelly of Poughkeepsie, who was a year behind me at Georgetown University Law School.

The Murphy's were bright, outgoing, articulate and fun-loving. The boys were raw-boned, muscular and of medium height, except for Donald, who was six feet tall. Their most distinguishing feature was their large, square-shaped heads topped with thick tufts of brown unruly hair. Each of

---

[88] When 'Packy' died in the early 1960s, his funeral cortège contained 21 flower cars and most of the limousines available for hire in New York City. The funeral procession tied up traffic on the west side of Manhattan with cars and police escort vehicles stretching the length of 10 city blocks.

them had a deep and resonating laugh and all were heavy drinkers. Tommy was a problem after a few drinks. He believed that with each swallow of Scotch he got smarter, while those around him got dumber. Initially, he was playful and mellow, but soon his mood darkened. The usual result was loud arguments, fistfights, and ultimately banishment from the premises. He was a classic Dr. Jekyl and Mr. Hyde[89] personality. Sober or high he was a thoroughly engaging personality and fun to be around. Drunk, you didn't want to be in his presence.

Over the years, the Murphy family would experience more tragedy than the Kennedy's. The four boys and their two sisters, Joan and Mary Ann, were orphaned at a young age. Kenny developed multiple sclerosis within three years of his discharge from the Army. Donald was killed at the age of 28 when a car smashed into the rear of his vehicle on Long Island. Tommy was 39 when he was hit by a truck and found dead in Long Island City, near the entrance to the Queens Borough Bridge. Patrick, the youngest, had poor health and died at 45. Joan, an attractive Navy Nurse, was killed instantly at the age of 29, a week before her wedding, when a car ran a red light and plowed into the side of her small car in Norfolk, Virginia. Mary Ann, the other girl in the family, died of cancer at a relatively young age. Kenny, the last surviving family member, eventually lost his sight and the ability to move about without assistance. He lived until 2003 and was cared for, motivated and sustained by his wonderful wife Colleen. She raised a large and successful family. Though proud of his family, Kenny was also proud that he overcame his difficult physical obstacles and acquired a bachelor's degree, two masters' degrees, and completed two years of law school. He maintained his wonderful sense of humor, compassion for others, and held his head high throughout his productive life.

---

[89] *Dr. Jekyl and Mr. Hyde,* Robert Louis Stevenson, 1886.

Murphy's Law

Murphy's Law establishes that "What can go wrong, will go wrong." That certainly was the case with Tommy, but he also carved out a special exception to this universal rule, which was invoked not against Murphy, but against whoever had the misfortune to deal with this unique character.

Uncle Packy had a large house on the east side of Greenwood Lake. Tommy would cruise over to the Long Pond Inn in Packy's sleek teakwood Cris Craft speedboat. His drinking would eventually lead to the loss of his boating privileges.

In his deep raspy voice, Tommy told me: "This is a great country. Where else can you jump in a boat and drive across the lake for a drink? I had no trouble getting the boat here, but getting home is another story. You can't imagine how difficult it is driving a boat in the dark when you've been drinking all day."

By the end of the summer, Murphy would also lose his house privileges. Packy was a patient man when it came to his blood relations, but he finally reached his limits with Tommy. The last straw was an incident involving a large dog.

Hatrick's Dog

One Friday later that summer, Tommy finished up on the docks in mid-morning and headed back to Queens. Shortly after 11 o'clock he stopped in Hatrick's, a popular bar on 48th Street and Broadway across the street from the east entrance of the 46th Street subway station. Bill Hatrick was a powerfully built and good-natured man, who easily handled trouble whenever it developed in his establishment. Tommy was the only customer that morning, enjoying his first of many drinks that day, when the liquor salesman arrived.

Hatrick was moving back and forth along the bar checking his liquor inventory while the salesman sat in a booth making notes in his order book. Meanwhile, Hatrick's large dog, a friendly drooling Boxer, was pacing back and forth with his leash in his mouth. The dog camped at the door and began to whine for his late morning walk. At first, Hatrick ignored him. The dog reacted to the lack of attention by barking and pawing at the door. At that moment, Hatrick made a serious error in judgment.

"Tommy, I'm going to be tied up here for a while, would you mind taking the dog for a short walk?"

"Sure Bill; I could use a walk myself."

Murphy leashed the dog and they began a journey that was long talked about in the surrounding neighborhoods. Murphy and the dog sauntered up Broadway towards Northern Boulevard while the dog made frequent stops at every hydrant along the Woodside Housing Project. Just down the street, at the corner of 53rd Place, was a bar called the Green Dolphin, where Murphy stopped for a beer. While Murphy was enjoying his beer the dog raised himself up on his hind legs to lick some spilled beer from the edge of the bar.

"So you want a beer too," Murphy said laughing. He ordered another beer and leaned down to allow the dog to lap it out of the glass. The dog finished the beer and Murphy finished his.

"Give me another, and one for the dog," Murphy said to the bartender.

"Tommy, is that your dog?"

"No, it's Hatrick's."

"That's what I thought. I don't think getting his dog drunk is a good idea. Suit yourself Tommy, but I don't think Hatrick's going to appreciate this."

"His dog certainly does," Murphy said, laughing.

"I'm serious, Tommy. I wouldn't fuck with Hatrick."

"Ah, let me worry about that."

Murphy finished his beer, looked at the bartender and laughing said, "We're going to have a good time. We're going bouncing."[90]

With the dog in tow, he left the Green Dolphin. Their next stop was a bar just up the street next to the Northern Boulevard subway station, where Stanley Bloom was tending bar.

"That dog looks hungry Tommy, why don't you get him a hamburger," Stanley suggested. At that, Murphy left the dog in the bar and got them each a cheeseburger at the White Tower next door. Following their greasy lunch and a few more drinks, Murphy decided it was time to visit Manhattan.

Well-primed with alcohol, Murphy put on his sunglasses, said goodbye to Stanley and left for "places unknown," as Stanley would tell Bill Hatrick later that afternoon. Murphy and the dog walked past the White Tower to the entrance of the subway station. Feigning blindness, a staggering Murphy led the woozy dog down the stairs into the station. Passing the change booth, he flashed his open wallet to the transit employee as he made his way to the exit gate used by students, subway employees, policemen and other people with special passes. As he did, he called out, "blind man." Once through the gate, Murphy pulled the now frightened dog down the platform to a wooden bench, where two middle-aged women were waiting for the 'GG' train.

Presuming that Murphy was actually blind, the women made room for him and told him they had done so. Murphy thanked them and sat down

---

[90] When a person went from bar-to-bar in the course of his or her drinking it was called "bouncing." Though "bouncing has a positive connotation, the term is derived from being bounced or thrown out of a bar and being impelled to move on to another one.

with the dog, who proceeded to sniff the ladies and the bench before lifting his leg to pee. Murphy whacked the dog in a failed attempt to stop him.

"You're not blind, you're drunk," one of the women said.

"You're blind drunk," said the other.

"Got this new 'Seeing Eye Dog' today – never been on the subway before."

"That's a lie. Those dogs are trained for everything. I don't believe you for a minute."

"Honest, lady. I'm blind – the dog's new at this."

"Don't give me that. You could see if you weren't drunk, I'm going to tell the man in the change booth to get the cops."

The arrival of the train saved Murphy, who boarded the last car with the dog and took a seat adjacent to the rear door of the train. The next station was 46th Street, where the train paused directly under Hatrick's. The women reported their concerns to the conductor, who delayed the train until he found Murphy. The conductor confronted him about his status, and again the frightened dog peed. The motorman came out of his compartment and walked back through the cars to join the discussion. By this time, Murphy was convinced he was blind and persuaded the skeptical subway employees to let him remain on the train. He exited the train a few stops later at Queens Plaza and boarded an 'E' train for the stop at 23rd Street and 8th Avenue in Manhattan.

Murphy introduced the dog to a number of his favorite bars in Chelsea and Hell's Kitchen. Early that evening, while Hatrick was searching far and wide for his dog, Murphy got a sudden urge to visit Greenwood Lake. He stopped a taxi, put the dog in the back seat, gave the driver a $10 bill, and told him to take the dog back to Hatrick's in Queens. The driver jumped out of the cab, returned the cash, and told Murphy to remove the dog. A long discussion ensued and a compromise was reached. The driver took them both to the Port Authority Bus Terminal.

Murphy, fully oiled after seven hours of drinking, was now quite confident in his blindness. He entered the terminal, purchased a ticket for Greenwood Lake, and moved cautiously towards his bus gate. On a Friday night, especially in the summer, the bus terminal is jammed with people, many the dregs of New York, so the sight of a drunk with a large dog wouldn't merit a second glance. Noticing the driver was not on the bus, Murphy led the dog up the stairs and proceeded to a window seat in the rear. The dog crawled under the seat directly in front.

As the sunlight began to set over the Hudson River, the fully loaded bus embarked for the Lincoln Tunnel. As the bus entered the tunnel its interior darkened, the dog panicked and started to bark incessantly.

"Jesus," Murphy muttered to the woman sitting next to him. "I think my dog's scared."

The bus exited the tunnel and pulled over to the side of road beyond the tollbooths. The driver rose from his seat and began walking towards the rear.

"Who's got a dog on this bus?" he asked.

Murphy raised his hand and called out, "It's a 'Seeing Eye Dog'."

"How'd you get on my bus?"

"I walked on."

"I didn't see you."

"I certainly didn't see you," Murphy said laughing.

"You'll have to get off the bus."

"I'll need the dog as a guide."

"I want you and the dog off the bus."

As Murphy and the dog made their exit, he tugged the driver by the arm and led him to the side of the bus. Again he asserted his blindness, convincing the driver of his status with a $20 bill, and a promise that the dog wouldn't cause further problems. The dog, now frightened by the roar of the heavy traffic, cinched the deal by peeing against the tire.

They re-boarded the bus and the dog slept all the way to Greenwood Lake. Murphy walked the dog to his uncle's house, explaining to Packy he had found it on the road. Sometime on Sunday, about the time that Packy was running out of patience with his nephew and the dog, Murphy ran out of money. In desperation, he hatched a scheme. He picked up the telephone and called Hatrick.

"Hello Bill, how's everything going?"

"Who's this?"

"It's Tommy Murphy."

"I'll kill you, you fucking bastard. Where's my dog?"

"The dog's fine. I took him bouncing with me, and before we knew it we wound up in the country. He loves it here."

"Where are you, Murphy?"

"Lend me a 'C-note' and you can pick up your dog."

"I'll kill you first."

"Bill, I'm sorry about this, but if you want to see your dog again, go to the Western Union office near Steinway Street and call me at this number."

Hatrick called 15 minutes later, whereupon Murphy instructed him to give the Western Union clerk the $100 and to put the clerk on the phone. Murphy instructed the clerk to immediately wire the money, in his name, to the Western Union office in Greenwood Lake, and requested that Hatrick wait for confirmation that he received the money. A half hour later, Murphy called to confirm he had the money and advised Hatrick where to find the dog. Murphy had a few beers at Eddie Chester's before tying the dog to a tree across the street from the Western Union Office. A relieved Hatrick retrieved his dog and returned to Queens. Murphy repaid the money a few weeks later, but he was banned from Hatrick's for more than a year.

The Bus

Though a bus played a significant role in getting Murphy and the dog to Greenwood Lake, it wasn't the only important bus in his life. Late one night the crowd gradually drifted out of the Shannon Inn. Surprisingly, and contrary to his normal practice, Murphy was one of the first to leave. One of the last to depart was Pete Moriarity a brilliant and unpredictable individual who graduated with honors from Bryant High School and later would distinguish himself at Columbia University.

Pete's car was parked outside the Shannon, partially in the bus stop lane. As Pete pulled out of his parking space, the bus was pulling in – resulting in a severe collision. Upon impact, Pete's car was propelled onto the sidewalk, where it rolled over into the large plate-glass window of Pat Abram's drug store. Shattered glass and Kotex boxes from the window display were strewn about the sidewalk. With considerable effort, Pete managed to extricate himself from the car. Upon doing so, he returned to the Shannon where he called Murphy, getting him out of bed. Within minutes Murphy managed to dress, run down Hobart Street and insert himself into the rear of Moriarity's overturned car. When the bus driver, and the police officer, who had just arrived on the scene, asked Moriarity why he left the car to run into the Shannon, Pete informed them he had called an ambulance for his injured friend trapped in the back seat.

The ambulance arrived a few minutes later and took Murphy, pleading for relief to his injured neck and back, to St. John's Hospital in Long Island City.

Following three days of X-rays and extensive probes of his body, Murphy was released from the hospital wearing neck and back braces.

Keenly aware that insurance detectives would follow him in the coming weeks, Murphy remained relatively sober and avoided physical exertion until the insurance company made its initial offer. He negotiated his settlement in the Shannon, accepting a check for $2,500. To seal the deal he insisted that the insurance agent include a six-pack of Rheingold Beer.

HFC

Murphy proved to be highly resourceful in acquiring money from large corporations. Late one Friday morning, a small crowd gathered in the Garden Grill in preparation for an outing at the Aqueduct Race Track. Murphy wandered in and was invited to join the group for a day at the races.

"I'd love to go, but I've insufficient funds," he lamented.

Just then, Benny the bartender said he had an idea and called Murphy over to the end of the bar near the telephone booths. After a few minutes, Murphy, smiling from ear to ear, inquired when the group would be leaving for the track.

"Tommy, we're waiting for Kevin Walsh. We won't leave for another hour," answered Wally Di Masi.

"I'll be right back. I think I know where I can lay my hands on some money," Murphy said, as he headed out the door. About 20 minutes later, when the telephone rang in the Garden Grill, Benny rushed to the booth.

"Why yes, Mr. Murphy works here. He just stepped out a few minutes ago. I believe he went to the fish market to pick up today's lunch and dinner order. He'll be back shortly."

"Oh, he's with you."

"Yes, he's the chef here."

"I'm not exactly sure sir. I've been here two years, and he was here then."

"Yes, he's an excellent chef, you should try his veal picatta."

"Of course he's a reliable employee, but you better get him back here for our luncheon trade."

"What seems to be the problem, sir?"

"Oh, I see, you just wanted to verify his employment. Well, why didn't you say so in the first place?"

"Who's this? I'm the day manager, Mr. Ronald Timothy," Benny said using the first names of the two owners of the bar.

Murphy returned 15 minutes later with a check for $150 from the Household Finance Corporation (HFC) office on Roosevelt Avenue in Jackson Heights. He cashed the check at the Pickwick Market and was soon off for a day at the races, with $50 of the $150 sitting in Benny's pocket.

12

Rabbit Makes the Hall of Fame

August began with Dad and a large neighborhood contingent traveling to Cooperstown, New York for the Rabbit's enshrinement into the Major League Baseball Hall of Fame. I wanted to make the trip, but I had used up all of my vacation time, and Dad made it clear that it wouldn't be proper to take a sick day for such an occasion. "What if you got your picture in the sports pages? Once they saw that you'd get fired." When I told Andy Rosasco where Dad was going that day he surprised me by telling me he would have given me the day off if he had known that I wanted to go. He told me he had seen Maranville play for the Boston Braves in the 1930s. He was fascinated that the Rabbit had lived downstairs from me and that I was there when he died.

Dad had contacted his drinking crony, former New York Yankees Pitcher Vernon "Lefty" Gomez,[91] and arranged for many of the Rabbit's friends to make the trip in a special train filled with sports writers and former players. As a favor to Dad, Lefty had appeared at a number of sports' nights at the Elks and the Jackson Clubs. Aside from being a great athlete, he was a character of sorts, and a terrific storyteller, whose presence always guaranteed a large attendance.[92]

---

[91] "Lefty" was the winning pitcher in Major League Baseball's first All-Star Game, was Joe Di Maggio's roommate, and, in 1972, was inducted into the Baseball Hall of Fame.

[92] Two of "Lefty" Gomez's funny stories linger in my memory. Referring to his hitting ability, he said, "I was the worst hitter I every saw." He followed this up with the time he surprised everyone, including himself, by hitting a double, only to be picked off second base. "What the hell were you thinking out there? his irate manager, Joe McCarthy, screamed when he returned to the dugout. "How would I know, I've never been there before," he responded.

A number of former Giant and Yankee players were on the train since Giant great, Bill Terry, and the Yankee's outstanding catcher, Bill Dickey, were also entering Baseball's Hall of Fame that day.

According to Dad, during the trip to and from Cooperstown, the Woodside contingent enjoyed themselves and hoisted many drinks in memory of their departed friend. Upon their return that night, the revelers made their way to the Oyster Bay, a bar and restaurant on Broadway in Astoria. When asked if there was a bar on the train, Frank "The Sea Lion" Dwyer exclaimed, "Jesus, Mary, and Joseph! The whole damn train was a bar!"

The U.S. Navy Reserves

The month took on a new meaning as the news media turned its focus from the first anniversary of the Korean Truce to a place called French Indo China. New war clouds appeared on the horizon. The French were dealt a crushing defeat by Vietnamese forces in the battle of Dien Bien Phu. Before they capitulated on May 7th, French Prime Minister M. Pierre Mendes-France pressured the United States to intervene on its behalf, but President Eisenhower decided that enough had been done for the French. It was a poorly kept secret that Eisenhower provided considerable assistance through the Central Intelligence Agency in supplying the French forces with over 600 airlifts of ammunition and food supplies.

The Cold War was now at its apogee, making military service a given for my generation. The Selective Service System continued to draft young men for the Army at Korean War levels to replace those being discharged in order to maintain troop levels in Germany to deal with the potential threat of a Russian invasion of Europe and to preserve the truce in Korea. In some areas of New York City, young men not attending college stood a chance of being drafted at 19. The draft was something that I was just beginning to think about. I had sat in class at Delehanty's with a number of wounded Korean War vets, mostly Marines, who were recovering at St. Alban's Naval Hospital. And, many guys from the neighborhood had served in Korea. I didn't relish the thought of combat, but war or the threat of war had been a constant for most of my life – military service was a certainty. Everyone in our neighborhood had either served or would be serving. There were no options about service, but you could make a choice to enlist. If you were drafted the chances were high that the Army would send you to Germany or to Korea, neither of which seemed appealing to me since both countries still had a long way to go in repairing their respective infrastructures that had been destroyed by war. Besides, serving in either of those places promised to be no more than an extended camping trip. If you enlisted, however, depending on the military branch you selected, it was likely that you would be sent to a first-rate technical school.

The thought of military service was foremost in my mind and those of my contemporaries when John McComb suggested that we protect ourselves from the Army draft by joining the Naval Reserves. It was something I had to face sooner or later – it was a rite of passage, and since I had been on an accelerated track all of my life, I felt it was time to see what the Navy would be like. Another selling point for the Navy Reserves was that John McComb was joining, and I wanted to be part of what he was doing.

Jackie Bennett, a friend from 50th Street, and a member of the Reserve unit in Whitestone, agreed to drive John, Howard Kelly and me to a drill meeting one night in July. The Naval Reserve Armory was located on the East River near the Queens' side of the Whitestone Bridge about a block from the Cresthaven Country Club. The meeting ended with a beer party, which cinched our decisions to join. The atmosphere was friendly and relaxing. Another member of the reserve unit was Richard "Red" Hilliard, who I knew from the Clover Inn on 52nd Street in Woodside. Red urged us to join by telling us that we would find it a rewarding experience.[93]

Howard "Howie" Kelly was a fun loving individual who lived in the other end of my apartment building in the Boulevard Gardens. We played basketball together almost every day and night either in the P.S. 151 school yard or the gym. Howie soon would have a new job driving a diaper truck.[94] His business cards carried a novel sales pitch, "Your Baby's Shit Is My Bread And Butter."

During our introductory drill meeting at the Whitestone Armory, we met with the executive officer and the senior enlisted men after we had filled out the requisite forms for processing our enlistment. Late in July, we were notified of our acceptance and requested to appear in August to be sworn into the U.S. Naval Reserve Surface Division 3-76 as Seaman Recruits. Dad was happy with my choice, since he was a member of the Naval Reserve in the late 1920s, where he won the Atlantic Fleet lightweight boxing championship.

The Reserves would prove to be an interesting experience in the coming months. We began our weekly meetings with inspections, followed by marching drills to develop teamwork and discipline. In the classroom sessions, which followed the drill instructions, we studied Morse code, signal lights and flags, knot tying, ship identification, and the principles of seamanship outlined in our basic text book, *The Blue Jacket's Manual*. We

---

[93] Red would remain in the Reserve Unit for 30 years. He became a New York Fireman and served until his retirement. In the mid-1970s, he and Harry Curley of Jackson Heights purchased the Garden Grill, where Red tended bar a few days a week until he and Harry sold the Grill in 2010. The new owner of the Grill drove away the customers and lost his license a year later. This once vibrant community hub is now a vacant store front.

[94] A few years later, Howie joined the police department and upon his retirement from the NYPD he moved to Naples, Florida and worked in hotel security. He succumbed to cancer last year at his home in Naples.

were paid $30 a month to attend the weekly meetings, and at the end of the month we finished early to share a cold keg of beer.

One night, driving home from a meeting, a motorcycle officer pulled us over to the side of Grand Central Parkway across from Saint Michael's Cemetery, where many of New York's Mafia legends, including Frank Costello, are buried. Jackie Bennett, the most cautious driver in America, was beside himself.

"Honest officer, I wasn't speeding," he pleaded.

"That's not the problem sailor. 'Ike's' coming by in a few minutes. We have to clear the Parkway."

"President Eisenhower?"

"He's the only 'Ike' that I know of."

"Can we get out of the car to see him?" Jackie asked.

"Sure; just don't do anything stupid."

A few minutes later, President Eisenhower drove by. The light was on in the back seat of his limousine allowing us to see him clearly as he waived to us and others who had pulled over on the side of the parkway. Little did I realize that 12 years later, I would be riding by that same location in a similar motorcade with President Lyndon Baines Johnson, in my role as a White House advance man.

Spuyten Duyvil

The work and play activities of August became a continuum of July. The weather was hotter than the Cleveland Indians, who were now leading the Yankees by seven games. The Giants were leading the National League, but the Dodgers were in close pursuit along with the Milwaukee Braves who moved from Boston to Milwaukee in 1953. New Yorkers expected to have a home team to root for in the October World Series. The Indians seemed to have the American League pennant sewed up, so even Yankee fans were not keen about the Braves making a run for the pennant.

The heat made work difficult in these pre-air conditioned days, and the listless application chasers were challenged to find a place to cool off. The building's roof was one option that we utilized from time-to-time. The elevator operators placed deck chairs near the top of the elevator shafts, where they relaxed during their smoking breaks while enjoying the cool breeze and the view of the top of the curved glass and steel canopy rising above the main hall of Penn Station, its 7th Avenue neighbor, the Pennsylvania Hotel and the Post Office building and the New Yorker Hotel on 8th Avenue.

On the roof one sweltering afternoon, Joe Gianinni announced, "Boys, tomorrow I'll provide the relief from this heat wave. Bring your bathing suits; we're going swimming."

"Where, Joe?"

"We'll drive up to Spuyten Duyvil for a swim in the creek." A swim in a cool creek sounded refreshing. I had never heard of Spuyten Duyvil before. I figured it was some place out in the country in Westchester County. I was soon treated to an interesting lesson about the geography and topography of New York City.

The top of Manhattan Island ends at Baker Field, the football stadium of Columbia University and the waters of the Harlem River, which separates Manhattan and the Bronx. At this point, the river is called Spuyten Duyvil Creek. It flows east from the Hudson River and then south into the East River at Randall's Island and the Triboro Bridge. Overlooking the river from the Bronx side is a large stone formation known as Spuyten Duyvil. Cut through the formation is a railroad pass for the northbound trains to Albany and beyond.

Following a busy morning searching for insurance applications, we left the office at 11:30 and headed for a parking lot on 8th Avenue and 31st Street. Joe lowered the top of his 1953 Mercury convertible and drove Artie, Dick, John and me up the Westside Drive and across the Henry Hudson Bridge into the Bronx. It was an exhilarating ride. The refreshing cool breeze from the Hudson River was enhanced by the speed of the car. We pulled up down the street from Joe's house in front of "Sugar" Ray Robinson's home. Robinson, the former welterweight and then middle weight champion, was one of the greatest boxers of all time. After we changed at Joe's place he drove us to the nearby freight yards, adjacent to the river. As we emerged from the rail yard, we came upon a group of young guys climbing up the rock formation and diving or jumping down into the swiftly moving water.

The top of the rock is about 80 feet high. I decided to watch for a while before leaping. After observing the jumpers and divers, I concluded that the water was deep enough to prevent injury from a properly executed jump or dive. As a further precaution, I entered the river and swam around the base of the cliff to determine how far out I should jump for safety purposes. Surprisingly, the side of the cliff was sheared straight down with no edges protruding out into the river. Since the current and pressure prevented me from diving too deep, I concluded it was as safe as the neighborhood kids claimed it to be.

Joe and I climbed up the side of the massive rock outcropping and realized that once we were up there it would be next to impossible to climb back down, given the traffic of divers and jumpers waiting behind us.

"Hurry up, you chickens, we haven't got all day."

"Chickens, chickens, go ahead and jump."

At that, Joe and I looked at each other; much like Paul Newman and Robert Redford did some years later in the movie, *Butch Cassidy and the Sun*

Dance Kid, before they jumped off a cliff to avoid pursuing lawmen. We jumped off together, hitting the cold water in a rush. When we surfaced we looked for each other, and burst into laughter.

"Mid-Town Manhattan Insurance Company Workers Drown in Bronx – how about that for a *New York Daily News* headline?" Joe said, as we swam back to the riverbank.

Though we had a hard time convincing the others to join us, Joe and I had a great time that day. Just as we were about to leave, one of the neighborhood kids asked us if we were going to stay for the arrival of the Circle Line tour boat. They informed us that the sightseeing boat, which cruised around Manhattan Island, was due in a few minutes and it was the neighborhood custom to mount the rock and moon or expose one's backside to the tourists aboard the boat. A few minutes later, the boat appeared and the captain tooted the horn to alert the rock climbers. We also learned that the Captain advised the passengers what was likely to happen. When the boat approached, it appeared it was going to capsize, with all the passengers having suddenly moved to the right side of the boat for a close-up view of our butts. Except for a group of startled nuns, all of the passengers cheered us as we showed our backsides before we jumped into the water.

We were back in the office by 3:30 that afternoon, made another search of the seventh and eighth floors, and handed in the applications we found, along with those we had stashed in our lockers. Not really a typical day at the office, but a fun day for all of us. This reckless pursuit indicated that my inclination for adventure still prevailed. Progress was slow – I still had a lot of reforming to do.

Lester Anderson

As the summer progressed, our group at Rockaway Beach grew larger and closer as we shared countless funny experiences. I had become better acquainted with Lester Anderson, thoroughly enjoying his outgoing personality. We initially met in the Sunnyside freight yards when I was about eight years old, during the price control and rationing days late in World War II. Meat, butter and sugar were deemed essential foods, and were rationed along with household goods such as soap. Our parents were issued coupon books and tokens that were required for the purchase of these items. Lester lived on 39th Avenue and 54th Street, just off Woodside Avenue, a few blocks from the freight yard's back entrance.

The Sunnyside Yards was the largest railroad complex in the world, running from Woodside Avenue almost three miles west to the East River tunnels at Hunters Point. Woodside Avenue is a continuation of Newtown Road, which was the main traffic artery in Queens during colonial times. It was once known as the Narrow Passage, surrounded on either side by the marshlands of the Wolf Swamp. The Pennsylvania Railroad purchased the land west of the swamp in 1905 and drained and graded it for a switching and train storage yard.

In 1776, an estimated 36,000 British soldiers, of the 42nd Highlanders, the Black Watch Regiment, under the command of Lieutenant General Henry Clinton, were camped in the dry land above the swamp, preparing to recapture Manhattan Island. Pursuant to the unpopular Quartering Act adopted by the British Parliament in 1765, the local farmers were required to provide a substantial portion of their production to feed the British troops.[95] Many of the troops were billeted below the hill in what is now the

---

[95] *"Woodside, Queens County, New York – A Historical Perspective 1652-1994,"* at pages 27-32.

Sunnyside Yards. The foundations of the 50-foot-long rectangular dugout huts, in which the British soldiers lived, were unearthed during the excavation and grading of the railroad yards.

Following the rout of General George Washington's troops and the recapture of Manhattan in September 1776, General Clinton became the commanding general of British Forces in America. While in Woodside, he utilized the farmhouse of Tory Loyalist, Nathaniel Moore, as his headquarters. The Moore homestead was located just north of where Northern Boulevard, Woodside Avenue and 51st Street converge at the location of the bus and trolley barns originally built as the terminal for the New York and Queens Railway. The Moore family cemetery is located on 54th Street by 32nd Avenue, near the Boulevard Gardens. One of the sandstone gravestones indicates that the person buried in that plot died in 1769.[96]

Long Island City in the 1940s and '50s was the largest light manufacturing area in the country and most goods were shipped by rail in that era, which predated the construction of the interstate highway system and the advent of long-haul truck shipments. The railroads were a dominant force in America and the freight yards were bulging with freight and passenger cars. Kids would walk the five blocks from the Gardens and spend part of the day having fun running through passenger trains and up and across boxcars. We rarely saw the railroad cops, who focused their patrols further up in the yards, where the freight and passenger trains were being loaded and assembled for their next trip.

I first came upon Lester Anderson, walking along a path next to the tracks pushing a baby carriage overflowing with boxes of Ivory Soap Flakes, a popular household product. Lester, along with his younger brother

---

[96] Ibid at footnote No. 1, pages 14-19.

"Buzzy," were supposedly minding their infant sister, Laurali, who was sleeping soundly under the boxes of soap. Curious as to where they had come from and where they were going, I followed them out of the yards and up Woodside Avenue to Blondie's, a small grocery store. Lester quickly negotiated a price for the soap with the storeowner and headed back to the yards.

"You can come, but you better keep your mouth shut," he said, as I continued to follow along. We reentered the freight yards and walked for some distance to a box car with its door slightly ajar. Lester pushed open the door and climbed into the car. In a flash, Laurali was covered with boxes of Ivory Soap Flakes that Lester had tossed down to us. Then, we made our way back to the expectant grocer. After three more trips, we retired for the day and enjoyed the soda and cupcakes purchased with the funds Lester realized from his great train robbery.

Lester remains one of the most likeable individuals I have encountered in life. He was tall, tanned and well-muscled with blond hair and blue eyes. A handsome Swede with all the classic Viking features, the girls flocked to him in droves. His playful nature and unpredictable antics, especially after a few beers, kept everyone in stitches. When he topped out with his fill of drinks, Lester, weary from his long workweek in his construction job, would collapse in a heap. Once he nodded out, at the beach or in a bar, it was slumber-land for at least an hour. Since it was difficult to awaken him, quite often the group's movement was delayed, while Lester caught up on his sleep. He was generous to a fault, and on many occasions he literally gave people the t-shirt off his back. [97]

---

[97] In the years to come, Lester's strict work ethic would pay off. He utilized the knowledge and the skills acquired in construction work to establish his own lathing and concrete company. His two sons now operate this successful business. Lester and his attractive wife Mary, a former American Airlines executive, now live in Yonkers after their initial retirement in Fort Myers, Florida.

Dave Richardson

One of the most the interesting persons I befriended at the beach was Dave Richardson, who lived in Woodside's Matthew's Flats on 52nd Street between Skillman and Roosevelt Avenues. Dave also had a connection to Blondie's, working there every afternoon while he attended Bryant High School. Reserved and serious minded, Dave, a few years older than I, served as an excellent role model. He was patient and deliberate and possessed a great, albeit subtle, sense of humor.

I found Dave's theory on pursuing women most interesting, "Neal, you must stay cool and show minimal interest," he advised. He believed that eventually the object of your desires would notice you, inquire about you, and be receptive when you made your move. Dave was unique in this regard, since most of us were under the impression that given our short time on earth, quick pursuit was the only way to go. Dave, smitten with Dottie McQuade, pursued her with his indifference and neglect technique.

"I don't think it'll work," I told Dave one night as he was waiting for the bus near the Hobart Theatre.

Looking at Dottie standing outside the Greek's, Dave smiled and said, "Not to worry, she'll come around."

The bus arrived and I walked back to the Greek's to rejoin the crowd. To my surprise, Dave's strategy was working. Dottie started asking questions about him.

"Where's he work?"

"Long Island City."

"What's he do?"

"I'm not sure. Something to do with adding machines or computers, I think."

"How old is Dave?"

"Twenty."

Dave's aloofness had sparked her interest. After a few weeks, they began to date. That's when Dave decided to buy a car. He bought a black mint condition 1936 Chevrolet sedan with a stick shift. It was a roomy car with jump seats that allowed it to comfortably seat eight people in the front and back. In the months ahead, it would become our primary means of transportation, taking us as far as West Point, New York and Fort Dix, New Jersey.

A good friend of Dave's, Bill Marquette, joined the group and our numerous good times in the remaining days of the summer and into the fall. Bill was kind enough to give me his old draft card. With the skillful help of a friend in Equitable's printing department the card was effectively doctored to include my name and my age as 18.[98]

Dave and Bill were helpful in other respects, in that they were quick to rein me in when I drank too much or became too boisterous. I don't know what it was about Dave and Bill or what they saw in me, but they took me under their wing. I listened to what they had to say. They would frequently advise me to use my intelligence and to consider other viable alternatives in life, like college or military service. These counseling sessions took place during the week, when we were more reflective in our thinking and not so influenced by the quest of beer and girls as we were on the weekends.

On most nights that August I played basketball in the playground in back of the Gardens or in the P.S. 151 school yard where we also played softball when a large enough group was on hand. While Dave and Bill were not active in sports they sometimes played softball and always joined the group for beers afterward.

---

[98] At a memorable 2003 get-together with Bill Marquette, Bob Houlihan, and our wives in Hilton Head, South Carolina we recalled his enabling my underage drinking.

Reflections

Our conversations usually focused on sports, a recent movie, our escapades at the beach, or girls. We didn't have plans or dreams about our futures at that time. We all had acquired the "security syndrome," a residue of the Great Depression. We were afraid to face the challenge posed by Eugene O'Neill,[99] of what to do with our "pipe dreams?" We didn't even have pipe dreams. We didn't have a clue about what to do in the years ahead. We never questioned ourselves about where we were or where we were going in life.

It was years earlier, but the only person I recall asking such questions was Sean Gallagher, but that was during our grammar school days. The Gallagher family lived in 'I' building in the Gardens. Sean and his two younger brothers, James or "Jay" and Jerome, were hard working and inquisitive. Sean and I frequently served mass together at Corpus Christi Church, and, along with Billy O'Donoghue, we walked together to St. Joseph's most mornings. Sean was six months behind me at St. Joseph's and Billy was six months ahead of me. Billy would go on to St. Ann's Academy and following his graduation he worked for an oil company before following his father's footsteps into the Police Department. Sean would attend St. Francis Xavier High School and then Fordham College and its Law School.

If I wasn't serving Mass that morning, I would leave for school at the 8:30 break in the Arthur Godfrey radio show after finishing a breakfast of Cornflakes or Wheatena. Walking with Billy and Sean we would talk about the things that young boys discussed: the New York baseball teams, movies, school and the interesting traits of our many friends from the Gardens and St. Joseph's or the how the nuns at St. Joseph's were treating us. Billy was a

---

[99] *The Iceman Cometh,* by Eugene O'Neill.

good athlete. We were both catchers and competed for time behind the plate while we both played for the baseball teams sponsored by the Gardens and Corpus Christi Church. Our rivalry was friendly, but occasionally we got cross with each other, usually when we played on opposing teams. We remained good friends up to the time of Billy's untimely death from a brain hemorrhage when he was in his late 20s. I believe that Billy, like Bob Houlihan, would have gone far in the police department.

Sean Gallagher was innately curious and always peppering me with questions about various subjects. What do you think about this or that? What do you want to be? Billy's questions were more sports oriented. Who do you think is better, Joe DiMaggio or Ted Williams? Sean is still asking dispositive questions, initially as a lawyer and now as an investment banker.

All of us were unselfish towards each other during this critical time in our lives. Growing up, our imaginations were shaped by radio shows and action comic book fantasies. I didn't discover books and cultivate my love for reading until I began high school.

Late each afternoon, in our childhood years, we were lured back to our apartments to listen to our favorite radio programs, *Jack Armstrong, Captain Midnight, Sergeant Preston,* and *The Green Hornet.* Depending on the day of the week, after dinner we could listen to *The Lux Radio Theatre, Inspector Keen, The Shadow, The Inner Sanctum,* or *Gangbusters, Duffy's Tavern,* and *The Life of Riley.* On Saturday mornings I never left the apartment until I listened to *Grand Central Station.* Sponsored by Pillsbury Flour, the program had a great opening sequence featuring the noise of a train whistle and the continual noise of its wheels clicking as they made contact with the tracks as the train rushed towards its terminus at Grand Central Station, which the announcer dramatically described as "the crossroads of a million private lives…"

The sound of the train was stimulating to one's imagination. It stirred up a desire to travel to places depicted on the programs you listened to. I would hear that whistle when day dreaming on fall days listening to football games later in the afternoon, particularly the broadcasts of the great University of Notre Dame football teams coached by Frank Leahy. They weren't day dreams of college studies, but of the far-away places I yearned to visit.

My parents, who came of age in the Roaring 20's and who survived the hardest of times experienced in the 20th century, were trapped in a Great Depression era mentality. It was all too fresh in their memories – a time when 13 million people, one-third of the U.S. workforce, were unemployed. At that time, there was no such thing as unemployment insurance or Social Security. Our parents still visualized the scenes of bread lines and 1.5 million people in New York, a city of 6 million, on a skimpy welfare program known as Home Relief. People were living in tents and shacks in Central Park and in other "Hoovervilles"[100] and shantytowns around the city.

Most of our fathers were too young to serve in World War I and too old for World War II, but they carried the baggage of those wars along with the Great Depression. We listened to countless stories of people losing their lives, jobs, homes, businesses, and savings. These human tragedies made a deep impression on each of us, as we attended grammar school during World War II and began high school at the outset of the Korean War. If we had a driving factor or a motivating force it was our instinct for security, given the stories of hard times that lingered in our memories and were always at the tip of the tongues of our parents and relatives.

---

[100] Named for U.S. President Herbert Hoover, who was in office at the onset of the Great Depression.

We were optimistic, but above all, we were security conscious. What to do with our lives was a conundrum. New York may have been the promised land to some, but few of us who grew up in its environs recognized it as the place for us to reach our full potential. I left New York to make the most of my opportunities in the Washington, D.C. area. It was our New York preparation, however, that enabled many of us to succeed in our careers.

College was not an option for many of us, though it was a dream that many of our parents wished would come true. The white, Anglo-Saxon, Protestant ruling class expected us to build or service structures, protect people from crime, fire and disasters or provide services such as transportation, gas, electricity, accommodations, food, insurance, printing, and banking. Family connections were expected to assist you in finding a good paying job in the building trades or driving delivery trucks, or as members of the police, fire or sanitation departments, in the New York Telephone Company, Con Edison, the various bus or subway systems, or in the printing trades at one of New York's many newspapers or printing houses. Simply put, we were working class, but we were much better off than our fathers and grandfathers, who faced harsh prejudice in seeking meaningful jobs.

The "No-Irish-Need-Apply" barrier had not as yet been surpassed and while the jobs reserved for the Irish may have paid well, there were few opportunities for advancement. The Irish learned something from their earlier treatment at the hands of the then ruling Protestants by establishing an "Irish-Only-Need-Apply" standard that would serve us well in many blue collar union jobs.

We measured our success or lack thereof based on how our

friends were doing. We were much like Ken Kesey's band of hippie friends known as the "Merry Pranksters." Kesey[101] observed that his friends had similar problems. "When you don't know where you're going you have to stick together just in case someone gets there," he said. That certainly described our collective thinking. We were not seeking affluence, since we had never observed it close up. Therefore we had no desire for something, which, at best, was an abstract concept that we only observed while watching a movie.

Though proud of the status that our parents had achieved, we knew there was something better, like a nice house further out on Long Island, but we were still unaware that it would be a considerable struggle to achieve more than that. Little did we know that the term working class would take on a new and favorable light when the children produced by our generation or their children would sacrifice their lives in the World Trade Center on September 11, 2001. It took a tragic event to finally give those who make New York function their just due, even though year in and year out they continually sacrifice themselves for others by building, servicing, and protecting a great city.

We were just out of high school with three to four critical years to find ourselves, waiting for our call to military service, falling in and out of love, and in my case in and out of trouble. We didn't have any idea what would become of ourselves. Our options were limited to our lives in our home boroughs and whatever opportunities were lying in wait in Manhattan. We didn't know of the opportunities that were there. Most of us had never heard of F. Scott Fitzgerald, no less what he wrote to his future wife, Zelda, soon after his arrival in the early 1920s, that in New York "anything was possible."[102] For the majority of us, our opportunities were limited, and

---

[101] Kenneth Kesey is the author of *One Flew Over The Cuckoo's Nest*.
[102] The letters of F. Scott and Zelda Fitzgerald.

given their Depression experiences, our parental role models pushed us towards job security. That is why I know a great many retired police officers, fireman, and civil servants and explains my enduring and interesting career in the cotton industry.

While the young men of my generation were confused about their potential, the young women were limited to seeking office or retail work and then restricted from any chance of success. A few went on to college, usually becoming teachers or nurses. They put in their time waiting for a good marriage proposal and departed the work force just before the arrival of their first child.

I don't know if it was the influence of Dave and Bill or John McComb's continual prodding to live up to my potential, but something was stirring in me. In five months at Equitable, doing the repetitive task of finding applications, I observed and talked to a number of people in supervisory positions. They might have been book smart and obviously more mature than I, but I didn't consider them any smarter than I was. They too were performing repetitive tasks that I thought I could do. There had to be a shortcut to putting in all this time and slowly moving up from one boring job to another. The shortcut was college, but my conundrum was how do I get there from here?

Considering College

Bob Perite and I would meet at 8:30 each morning at the entrance steps to the Gardens in front of 'A' building and walk the two blocks to the Northern Boulevard subway station. John McComb would board our train at the 46th Street stop and we would ride together to Queens Plaza, where we forced ourselves into the first Manhattan bound train arriving at the express platform.

Bob was still talking about college, and after work one day he convinced me to accompany him to Brooklyn to visit the Pratt Institute of Technology, a highly regarded art and architectural school that offered a few pre-engineering courses. Most of my Brooklyn Prep classmates and some of my Delehanty classmates were preparing to set off to college in a matter of weeks. While that stirring was there, levity still reigned. I was having too much fun to reflect on college until Bob raised the issue.

While Bob was filling out admission application forms, I perused the available literature and the course catalog and wandered about Pratt's hallways thinking about it. I continued to read the literature going home on the subway, and as I did, I began to think that if Bob could do it, so could I.

When I arrived home, I reviewed the Pratt material again and left it on the kitchen table. The next morning it was gone. Puzzled, I thought I had misplaced it and would find it later. Dad was waiting, when I returned home from work. What's with him? He should be drinking in some bar, I thought.

"Son, I'd like to talk to you about your future."

Uh-oh, what brought this on? I wondered.

"Son, I always wanted you to be a college man, an engineer. I was very happy when I found the materials from Pratt this morning." Dad explained that he took the Pratt catalog and brochure, and reviewed them with the civil engineers at the construction site where he was working.

"It's a terrific school. I'll help you with the tuition," he announced.

He was in an expansive mood and beaming with pride. I knew this was special, since my conduct and scholarship up to this point in my life produced few, if any, such moments. I had finally done something right. His feeling good was gratifying and encouraging. His encouragement and praise was the first I had received in too long a time.

We discussed the preparatory courses that the engineers recommended I consider taking, and I began to believe that I could really do this. I was going to college, if they would accept me.

The following day, I visited the personnel office and learned that Equitable Life would pay half my tuition if I maintained an acceptable grade point average. There was no backing out now. I returned to Pratt that night to begin the process of applying for admission and arranging for the mailing of my transcripts from Delehanty's and Brooklyn Prep. Two weeks later, a letter arrived announcing I was accepted for admission to their night session for the fall semester. Wow. A college, a good college, had accepted me. Maybe I wasn't so bad after all, I thought. Enclosed with the letter was a list of recommended courses. As the summer began to fade, I began to focus on my future.

13

Labor Day

 Labor Day was filled with promise. For many of us, it would be our last opportunity to gather together and release our pent-up adrenalin and overactive hormones. The anticipated pleasures of an exciting weekend had me and every other guy and girl in high spirits, ready for that final fond embrace and goodbye to summer.

 My experiences at Rockaway taught me the importance of getting a decent place to stay. John McComb, Bob Houlihan, Kenny Reich and I rented a room near the Cross Bay Bridge. It was relatively clean and affordable. More importantly, having a nice room enabled us to have a larger wardrobe and a place to sleep and clean up. Kenny Reich was another friend that I had acquired that summer. He, too, was a member of our Naval Reserve Unit. He lived on 92nd Street in Elmhurst and attended St. John's University. Tall and preppy with blonde hair, Kenny was a person in whose company you felt comfortable. Conservative in manner, like Bob and John, he helped monitor my exuberance.

 The weekend was another three days of sun and fun, though the fear of the impending hurricane "Carol" trimmed the number of people making it to the beach. The storm moved east beyond Montauk Point, leaving us with ideal weather. One vignette from that weekend stands out in my memory. On Sunday morning, Bob Houlihan and I were walking up Rockaway Boulevard to meet Jack Sherman and a group of BICs from Parkchester to attend Mass at Saint Camillus' Church. As we approached the awning over the entrance to a bar in the vicinity of Playland I instinctively took note of its ragged condition and jumped up and punched at the ripped edge of the canvas. No sooner had I landed from my jump when a man dashed out of the bar and punched me square in the jaw, sending me flying onto the hood of a car parked at the entrance. My head ringing and jaw aching, I slumped down to the sidewalk reflexively admitting it was a stupid thing to do. Looking up at his angry face I listened to a lecture on respecting the property rights of others. Then, he reached down and pulled me up from the side of the car asking, "Are you all right?" "Do you need any ice?"

Politely, I declined his offer as I checked to see if I had all of my teeth. I apologized again as I rubbed my jaw before we moved on. Walking away, I did something I never thought I was capable of doing – I admitted to Bob that I was wrong.

"I really screwed up. I never should have done that." Bob agreed, and like me, was amazed at the quick reaction of the man cleaning the bar.

"That guy came out of nowhere. You were smart to apologize."

"It happened so fast. I'm surprised by each of our reactions." Massaging my jaw as we walked towards church, I thought about my foolish act and my tactical surrender. A foolish and immature act quickly followed by a well-reasoned and sound decision based on fear – perhaps my first experience that many wise decisions are often generated by fear. In my case, the fear of having the bar owner wipe the street with me. I have not forgotten that incident. It flashes back whenever I approach an awning entrance to a bar or restaurant.

I often look back on the summer of 1954. It was a laboratory experiment in human relations. Above all, and aside from my scare from my involvement with TG, it was a summer of wonderful friendships and enjoyable times that brought me together for the first time with a large group of people beginning to find their way in life, testing boundaries, experiencing passion, developing loyalties, and learning to look out for one another. The guys and girls in our ever-expanding circle could depend upon one another for both friendship and support. We enjoyed our newfound freedom. We did so with gusto, taking great care to respect each other. We returned to the beach each week to see our new friends, strengthen these friendships, and savor these great times together. Yes, many of us were interested in the physical aspects of socializing. Occasionally we got lucky, but what really lured us back each week were the wonderful friendships.

Changes At Equitable

The Lay Underwriting Department's team of application chasers, Gianinni, Gillen, O'Rourke, Pertrowski, and Wassen was about to be changed by the promotion of John O'Rourke. Chris Burns from 30th Avenue and 45th Street in Astoria joined our team. Chris was in the class ahead of me at St. Joseph's with Dottie McQuade and Joan Dean. He was not satisfied with his initial job out of high school at General Motors and decided to make a change. He couldn't believe what we were up to, and how we went about doing our job. Chris had a funny way of shaking his head and rolling his eyes when we outlined our activities for the day. "No one in Astoria will believe what we're doing here," he would often exclaim.

John O'Rourke's promotion was well deserved and everyone was happy for him. He would be working for Andy Rosasco and also assisting Grace Van Sicklin. His salary was increased by about $10 a week with the assurance of overtime. Chris Burns was initially skeptical about whether O'Rourke's knowledge of how we went about our job would be revealed. We assured him it wouldn't, as did John, and Chris quickly learned the ropes of application chasing, all the time shaking his head in disbelief.

September also brought with it an increase in activity in insurance applications as the economy continued to burgeon. This meant overtime almost every night, which raised my take home pay into the $50 range. It would have been higher, but my Naval Reserve and college obligations limited my availability in the evenings.

The overtime work gave me a chance to meet the part time college workers, who arrived late in the afternoon and worked into the evening. Many of them were attending college under the Reserve Officer's Training Corps (ROTC) or the Marine Corps' Platoon Leaders (PLC) program, including Harry Bailey from the Gardens. They received commissions as Army or Marine officers upon their graduation. In Harry's case, it was the Marines. Others, like John Chianese, were members of the Army National Guard. John was a member of the Seventh Regiment's honor guard. His dress uniform was similar to that of the West Point cadets, gray cutaway jackets with rows of brass buttons across the chest complete with tasseled epaulettes on the shoulders and wide white leather belts around the waist. An observant *Life* magazine photographer enshrined John in history the following year, when Jayne Mansfield, the heavily endowed actress, reviewed the honor guard at a film preview. While Chianese was steadfast at attention, his head looking straight forward, the camera lens captured his large eyes bulging sideways from their sockets in amazement and admiration of Miss Mansfield's bountiful cleavage.

The college workers held regular Saturday night parties at a suite in the McAlpin Hotel on Broadway and 32nd Street. The parties were civil, instructive, and enjoyable. At these soirees I found myself almost equal to the group since I was a member of the Naval Reserve and was about to begin my life as a college man. Though every guy in attendance was destined for the military, not one of us gave any thought to the foreign policy obligations of the U.S. beyond Europe and Korea.

On September 8th, an additional burden was added to our generation and those that followed when the U.S. joined the South East Asian Treaty

Organization (SEATO),[103] a defense alliance organized to affirm the rights of the Asian and Pacific people to self-determination and equality. In the years to come, however, the U.S. would pay a high price for its SEATO obligations – some 58,000 lives in Vietnam, including those of John Ryan and Jimmy Hanley from the Boulevard Gardens.

Pratt Institute of Technology

The Pratt Institute of Technology is located in the Fort Greene section of Brooklyn on Myrtle and Clinton Avenues near the Classon Avenue station of what was then the 'GG' train. Getting there and home was a logistical task. Bob Perite and I would take the downtown 'A' train from 34th Street 10 stops to the Hoyt & Schemerhorn station and transfer to the Queens bound 'GG' train for three stops, and exit at Classon Avenue. One the way home I followed part of my old Brooklyn Prep route for 14 stops to the Northern Boulevard station. The long ride gave me the opportunity to catch up on my reading.

Introductory Physics and Trigonometry were my initial course offerings that fall. Since my weekends were less taxing than those of the summer, my brain synapses were functioning somewhat better, at least in the physics course, a subject that I had enjoyed in high school. The classroom number was the only thing I was sure of in trigonometry, as I was in over my head. I should have taken a refresher course in algebra since everything sounded like Chinese. My first quiz mark in physics was respectable, but my trig grade was a 65, a charity grade that probably included points for personality and perhaps spelling my name correctly. Nonetheless, I kept to my schedule of working overtime at least two nights a week, fitting in the weekly Navy Reserve meeting, and going to school the

---

[103] The initial members of SEATO were England, France, Australia, New Zealand, the Philippines, Pakistan, and Thailand.

other two nights. The pace set at Pratt was challenging, and the overtime at Equitable enabled me to put aside money and begin to assemble a decent wardrobe.

The Pennant Race

Since the Yankees had no chance of catching Cleveland in the American League, like everyone else in New York, I was caught up with the standing of our two National League teams. As the weather turned cooler, the National League pennant race was still hot as the teams came down to the wire. In the end, the Giants finished five games ahead of the Dodgers by virtue of their sound pitching and solid hitting. Johnny Antonelli led the league in earned runs with a 2.30 average, and his 21 wins and 7 losses gave him the league's highest winning percentage of .750. The other Giant pitchers had mediocre years compared to the pitching staff of the Cleveland Indians. Rueben Gomez was 17 and 9, Sal "The Barber" Maglie 14 and 6, Don Liddle 9 and 4, and knuckleball pitcher Hoyt Wilhelm 12 and 4. Willie Mays led the league in hitting with a .345 average, in slugging with a .667 average, and captured the Most Valuable Player award. Don Mueller led the league in total base hits with 213 and lost out to Mays on the last day of the season in his quest for the batting title, finishing the year with a .342 batting average. Despite the Giants' excellent record, it appeared that they would be cannon fodder for the awesome Cleveland Indians, who wrapped up the American League Pennant relatively early, winning more games than any team up to that time. They banished the Yankees from the World Series for the first time since 1948, which was also the last time the Indians had won a pennant.

Cleveland's pitching was spectacular, with three of its four starting pitchers, Bob Feller, Bob Lemon, and Early Wynn, destined for the Baseball Hall of Fame. The four starters won a total of 79 games. Bob

Lemon and Early Wynn led the league in pitching with respective records of 23 and 7, and 23 and 4. Mike Garcia had the league's best earned run average of 2.64 runs per game and a record of 19 and 8, while Bob Feller was 13 and 3. Second baseman Bobby Avila led the league in hitting with a .341 average, and Larry Doby, the first black to play in the American League and a future Hall of Fame outfielder, won the home run crown with 32 round trippers and led the league with 126 runs batted in. In addition to Doby, Al Rosen was a feared hitter who had previously led the league in home runs. Also, Cleveland's acquisition of Vic Wertz from Baltimore gave them another serious long ball threat.

Wertz was one of my favorite players. During his 1951 and 1952 seasons with the Detroit Tigers and the St. Louis Browns he gave the Yankees fits because of his ability to pull balls down the short right field line. On the weekend games that I worked when Detroit and St. Louis came to town, I always got to my job in Yankee Stadium early enough to be dressed in my white vendor's uniform and on time for the morning batting practice. Wertz would put almost every pitch over the low wall in right field, in the vicinity of the foul line and the bullpen, where the distance ranged from 293 to 310 feet. Many of the other vendors had the same idea. We carefully positioned ourselves when Wertz took his swings. I got lucky one weekend, ending up with five practice balls that Wertz smashed into the right field seats.

Hurricane Hazel

"Look out folks. This could be the big one," said Tex Antoine in his evening Con Edison weather forecast in mid-month. "This one's called 'Hazel.' She's tearing up the Carolinas, and heading our way," he warned.

His forecast was as accurate as it had been around Labor Day when he predicted that hurricane Carol would blow out beyond New York City in her trip up the East Coast.

Hazel turned out to be a real killer, wreaking havoc up and down the entire East Coast. Communities were bruised and battered in her wake. It was one of the most violent and damaging storms in history, resulting in the death of 99 people in the U.S. and 240 in Canada. The rain fell in buckets. The neighborhood's many sailors, home on leave or on weekend passes from destroyers and cruisers based in Boston, Newport, and Norfolk were stranded. Train and bus transportation came to a standstill because of washed out tracks and roads up and down the coast.

Everything came to a halt in New York as well. The subways were partially flooded and many bus routes were diverted. I made it into work each day and presumed that the Naval Reserve meeting would be cancelled that week. Jackie Bennett, never one to miss a meeting, called John McComb and said we should try and make it. Jackie took a circuitous route to get to the Whitestone Armory since the Grand Central Parkway was flooded. He was determined to get there, and when we all did, after navigating through the heavy rain and flooded streets of Flushing and Whitestone, we found few people in attendance. All you could do was wait it out, and hope for the best.

That Friday, John McComb and I went to a dance at a Czechoslovakian hall in Yorkville. Someone from Equitable told John there would be a number of terrific looking Czech girls in attendance. That information was as bad as the polka band playing havoc with our eardrums. We had made it to the place during a lull in the storm, but once we arrived we were literally marooned when the torrential rains resumed. The few people in attendance were middle aged and the music was driving us crazy. Regardless of the relentless rain, we were leaving. I poked my head out the door to discover the streets were deserted, not a taxi in sight. Since we had no raincoats or umbrellas, we were forced to innovate to protect ourselves from the tumultuous downpour.

"Let's find some cardboard boxes," I suggested.

"Good idea, we can hold them over our heads," John responded.

Luck prevailed, as we noticed an abandoned mattress lying on top of a row of garbage cans in the alley adjacent to the Czechoslovakian hall. Ignoring the mattress' ammonia-like stench of urine, we raised it over our heads and walked four blocks to a subway station on Lexington Avenue. Safely down the subway stairs, and relatively dry, we offered the mattress to a few people about to exit the station. They looked at us as if we were crazy.

"Smart bastards. After a few feet in that rain, they'll be glad to pay for the mattress," John said.

If there was a lesson gained from that experience, it was hunker down in bad weather, and it's best to play in your own backyard. For many years, John and I would recall that night. I guess if there was another lesson to be learned it was that in your travels make absolutely sure the mattress you are sleeping on is clean.

14

The Catch

The Cleveland Indians won the American League pennant with surprising ease, putting up huge numbers on the scoreboard on their way to an incredible record, winning 111 games with only 43 losses. Though the Giants had an excellent season, winning 97 games against 57 losses, the betting odds were clearly stacked against them. None of the baseball experts gave them a chance. What did the Giants do? They swept the series in four straight games.

The first game really decided the series. Cleveland took a two run lead in the first inning, when Vic Wertz hit a Sal Maglie pitch for a triple. The Giants came back to tie the score in the third inning, getting to Cleveland's Bob Lemon for a walk and three singles. Thereafter, the pitching tightened up and neither team scored until Cleveland came alive in the top of the eighth inning when Sal Maglie started to tire. He walked Larry Doby and gave up a single to Al Rosen. With two men on base and none out, Manager Leo Durocher did the obvious, he walked to the mound and asked Maglie for the ball since the next batter was Vic Wertz. Everyone watching the game with me in front of a 32nd Street appliance store agreed with Durocher's decision. Wertz owned Maglie that day with three hits to his credit. Durocher brought in Don Liddle and pulled in his outfield in order to cut off Doby from tagging up on a fly ball or from scoring on a single. Liddle promptly served up a pitch that Wertz hit some 450 feet to the deepest part of the Polo Grounds in right center field. The ball had win written all over it as the two Cleveland runners took off for home in expectation that the ball was going out of the park or would end up as an inside-the-park home run. Amazingly, Willie Mays, running at full speed, caught the ball over his shoulder with his back to home plate.

Monte Ervin, the Hall of Fame left fielder, said "I knew Willy would catch the ball, when he paused slightly and punched his right hand into his glove before he took off on the run for the ball." No one else watching the game at the Polo Grounds or on television thought that Mays would ever catch up with Wertz's long drive. Equally amazing, is that Mays had the presence of mind to turn, plant his legs, and throw the ball to shortstop Alvin Dark, who had run into center field for the cut-off throw. Dark's relay-throw to the infield, though not in time to double-up either of the runners, did prevent Rosen from advancing to second. Doby with good speed managed to get back to second base and then tag up to advance to third. Had Doby stayed close to second base and tagged up when the catch was made, he probably would have been able to score from second base. To this day in baseball lore, Mays' feat that inning is known as "The Catch."

Durocher promptly yanked Liddle and brought in Marv Grissom, who walked the next hitter to load the bases. The fans on 32nd Street were holding their breaths, expecting their dream to end. To everyone's delight, Grissom bore down and retired the next two Indians. But the Giants failed to score in the ninth inning and the game remained tied.

Vic Wertz was not done for the day — he hit his second triple in the top of the 10th inning, but was stranded on third as Cleveland squandered another scoring opportunity. In the bottom of the inning, Bob Lemon retired the first Giant batter, and after a struggle walked Willie Mays. Durocher gave Willie total freedom to run, and run he did, stealing second base. The dangerous Hank Thompson came to the plate and Lemon was instructed to walk him intentionally to set up the double play. The next batter, James Lamar "Dusty" Rhodes, a journeyman utility player, promptly hit a Lemon pitch into the short right-field stands for the game-winning home run. New York City exploded – the people on 32nd Street were delirious with joy. Horns were honking, and people were running about and jumping up and down. On the subway home that night everyone had a smile on his or her face.

In game two, Cleveland again took the lead in the first inning on Al Smith's home run off Johnny Antonelli, who the Giants had secured earlier in the year when they traded their 1951 playoff hero, Bobby Thompson, to the Braves for Antonelli and a seldom-used catcher named Sam Calderone. Rhodes was the improbable hero again, driving in two of the Giants three runs with a single and a home run. Though Antonelli allowed 14 Indians to reach base on a total of eight hits and six walks, Smith's homer was the only run he gave up. For the second consecutive day, New York City was in a giddy state of total disbelief.

The next day, the scene shifted to Cleveland for the third game. It was over early as the Giants scored one run in the first inning, three more in the third, and one run in each of the fifth and sixth innings with Alvin Dark and Don Mueller getting a bunch of hits. Again, it was Dusty Rhodes who ignited the Giants in the third inning. With the bases loaded and home run threat, Monte Ervin due to bat for the Giants, Durocher confounded the sports writers and the fans by sending out Rhodes to pinch hit for Ervin. Rhodes promptly smacked a hit to right field scoring two runners. For all intents and purposes, the Cleveland Indians were dead Indians. The Giants had scored six runs before Cleveland got on the scoreboard in the seventh inning on a home run by Vic Wertz. Rueben Gomez, the Giants' starting pitcher, allowed only four hits in the first six innings. Hoyt Wilhelm came on in relief in the seventh inning and preserved the victory for Gomez.

New York was approaching pandemonium. Three games won and one to go. The confounded baseball experts were now talking sweep. Was this possible? I couldn't believe what was happening. At Equitable Life, Ace

Corcoran was beside himself. He had bet $100 on the Giants at seven to one odds and was contemplating how to spend his winnings. The Ace had his eyes on a new convertible and more garish clothes. "I coulda gotten a hundred to one on a Giant sweep last week," Ace told everyone.

The next day's fourth and final game was anticlimactic. The Giants gave Don Liddle a seven-run cushion in the first five innings, and he returned the favor by pitching almost five scoreless innings. Hank Majeski's three-run, pinch-hit home run in the bottom of the fifth was not enough. Cleveland could only manage one more run in the seventh inning. Johnny Antonelli took over for Hoyt Wilhelm and finished the game.

For a disappointed Yankee fan it was an incredible series. I was especially happy for Bob Perite, a defiant Giant fan in a neighborhood overpopulated with Yankee rooters. All of New York cheered on the Giants in that incredible Series, with the understanding that real Giant fans were entitled to special recognition for the victory and their team loyalty. To their credit, they didn't gloat in victory as Yankee fans were prone to do, instead they graciously allowed us to share in their joy.

The Giant pitchers gave up only six earned runs in the four games, compiling an incredible 1.46-combined earned-run average. At bat, while the Giants had only six more hits than Cleveland (33 to 26), they out-scored Cleveland by 11 runs (21 runs to 9). Five of the Giants accounted for 26 of the 33 hits, Alvin Dark and Don Mueller had seven hits each while Willie Mays, Hank Thompson and Dusty Rhodes, the Series' Most Valuable Player, each had four hits.

It was a thorough and sweet victory for the Giants. The bars were overflowing after the third game on Friday afternoon. The beer and whisky was liberally consumed late into the night and early the next morning in anticipation of the final game on Saturday afternoon. When the Giants won on Saturday it is safe to say that the bars probably did a record business for alcohol consumed and money made.

In that week, the Giants did more for New York's pride and morale than any of its sports teams had ever accomplished. It was an auspicious beginning to the brightest of fall seasons for me, but for others, it was not to be.

"Hey, Ace, what are you going to do with all that money?" Joe Gianinni asked him on Monday.

"I can't talk right now," he responded with a pensive look on his face.

"What's wrong, Ace, can't you find your bookie?"

For the next few days the Ace was evasive when questioned. His elation on Friday dissipated into despondency by Monday. Joe was right – the Ace was unable to contact his bookie on the telephone or find him in his usual haunts. By mid-week, Ace learned that his neighborhood bookie had flown the coop. Ace's experience was not unique. It turned out to be a common occurrence throughout the city. Die-hard Giant fans bet with their hearts. Their huge anticipated winnings vanished that week, like Marilyn Monroe did from Joe DiMaggio by filing for divorce.[104]

Months later, unconfirmed reports circulated that a number of fresh bodies were fertilizing the marshlands of Jamaica Bay, Classon's and Old Ferry Points in the Bronx, and the meadowlands of Secaucus, New Jersey. The missing bookies burned too many people, including a few of the big boys, who had methods of recourse not available to the Ace.

---

[104] A short time later, she stunned the world again when she showed up on the arm of her new lover, Arthur Miller, a nerdy looking intellectual and acclaimed playwright, and announced their engagement. Among Miller's highly acclaimed works are *Death Of A Salesman* and *The Crucible*.

The Call

October continued to be a harsh month for Ace Corcoran. A guy named Mike from the sixth floor was now dating TG. Ace picked up on it and made inappropriate comments about the relationship. TG felt that the Ace had crossed the line and reported the incident to her brother.

Early one morning, while we were working on the eighth floor, Joe Gianinni rushed up to me all excited.

"The Ace is really in deep shit this time."

"What are you talking about, Joe?"

"It's TG's brother, he's coming after the Ace."

"No shit. He's coming to the building?"

"We're not sure. Ace requested that you and I intercede with her. He's willing to apologize."

Ah, revenge is so sweet, I thought as I broke into a grin. "No way, Joe. He deserves to get his ass kicked."

Artie Wassen walked in on our conversation and Joe filled him in. Since Artie went to grammar school with TG and knew her brother, he volunteered to talk to her. I pulled Artie aside. "Why do you care so much about the Ace after all the shit he's given you?"

Artie smiled. "Now, he'll owe me. That's why."

I smiled in return. "Good thinking, but I was hoping that he'd get his ass kicked."

"Believe me, Neal. This is better. Now he'll treat us differently."

Artie approached TG and discussed the proposal. Later that day, she tracked down Artie and asked for a number where Ace could be reached between 6:30 and 7 o'clock that night. Artie gave her our number in the Underwriting Department and everything was set.

Ace appeared in our office at 6:15 and took a seat near the filing cabinets. Staring past those waiting with him, he didn't respond to the kidding of Joe Gianinni. His eyes were blank and lifeless. His face had an ashen gray pallor, his jaw twitched nervously. Sweat poured out of him as he awaited his fate. He looked and smelled like death in waiting as the sweat rings in the armpits of his powder blue, gabardine, wrap-around jacket spread. Joe Gianinni was having fun with the situation.

"This guy is so fucking tough that people shit their pants when he looks at them."

"Come on, Joe. I'm going to apologize for what I said to her."

"Apologies don't cut it with this guy – he's going to play with you like a cat with a mouse. Then, he's going to break your neck."

I enjoyed watching him suffer. As far as Artie and I were concerned, he was reaping what he had sown and was most deserving of his fate. Just then the telephone rang. It startled us. The room became quiet and we looked at each other in varying degrees of anticipation. For Ace it was fearful anticipation. Ace swallowed hard. Joe, with a gleeful look on his face, deliberately hesitated, looking at the phone.

Ace began to panic, "Joe, please, please pick up the fucking phone," he pleaded.

Joe coolly picked up the receiver on the third ring, as did Artie and I on other extensions.

"Hello, Lay Underwriting Department, how can I help you?"

"I'm calling to speak to Ace Corcoran," the deep and tough sounding voice announced. It was TG's brother.

"The Ace. You want the Ace. He's right here," Joe said, handing the phone to Ace, while running a finger across his neck in a slashing motion. Joe also picked up another nearby phone to listen in on the conversation.

"Hel-lo," he said in a tremulous voice.

"Is this Ace Corcoran?"

"Ye-a-s," he responded haltingly.

"Listen, you fucking piece of shit. I'm not going to tolerate your remarks about my sister. She has to be shown some respect. Is that fucking clear?"

"But you gotta understand it was all in fun …"

"Fun? Fun? Fun my fucking ass! I know all about you. You fucking piece of shit. You're always insulting people."

Joe, Artie, and I, listening to the conversation with our hands covering the phones' mouthpiece, had never enjoyed a conversation as much as this one, but we were just as terrified as the Ace.

"Please, you must understand. We kid around all the time. I didn't mean anything personal. I didn't intend to disrespect your sister. Honest."

"You're a fucking lying creep. If I hear of one more insult or any sign of disrespect, I'm going to come down there and de-nut you. You hear me?"

"You – you've got my word on that. I'll respect her. I'll apologize to her tomorrow."

"Don't even go near her. You understand that you fucking creep? Don't you ever go near her again. You're a fucking piece of shit. You go near her again, even to apologize, and you'll be East Harlem's only eunuch. You understand that?"

"Ah, yes. Yes, I do. I appreciate your listening to me. I'm very sorry."

"You're not sorry. You're just scared shitless. You betta remember what I just said. You're a marked man. You piece of shit."

When the conversation ended, Joe was convulsing in laughter. "You're finished in this building when the word gets out," Joe said to Ace.

The Ace looked around. "You guys betta not say anything about this."

Artie and I looked at Ace with half smiles. Each of us nodded our heads as we hunched our shoulders and opened our hands indicating that we couldn't promise him that we would keep quiet about his dilemma.

Both Artie and I found the phone call to be a sobering experience. Each of us believed that TG's brother would back up his words with deeds. Thereafter, Ace avoided TG like the plague. She walked about the building with an extra bounce in her step. She was now a more confident person having prevailed in a showdown with the Ace. Proud of her brother for putting the Ace in his place, she was now protected from his nasty remarks. The Ace suffered alone. For some weeks he was not his usual self, obviously still in shock from his rude awakening.

West Point

Dave Richardson was now dating Dottie McQuade in earnest. She suggested that Dave drive a group of us to West Point for Army's football game with Dartmouth. I joined Lester Anderson, Billy "Doc" Doherty, Bill Marquette, Maureen Connaughton, Dave, and Dottie for the trip that Saturday morning in Dave's 1936 Chevrolet.

When Dave arrived at the Gardens to pick up Dottie, Maureen and me, Lester and Doc, still hung over from the previous night, were sitting in the back of the car sharing a quart bottle of beer to ease their pain. Bill Marquette was sitting in the front seat alongside Dave, who was not too happy with the antics of Lester and Doc. Bill possessed a great sense of humor, and a reassuring manner. As the trip progressed he helped keep Dave's blood pressure at a reasonable level. Bill was six foot two and weighed about 210 pounds. He had thick arms and a large barrel chest to go with a kind and generous disposition. He was fully capable of restoring order in the event that Lester or Doc became disorderly. At that time, Bill was working with his father, at the BPS Paint Company on Van Dam Street in Long Island City, along with Jack Dadian, Matty Martin, and John Renck.

Doc Doherty was a handsome, freckled faced, fun loving guy with a permanent smile sitting below a shock of thick brown hair on a solid and strong frame. He was friendly, generous, and enjoyable to be around. Like Lester, he was totally unpredictable. Doc was home on leave from the Marine Corps and getting ready to ship out to Port Lyautey, French Morocco. Another St. Ann's Academy product, Doc had a tremendous capacity to drink, a quick mind, a warm smile, and a gift with words that made him irresistible to women. I speak with experience, as a few years later I fell for a wonderful girl who happened to be crazy about Doc. He was dating Ann Sutton from Flushing and then stopped seeing her. About a month after their breakup I ran into Ann and some of her friends in the Melody Lounge in Sunnyside. I asked her out and we began to date. Ann was attractive with a quiet manner and a sweet nature. After a few months of dating, and getting to like her more and more, I began to peel back her protective shell. What I discovered was a sensitive young woman who had someone else in mind. Ann was head-over-heels in love with Doc. Just about that time he was injured at his construction job. I went to visit him in St. Clare's Hospital on West 51st Street in Manhattan. He was happy to see me and we had a good visit. Just before I left, I told him of Ann's continued interest in him. Doc didn't seem surprised. I stressed that I had no idea about her feelings when I started dating her, as I had thought that it was over with them. Given her feelings, I told Doc that if he had any sense he should call her. He did, and six months later they were married. Doc and Ann were married for 51 years until his death in 2010. He was very successful in the construction business. When I visited them in 2006 they were living in a fabulous home in Amagansett, Long Island.

Dave Richardson's car had gray felt upholstery with an aged and musty smell from the dampness it had accumulated in its 18-year life. The seats were comfortable, even the jump seats, and there was more than enough foot room between the rear seat and the jump seats. It could move at a good clip on the open road. Its sole problem was a rattling noise from the undercarriage, which occurred at speeds in excess of 55 miles per hour. The rattle was an excellent safety governor, since 55 to 60 was considered fast driving at that time. But Dave was a careful driver and we always traveled with the assurance of a good time and a safe ride.

"I hope someone has good directions," Dave said as we entered the car.

"My father said it is just above Bear Mountain," Dottie replied.

"Great. Now how do we get to Bear Mountain?" Dave asked.

"By boat," we all answered in unison, since this was the usual way people traveled there on their school and church outings.

We stopped at a local gas station, conferred with the owner, and headed for the Triboro Bridge, made our way along the westside of the Bronx on the Major Deegan Expressway, crossed the Alexander Hamilton Bridge over the Harlem River into Manhattan, and then onto the George Washington Bridge, which carried us into New Jersey. Once in the Garden State, we headed north on route 9W for the 45 mile drive to West Point.

Route 9W curves along the Hudson River at a considerable height above the water along the Palisades, where the view is spectacular. During the drive Doc regaled us with his inventory of salty songs, including one that I still remember. Only part of the lengthy verse is suitable for print. It goes as follows:

Ay, ay a yay
In China they never eat chili
So here comes another verse
That's worse than the other verse

So waltz me around again Willie
There once was a man from Mersass
His balls were made out of brass
When he banged them together
They played Stormy Weather
And lightning shot out of his ...

After an hour of driving and singing, the hunger and thirst of the passengers became the priority over the destination. Just outside the West Point gates, in the town of Highland Falls, Lester and Doc insisted they be let out of the car. Frustrated, Dave stopped the car and said they would have to get to the game on their own. "Not to worry," said Lester, as they made their way in search of a bar or restaurant.

Dave was fuming as we drove to the main gate for information about the football game. Learning that the game wouldn't start for three hours, we stopped and looked around Highland Falls for a while before we drove off. "Where are we going?" Dotty asked Dave. "Good question," Dave said, before he stopped to ask an old man working in his front yard where we could get a sandwich and something to drink. His instructions took us to a road side bar and restaurant about a mile from West Point. The girls expressed their concerns about the whereabouts of Lester and Doc, but Dave, still peeved that they had left us in Highland Falls, said, "Don't worry about those two, they'll find their way."

Famished and thirsty, we alighted from the car and walked into the bar. Our faces lit up in surprise and delight when we saw who was sitting at the bar. There was Lester and Doc. As luck would have it, their antics in Highland Falls got them a quick ride to the place. Lester explained that once they got out of the car in Highland Falls they found a one-horse shay,[105] without the horse, sitting outside an antique shop. Lester jumped into the seat and Doc grabbed hold of the wooden stays, which are normally harnessed to the horse, and jogged off with Lester waving to passersby as they moved through town. They were stopped in short order and literally driven out of town by the local constable. We celebrated our reunion by ordering food and drinks, loaded the jukebox with quarters, and introduced the Hudson River Valley to the Savoy.

We were having a great time, and as kick-off time approached, the guys debated whether we should attend the game. The girls summarily informed us that attendance was not an option, that they really didn't come to see a football game, but they were interested in the pre-game color and pageantry, particularly the thousand cadets. The Long Gray Line won out, and we headed back to Highland Falls and West Point.

The game proved to be a wonderful experience. It was sunny and clear, a touch of fall was in the air and our seats in the sun, adjacent to the Corp of Cadets, were comfortable. Unfortunately, we had to quench our thirsts on soda, as Mitchie Stadium did not dispense beer. Our section of the stands was euphoric when Army overwhelmed Dartmouth that day 60 to 6. Don Hollender, Army's consensus All-American, sparked the Cadets by catching a 67-yard pass from Pete Vann in the first quarter, and caught another Vann pass for a touchdown in the second.

Hollender was one of Army's all-time greatest players. His versatility made him invaluable. In his senior year, the fabled Army Coach, Colonel Earl "Red" Blaik, switched Hollender to quarterback. It was a tough transition to make for someone who was left-handed and had never played the position. Mid-way through Army's tough schedule, he and his teammates made the adjustment. He capped off the season with a virtuoso

---

[105] A light or small carriage pulled by a horse.

demonstration of his skills in Army's victory over Navy. A few weeks later, playing at the end position, he was named the Most Valuable Player in the North-South collegiate all-star game. Hollender was tall and solid, with a firm jaw and movie star looks that are fully evident in a 1955 Sports Illustrated cover photo.[106]

Hollender went on to distinguish himself in his military career. He turned down a choice assignment in Europe to serve in Viet Nam. Unfortunately, in his first combat action on October 17, 1967, as the operations officer of his regiment, he was killed attempting to rally troops falling back in retreat from a severe crossfire. Following his untimely death, a classmate, Perry M. Smith, aptly described Major Donald Hollander in the West Point publication, *The Assembly*:

> "He was, of course, much more than a great football player, athlete, and competitor, but his athletic feats do reflect the strength of character, the perseverance, the maturity, and the inward forcefulness that made him a man among men. He died very much as he lived, with the total commitment to the team of which he was a part, and we are all much richer for having known him, admired him, and loved him."

Seeing Hollander play that day made me realize that he was something special. Everyone with me felt he was destined for greatness as a leader. We were certainly aware that all of these young men were being trained to defend the interest of our country, but we didn't focus on the possibility that some of them would die in combat in the coming decade.

The West Point visit was a wonderful day capped off by Dottie McQuade being passed overhead through part of the Cadet seating section.

---

[106] *Sports Illustrated*, November 28, 1955.

This early version of the mosh pit started with Dartmouth Cheerleaders body surfing through the crowd during a meaningless second half. Army was scoring at will on the hapless Dartmouth team, and the Corp of Cadets was swelling with enthusiasm as the bench continued to empty with every player getting into the game. Four quarterbacks were used, and all led scoring drives totaling 600 yards on offense. The Army mule was suffering from fatigue from being continually galloped around the perimeter of the field, and the men loading, shooting, and unloading the artillery cannons after each score never had a busier day. Dottie got caught up in the enthusiasm and could not resist the opportunity to perform. Following the game we returned to our roadhouse bar and savored this memorable experience.

Soon after our West Point visit, Lester Anderson learned he had reason to root for Army. Out of the blue, he received his draft notice, and our crowd went into shock. This was too much to take. One of the most popular guys in the Woodside-Sunnyside area was being removed from the scene for two years. We went into mourning, doing what the Irish do best at such times – drinking, and trying to think it through.

Lester's fate caused those who frequented the Clover on Roosevelt Avenue, the Shannon Inn near the Boulevard Gardens, and the Avermore on 30th Avenue to mull over their individual fates. Since none of us qualified for deferments, it was a waiting game. There were draft deferments for men who were married and had a child or were in college or graduate school. In the former case you would likely never have to go, and in the latter, you were drafted as soon as you received your degree. The only other option was a 4F classification for a physical or mental incapacity. Most of us did not have any of these options available.

Pratt Realities – Sound Advice

Well into October it became apparent that my efforts in Trigonometry fell short of my relative accomplishments in the Physics course and the expectations of my patient and capable teacher. At a smoking break just prior to the midterm examination, he approached me.

"Mr. Gillen, could you please tell me who the hell's paying your tuition?"

"Well, ah, my father and Equitable Life."

"As far as I'm concerned, they're wasting their money. Have you thought about the GI Bill?"[107]

"Well, I haven't. What'd you mean, sir?"

"The fact that you don't seem to have a clue what we're doing in class, the sooner you get yourself into the military, the sooner you'll straighten out."

I asked him if we could discuss the matter further. He invited me to meet with him after class in the teachers' lounge, where for 15 minutes he quizzed me about my life, the type of work I did, and what I expected of myself.

"Neal, why'd you come to Pratt?"

"Well, I actually agreed to accompany my friend, Bob Perite, who was registering. I picked up some literature, looked around, and thought about coming here. My Dad always wanted me to go to college to be an engineer. He was really enthused about my enrolling."

"I'm trying to determine your motivation. I don't see any. It's all about your friend Bob enrolling and your father wanting you to be an engineer.

---

[107] The GI Bill, formally known as The Servicemen's Readjustment Act of 1944 (P.L. 78-346), provided a range of benefits for returning veterans, including low-cost mortgages, loans to start a business or farm, cash payments of tuition and living expenses to attend college of $110 per month, and for those who could not find work, one year of unemployment compensation – $50 per week for 52 weeks. It was available to every veteran who had been on active duty for at least 90 days and had not been dishonorably discharged.

Besides, we don't offer an engineering degree at Pratt. You're a smart kid, but I don't really see any direction on your part. Tell me, what do you want to do?"

"I don't know," I responded. I was so damned confused. I closed my eyes and took a deep breath, attempting to get a grip on the situation and myself. Then, it hit me, this sudden realization coming from such a simple, but albeit dispositive question. My response, "I don't know," rocketed throughout my brain. Everything came into clear focus.

I was wasting my time at Pratt.

I lacked an adequate foundation in higher mathematics.

I lacked the proper attitude to listen and learn.

I lacked so much of everything.

I'm involved in a great charade, fooling my father and myself.

It became all too clear that I should be considering other alternatives in life.

My trigonometry teacher volunteered to talk to my father and promised to find out when the GI Bill was expiring.

When I reluctantly discussed it with Dad, he was disappointed, but surprisingly, he took the news calmly. At my next and last class at Pratt, I was informed that the GI Bill was expiring on January 31, 1955. The clock was ticking.

Although I don't remember his name, I consider that assistant professor one of the more influential people in my life for taking the time and trouble to point me in the right direction. His bold and forthright nature made a considerable difference in my future. I often wonder what turns my life would have taken if Bob Perite had chosen a school with less rigorous requirements for me to follow him to.

15

The New Sunday Ritual

When Freddy's Gay Café opened on 37th Avenue in Jackson Heights, Dottie McQuade suggested that we gather there on Sunday afternoons for drinks. John McComb was concerned that it was a gay bar and that we might not be welcome. That certainly was not the case at the nearby Flora Dora, on Roosevelt Avenue that attracted a sizeable gay crowd. It featured a corpulent, raucous, middle-aged, peroxide blonde playing a piano set back above the middle of its long bar. A wonderful entertainer, she told racy jokes and sang a medley of Broadway hits and risqué songs. I remember her effective use of an old vaudeville line. She would ask the question, "Tell me, folks – what did the virgin have for breakfast?" Pausing briefly, she would respond to laughter and applause – "Well, I had bacon and eggs and …"

John McComb called Maureen Connaughton, who lived a few blocks from Freddy's, to ask her about the place.

"Maureen, is it a gay bar?"

"Hmm. Girls, don't think of questions like that, John."

"It's the name, Maureen. Doesn't that tell you something?"

"All I know is that Freddy's can't attract any business. The place is dying, and it's a nice place. To generate business, he's offering 50-cent mixed drinks at two for the price of one from two to five every Sunday afternoon."

"Did you say 25 cents for a mixed drink?

"Yes."

"In that case, I don't care what kind of place it is - we'll be there at two – promptly, at two!"

Within a few weeks, Freddy had a huge success on his hands. The booths were filled by 2:15 every Sunday afternoon, and it was three deep at the bar for months to come.

It was at Freddy's, sitting in a booth with Dave Richardson and Bill Marquette, that I firmed up my decision to enlist in the Navy. The personnel officer at my Naval Reserve Unit informed me that I couldn't be activated from the Reserves, since I hadn't completed Boot Camp.

Dave and Bill helped as I struggled with my limited options. Most of all, they reminded me I was only 17. In comparison, they were 20 and still waiting for their draft call. But they knew it must be close at hand since Lester Anderson was 19 when he was drafted.

"Don't be like us," Dave said. "Don't wait for the draft. You'll be jumping from one dead-end job to another, like me."

"We're both almost 21, and we're still waiting to be called," Bill said, shaking his head in frustration. At that time, only dead-end jobs were available for people who had not yet served in the military. Few companies were willing to spend time and money in training someone for a good-paying job only to see them end up in the military. They avoided a continuing training cycle by hiring people after they had completed their military service.

"Shit, I can't wait that long. I'll just screw up my life some more," I responded. Then and there, I made up my mind – I was enlisting. Little did I realize that they would soon be following me into the military.

Following Freddy's, in high spirits, fueled by his generous drinks, we usually visited someone's home for dinner. A few times I invited members of the group for one of Mother's Sunday specialties – roast pork with applesauce, sauerkraut, and mashed potatoes and gravy. Following the first such unexpected drop in, Mother made it clear that my friends were more than welcome, provided that I gave her ample warning to prepare for such a ravenous crowd.

After dinner, we regrouped for a night of dancing at the Ascension Parish Hall on Grand Avenue, just above Queens Boulevard in Elmhurst. These well-attended dances featured an excellent band and Bobbie Breen, an attractive and talented singer. I still vividly recall her singing *Moonlight in Vermont* and *Goodnight Sweetheart*, like it was yesterday. She made the slow dances meaningful with her soft and sexy voice.

I often wonder about a super young woman named Mickey who attended the dances on a regular basis. She resembled the beautiful Hollywood star, Cyd Charise, and like her, Mickey was a dancer, hopeful that someday she would become a Rockette. Though she had a lazy eye, it was never a distraction, given her pleasant manner, quick smile, personal confidence, and the way she carried herself. If anyone deserved to make it to Radio City Music Hall, she certainly did. I hope she was able to live out her dream.

On Sunday nights at Ascension dances, "pick a winner" had a distinct meaning. It referred to our Pick-a-Pig or the Beast-of-the-East contest. Like most dances, chairs lining the walls were usually occupied by unattractive girls with an unlikely chance of being asked to dance unless they did a fast dance with a girlfriend. We gave them their chance. While engaging them in innocuous conversation, we glided them by the front of the stage, where members of our crowd stood ready to pass judgment. It was done with a maximum of subtlety to avoid embarrassing the contestants. I'm not aware that any of our victims ever knew or suspected what we were up to – the night's winner was never informed of her achievement.

The following summer, Pig of the Week sweatshirts appeared on the Rockaway scene. Reportedly, Jack Sherman, a retired CPA and college professor, can still be seen jogging in such a shirt, albeit tattered, in the suburbs of Dallas.

Looking back, regretfully, on what can only be judged to be inexplicable meanness, reminds me not to be surprised, whenever I see similar, insensitive acts perpetrated by today's teenagers, who, not unlike us in 1954, amuse themselves at the expense of others.

Enlisting in the Navy

Acting on my decision to join the Navy I visited the Third Naval District Headquarters at 90 Church Street the week of "Armistice Day"[108] and reviewed my enlistment options.

The massive federal structure, which 47 years later survived the destruction of the neighboring World Trade Center, houses many U.S. Government bureaus and agencies. Following inquiries in the lobby, I was referred to a friendly chief petty officer in the Navy Recruiting Office. He was impressive sitting behind a large gray metal desk in a dress blue uniform with four rows of ribbons on his chest and gold hash marks on his left sleeve, indicating his lengthy and honorable service.

The Chief inquired why I wanted to join, and what I expected from the Navy. He outlined various areas of potential interest and opportunities to learn and travel. When I exhausted my list of questions, he indicated it could be arranged for me to be called any time from late November through January. He cautioned that in any given week I could be sent to either the Great Lakes Naval Training Center on Lake Michigan, north of Chicago, or to the Bainbridge Naval Training Center in Perryville, Maryland. He also noted that were I to be sent to either place in January, "You'll freeze your ass off." If I wanted to leave in the coming weeks, he

---

[108] That year Congress changed the name of the November 11th holiday to Veteran's Day.

told me I would miss the extreme cold common to those locations in mid-winter. I told him that I would risk the cold, since I needed the additional time. I thanked him, took the enlistment papers, and returned to the Equitable Life building.

I went over the forms with Mother and Dad that night and completed them at the office the next day. Later in the day, I jumped on the subway and delivered them to the chief. Upon reviewing my paperwork, he learned that I was only 17. He had presumed that I was 18, since I had worked for almost a year and was a member of the Reserves. Returning my enlistment papers, he asked that I get a signed and notarized permission letter[109] from one of my parents and submit everything together. Mother took the parental authorization letter I had typed for her and took it to her bank near Steinway Street where she signed it and had it notarized.

It was time to go. I was certainly ready, since the ennui of the work routine created a desire for greener pastures. Also, the drop in the temperature was making it increasingly difficult for an application chaser to wander too far from the building without a coat.

At a beer racket in Astoria's Kneer's Ballroom that weekend, Johnny Kosnar, a Navy Hospital Corpsman and a friend from the Woodside Projects who was home on leave from his Marine Corps unit advised me not to go until after the Christmas Holidays.

"Neal, you want to be home for Thanksgiving, Christmas and New Year's. God only knows where you'll be next year."

I thought it over, discussed the issue with a number of people, and decided to take Kosnar's advice. Everyone I talked to at Equitable convinced me that Kosnar was correct. They stressed that if I were to leave in early December, I would miss out on an unbelievable week of Christmas parties. Further, they noted it would give them more time to organize a

---

[109] In contrast, my Navy Reserve enlistment did not require parental permission.

proper going-away party and the traditional office collection for those entering military service.

Johnny Kosnar's advice was right on the money. As it turned out, I'd be overseas for the Christmas holidays for the next three years: 1955 in Guam, 1956 in Okinawa, and 1957 in Naples, Italy.

I returned to 90 Church Street, submitted my enlistment papers, and notified my naval reserve unit of the ongoing process. A few weeks later, I received a notice to report to 120 Whitehall Street for my physical.

The Whitehall Street facility is an historic federal period building, where since the post-Revolutionary War era millions of young men from New York City have lined up in its drafty rooms and corridors for their physical exams and military inductions. That morning, about 100 of us were being examined for all branches of the military. At one point during the examination process, clothed only in a pair of jockey shorts, I literally bumped into Gerry Andrews as we were exiting our respective examination rooms. Gerry and I were told we had passed our physicals and the Navy would soon notify us when to report for duty.

Visiting Lester

Just before Thanksgiving, Dottie McQuade suggested that we visit Lester Anderson at Fort Dix. She convinced Dave Richardson to provide the transportation and we set out at noon one Sunday to see Lester. It would be my first of countless drives on the New Jersey Turnpike, which had opened to much acclaim in 1951. Equipped with beer and song, we headed for exit seven on the Turnpike. Fort Dix is a massive military installation adjacent to Maguire Air Force Base in Wrightstown, New Jersey. It's also close to the Lakehurst Naval Air Station, the site of the tragic 1937 explosion of the German passenger dirigible, the "Hindenburg."

The Army's largest basic training installation on the East Coast, Fort Dix is named in honor of Major General John A. Dix, best known for leading 10,000 federal troops into New York City in 1863 to quell the Irish Draft Riots. It's ironic that when millions of those rioters' descendants were drafted to serve in World Wars I and II, the Korean War and Vietnam, they were sent to Fort Dix – the base named for the person responsible for the killing, wounding or jailing of many of their forbearers rebelling against a corrupt conscription system requiring their service during the Civil War.

Once basic training got under way, Army recruits were given a few hours off on Sunday afternoons to see friends and relatives, visit the canteens and recreation halls, or drink beer with a 3.2 percent alcohol content in designated fenced-off beer gardens. When we arrived at the beer garden near Lester's Company that Sunday, we couldn't find Lester. Dave asked around and we found him outside his barracks hosing and scrubbing down trash cans. Lester was embarrassed and we convulsed in laughter. He was happy to see us and asked us to wait while he hauled his clean and shiny cans to the rear of the barracks. He made his official debut 10 minutes later in his ill-fitting dress uniform and we headed for the beer garden for a good time. We brought along real beer and scotch, which Lester appreciated. We returned to New York in time to attend the Ascension dance. A few weeks later, we made a second visit to see Lester and experienced another enjoyable day with this unforgettable character.

Thanksgiving

Thanksgiving Day turned out to be an enjoyable family affair with the usual abundance of food and ample fatherly and grandfatherly advice about my upcoming naval service. Mother always made a great effort on these occasions, while Dad usually spoiled them, coming home late in the afternoon with a number of drinks under his belt, but on this occasion, he was on his best behavior. His only outburst came when it was reported on the television that Alger Hiss, the convicted perjurer and alleged spy, was being released on parole from the federal penitentiary in Lewisburg, Pennsylvania in the coming week.

"That lying, commie, pinko bastard. He's a spy. I can't believe it. They're letting him out. He should spend the rest of his life in the can," Dad said.

My grandfather nodded in agreement. It was all above my head at the time. I didn't know much about Hiss until after Dick Oliver and I had sat next to him and his wife at a Manhattan party in 1969 on the night that John Lindsay was re-elected mayor of New York. Following that, I read up on his case, talked to a law partner of my wife who was involved in the prosecution, and concluded that Dad's views had traction.

Thanksgiving was a busy day for the neighborhood bars, which were packed with husbands avoiding the situation at home. As the preparation of these massive meals progressed, the tension increased. The safe thing to do was exit the premises.

Every titular head of the household knew it was only begging trouble from the real head if he dared to get in her way during the seemingly endless dinner preparations. Since they were damned if they stayed home, they went out. And when they came home, they were damned again for being out with the boys on a family day.

To this day, I equate turkey with tension. Further, I share Damon Runyon's opinion that turkey "is the most overrated critter for eating purposes in kingdom come, but the most striking example we have of the power of propaganda."[110]

A number of traditional high school football games were played on Thanksgiving morning with Brooklyn Prep always lining up against St. John's Prep at Ebbets Field before a large crowd. But the big event was the Macy's Day parade down Central Park West and Broadway to its terminus at Macy's on 34th Street. Fathers with younger families usually took their children to the parade, returned them home, and made their way to the local bar until the designated meal time.

The traditional televised football game pitted the then dominant Detroit Lions against the Green Bay Packers. Since neither team was popular in the New York area, the game provided little more than background noise in the neighborhood bars. In 1954, the legendary Vince Lombardi left his position at West Point to became the offensive coach of the New York Giants. Only when Lombardi moved to Green Bay four years later did the NFL's Thanksgiving game begin to pique the interest of New York fathers biding their time in the neighborhood bars.

Reindeer on 32nd Street

Just after Thanksgiving, during a morning saunter through Gimbel's, I came upon a Rockaway acquaintance and a Sunnyside character of note – Emanuel "Manny" Charles Luxenberg. Manny was a svelte six footer weighing about 175 pounds. He had blue eyes and curly blond hair set on a large and handsome head. Manny's mother was Catholic; his father was Jewish. Out of respect for their ecumenical marriage, he wore a large gold chain to which was affixed a gold Crucifix joined to a gold Star of David.

---

[110] *Talking Turkey,* from *Short Takes* at page 303, Whittlesey House, 1946.

Manny had the unusual job of caring for and feeding a team of reindeer lodged in a fenced-off area of Gimbel's Toy Department. Aside from the job being unique, it was unusual to find Manny gainfully employed. While the position had cachet, Manny did not anticipate it would be so labor intensive, which Manny was not. The reindeer ate and drank continuously requiring constant care. He quickly discovered that though they were cute, reindeer could be moody and unpredictable creatures when cooped up in an overheated department store. "Cupid," belying his name, did not endear himself to Manny, providing him with a potential workmen's compensation case for the love bite he inflicted at feeding time. This incident would be the last time Manny missed an opportunity to take advantage of a government benefit.

Another drawback to tending reindeer was their need to relieve themselves with considerable frequency. Gimbel's wanted it both ways, well-fed reindeer and spotless pens to allow children to be photographed with them. The labor requirements eliminated the initial glamour and allure associated with the position, particularly the constant hosing down, mopping up and waste removal.

I dropped in on Manny every day to hear him expound on his care and feeding of reindeer. Among other things, he thoroughly understood their digestive cycle – he could predict to the minute when they would relieve themselves. Also, given the high temperature in Gimbel's, the reindeer were consuming considerable amounts of water, resulting in more clean-up work for Manny, which led to his suggestion that the area be cooled down to make the reindeer more comfortable. His real concern was the extra work, not the welfare of the reindeer. When his suggestion was ignored, Manny took matters into his own hands and anonymously called the Humane Society. That changed things in a hurry. The next thing you know, the area containing the reindeer pen had North Pole temperatures. While the reindeer liked it, Manny then complained about his freezing working conditions.

As life would pan out for Manny, except for a position as assistant to a rabbi while he was a guest of New York State for a legal transgression in the early 1960s, this Christmas holiday position was one of the better jobs he held in his lifetime.[111]

The luminosity of Manny's personality and his intelligence, unmatched in Sunnyside and Woodside, helped to mask his glaring imperfections. Suffice it to say, Manny was devoted to women, music, theatre, and literature, but not gainful employment. His love for the finer things in life prevailed, and, amazingly he somehow managed to acquire them with minimal effort on a limited income. An avid reader, film buff, and a polished speaker, Manny was a resource for information on all things cultural, including fine furniture and antiques. His intellectual gifts

---

[111] Manny remained single until his death in 2010. For the entirety of his life, except for brief sojourns crashing with Jack Kehoe on the Westside and in Hollywood, Manny resided in the rent-controlled Sunnyside apartment of his deceased mother, Stella. He had enjoyed a unique and loving relationship with her, who, during her long lifetime, faithfully maintained his room, and tended to his every need when he happened to be home. In Stella's memory, Manny kept all of her clothes hanging neatly in her closet. The apartment, which Doc Doherty compared to the infamous Collier brothers' mansion, was cluttered with memorabilia, most issues of *Life* magazine, stacks of 33 and 45 rpm records, music and video tapes and virtually all of Manny's clothes dating back to his high school days were all neatly hung or stacked in size and color categories on clothes racks made from steel pipes that Hank Rice and other caring steam-fitters had affixed to the ceiling in the two bedrooms in his apartment. Stuffed under his bed was every pair of shoes he ever owned, including a pungent selection of sneakers dating back to his days at Bryant High School.

In the mid-1990s, when Manny received his initial personal earnings & benefit estimate statement from the Social Security Administration, he shared the information with neighborhood friends. Incredibly, his lifetime reported earnings barely totaled $34,000. Most people his age in marginal minimum wage jobs have earned more than 10-times that amount in their employable years, and most people have made Social Security payments twice that amount. Unfortunately, Manny's aversion to sustained employment and a preference to be paid off the books in cash when he was employed limited him to the minimum Social Security benefits, which necessitated his enrollment in the Food Stamp program.

He had survived a stroke, had a lung removed following a bout with cancer, and was struggling with diabetes in the years before he died, but his activity was not limited. In his final days, Manny's health had faded, but he continued to stand out due to his long white hair. He was a minor celebrity of sorts, his photo appearing in an edition of the *Irish Echo* a few months before he was found dead at his kitchen table.

combined with his pleasant manner resulted in his being a frequent dinner and houseguest of many people, who either enjoyed his good company or were sympathetic to his plight. Lester Anderson and Doc Doherty spent considerable time with Manny, though they lived far from Sunnyside. They affectionately referred to him as "America's guest."

Perite Joins the Army

The following week, I watched the Army-Navy game at Billy Thomas' apartment on 47th Street near Greenpoint Avenue. I was proud of my choice of military service when George Welsh,[112] the Naval Academy quarterback, led Navy to a 27–20 victory after it had been down 20–14, sending Don Hollender and Pete Vann of the fifth-ranked Army team home to brood over their defeat that long cold winter.

During the game, Billy Thomas, John Power, Bob Perite and I talked about the changes taking place in Major League Baseball and the new 1955 model cars being shown in the television ads.

Bob was still walking on cloud nine about the Giants sweep of the Indians. We had learned that morning that Connie Mack, the great owner/manager of the Philadelphia Athletics, was selling the team to a group in Kansas City for $604,000. Kansas City was the home of the Yankees' triple-A farm team, and as part of the deal the Yankees sold their stadium to the new owners at a nice profit. The law of unforeseen consequences was in play, since the stadium was also the home of the Kansas City Monarchs, the great Negro League team. Lacking a place to play, the Monarchs took to the road, and folded in a few years, bringing an

---

[112] In the years to come, Welsh would build a distinguished coaching record at the Naval Academy and the University of Virginia.

end to the barn-storming era of baseball. Also adding to the Monarch's demise was the increasing acceptance of African American players by Major League Baseball teams.

In 1953, the National League's Boston Braves moved to Milwaukee, and in 1954, the St. Louis Browns, after losing 100 games and drawing only 297,238 fans to their home games, moved to Baltimore to become the Orioles. One of the possible locations the Browns had considered was Woodside. Rabbit Maranville, Lou O'Neil, a sports writer for the *Long Island Star Journal*, and Dad were present in the fall of 1953 when surveyors inspected and measured Queens Park adjacent to the Boulevard Gardens. While the Browns liked that site and others in Queens, including Dexter Park a block from Jamaica Avenue in the Woodhaven section of Queens, it would have made New York a four-team town. It was not to be, since the other New York teams opposed the move and Baltimore's stadium along with a solid fan base was ready and waiting.

Within four years, the Giants would move to San Francisco and the Dodgers would quickly follow moving to Los Angeles. Dodger owner Walter O'Malley would make two other key decisions that month. The first was a move of total stupidity. In a telephone conversation with former Dodger General Manager Branch Rickey, who was then in that position with the Pittsburg Pirates, O'Malley lost his temper as they discussed the tentative deal that Rickey had made with the Dodgers' AAA team in Montreal to draft pitcher John Rutherford. As a result of O'Malley's intemperate remarks, Rickey voided the deal and instead drafted a 19-year-old Puerto Rican prospect, Roberto Clemente, who the Dodgers were grooming for the big leagues.[113] The second decision, however, was one of

---

[113] When the Dodgers signed Clemente as a bonus player with a payment above $10,000 he was required to be part of the Dodgers Major League roster. Since he would not have been a regular player in Brooklyn given the Dodgers strong roster that year, he was sent to Montreal. In doing so, however, the Dodgers risked him being drafted by another team at

total genius. He signed Sandy Koufax for $14,000. Koufax, a University of Cincinnati walk-on basketball player from Brooklyn, had had limited experience for the Bearcats with a 3 and 1 record in his initial year as a collegiate pitcher. Both players had remarkable careers and are members of the Baseball Hall of Fame.

When we started talking about cars, I took more than my share of kidding about my previous encounters with the law. We all had dreamed of owning a car, which we knew would not happen for many years, given the expense of buying and then maintaining a vehicle in New York. Once you owned a car, you were faced with high insurance rates and serious parking dilemmas. Our conversation was keyed by a General Motors promotion celebrating the production of its 50-millionth car. GM rolled out a gold-plated Chevrolet Sports Coupe at its Flint, Michigan plant, generating considerable media coverage. As luck would have it, Billy Thomas,[114] Johnny Power, and Bob Perite were among the first of my friends to own cars. They were extremely generous in providing rides on double dates, to and from the beach, and to group picnics on many occasions in the coming years.

At the conclusion of the game, as we were preparing to leave Billy's apartment, Bob Perite revealed that he had joined the Army. We were taken aback by his announcement, particularly his service choice. We told Bob he was crazy, that no one joins the Army, unless he wanted to go airborne like crowd from the Sugar Bowl and the Avermore. In 1954,

---

the end of the season. Dodger General Manager Buzzie Bevasi, who had an excellent relationship with Rickey, got Rickey to agree to draft Rutherford. Had that happened Clemente would have remained with the Dodger organization since a minor league team could only lose one player to the draft under baseball's rules in 1954.

[114] In 2003, upon the publication of my first novel, *Sugar Time*, John Power asked me to autograph a copy for Billy. I sent him the book along with a photo of him sitting in his first new car, a white and baby blue 1955 Ford Fairlane. In return, Billy sent me a Queens Boulevard street sign that he had removed from a lamppost early one morning in the late 1950s after a long sojourn at Gildea's in Sunnyside. The sign now rests in a prominent position in my home office. Billy died after a long illness in 2012.

young men were drafted into the Army. Those who enlisted on their own free will joined the Navy, Air Force, Marines or Coast Guard. Billy and John were members of the Naval Reserve surface unit in Manhattan, so it was three against one, arguing against the Army.

"You're out of your mind," Billy said.

Bob stood his ground. He explained that he wanted to see Europe. "They guaranteed I'd be sent to Germany."

"You believe the Army?" John asked.

"What if they send you to Korea?" Billy said.

"I've made up my mind. I report for duty next week."

Jesus – next week. That hit me hard. Bob would be gone before I was. I knew Bob had had something on his mind, ever since we both decided to drop out of Pratt Institute, but he had never said a word about the Army during our subway rides to and from work each day. As well as I knew Bob, I thought he might have told me what he was thinking. When I later asked him about it, he smiled and said, "I was afraid you'd try to talk me out of it."

Bob's decision came quickly. He had heard Bill Marquette and John Renck discussing their futures over a beer in Murphy's. Their discussion had started in the paint factory where they worked in Long Island City. Once they decided that it was time to face the music and get their military duty behind them by expediting their draft status, Bob decided to join up with them if something could be worked out to allow them to serve together. He was told that they could enter the Army together under the Buddy System. An arrangement was made with the Army and the local draft board for Bob, who enlisted for three years, to report on the same day as Bill and John who would serve for two years as draftees. It seemed that everyone was leaving for the service.

Mister Sandman

That weekend, the number one song on the Lucky Strike Hit Parade, a popular Sunday night television program, was *Mister Sandman*,[115] sung by the Chordettes.

I had skipped the Sunday night Ascension dance, and, after a few drinks in the Clover Inn, I ended up with Matthew "Matty" Martin in the Sunwood Tavern on Queens Boulevard – so named because it was located on the Sunnyside/Woodside border. The Sunwood was a quiet place where a talented blind black man sang and played an organ on a raised platform at the end of the bar. We were about to order our second drink when suddenly the door flew open and in walked four attractive women in their 20s, dressed to the nines. Accompanying them was a heavy-set, swarthy looking guy in a shiny mohair suit.

"Can you please turn on the television? Please? We have to watch The Hit Parade," they asked the bartender as the blind man played away at the organ.

The man accompanying them announced, "Please, buddy. These girls are the Chordettes. They're anxious to know if their song is still number one."

"What song is that?" the skeptical bartender asked.

"*Mr. Sandman*. It's been number one since September."

Obviously impressed, the bartender walked over to the organ player, told him who was in his presence, and asked if he would mind taking a break.

The organ player climbed down from his platform and groping the side of the bar made his way over to where we were standing in the middle of the bar. He extended his hand to meet everyone. The man with the

---

[115] *Mr. Sandman* – Lyrics and music by F.D. Ballard.

Chordettes identified himself as their manager and publicist. After the introductions, the organ player asked, "Are these girls as pretty as they sound?"

"They sure are," Matty responded.

"Well, if you girls are the Chordettes, can you give me a few chords?" the organ player asked.

The girls looked at each quizzically, then one of them began to hum "bung, bung, bung, bung …" and in unison they began to sing:

> *Mr. Sandman, bring me a dream.*
> *Make him the cutest that I've ever seen.*
> *Give him two lips like roses and clover.*
> *Then tell him that his lonesome nights are over …*

The bartender turned on the television and the manager bought a round of drinks. The girls, still excited from their frantic car ride, explained that they had appeared in an early dinner show on Long Island, and hoped to be back in Manhattan in time to watch the Hit Parade at their hotel. They were delayed in traffic, and, to our delight, they decided to stop and catch the show in Sunnyside.

The Hit Parade format built up the audience's suspense by opening with the 10th place song and finished the show with the song in the number one position. *Mr. Sandman* remained number one on the charts for a long time and became the Chordettes' signature song.

The Chordettes were fun to be with. It was enjoyable trying to teach one of them the Savoy. I got to dance with Lynn Evans, the lead singer. She was the tallest of the four girls. I still remember her long attractive face. She had big eyes, a great bone structure, full wide lips, and a jutting jaw. She was a genuinely nice person. Best of all, she was a good sport and a fun person to be around. Matty Martins was more of a mauler than a dancer. He did not get far trying to put his arms around the girls at the bar. Their manager enjoyed watching Matty trying to hustle his famous clients. The girls were elated when they learned they were still at the top of the chart, and a second round of drinks was ordered to celebrate. Meeting them was a great surprise, turning an otherwise quiet Sunday night into an unforgettable evening and making November a memorable month.

Understanding the Alternatives

Finally, I was beginning to learn about life and myself. Looking back on the previous year's reckless behavior gave me reason to pause and contemplate that there was so much more to learn. I was still prone to foolish behavior, didn't take my job seriously, gave insufficient thought to determining if I was fit to pursue higher levels of education, and drank too much on too many occasions. But more importantly, I discovered there were people outside my family who believed in me, thought I had potential, and cared enough to point me in the right direction. True, like my many new friends, I was curious in learning how far I could stretch the envelope in any given endeavor. When you test the rules at that age you sometimes say and do things you soon regret. As the year ensued, I was learning to apply the brakes a lot sooner than I previously would have, though some may remember me as too adventurous, always flying high with the throttle wide open.

Free from parental constraints, I was finding myself through supportive co-workers and friends, who took the time to nurture me with more patient guidance. There was still a long way to go, and little did I realize that it would take many more years. My head was clear as November came to a close. I was upbeat and looking forward to my final month as a civilian.

Simply put, I was tired of the current in my life that had turned monotonous – work, drink, get lucky sometimes – all the while going nowhere. I was grabbing onto the hope that my enlistment in the Navy would save me. I hoped it would not be the end of me, like the new and increasingly popular television jingle for Roto Rooter – "And away goes trouble down the drain."

It was all too clear that I must give up my lifestyle. While I couldn't express myself as I have in this memoir, I knew that I would never achieve excellence through the ordinary. Most of my friends experienced the same predicament.

What was to become of us?

Was military service the answer?

What will we do in the years ahead?

More importantly, were we asking the right questions as we began to realize the time was upon us to consider other alternatives?

Our daily routine, while enjoyable, was avoiding the realities of life. It was time to test the waters and determine what we were made of.

16

December

The departure of Bob Perite, a reliable and loyal friend since childhood, started December off on a sad note. The Friday before he left for Fort Dix, there was a goodbye party for him at Equitable. Following that, a group of us got together at the Little Penn Tavern. Bob was looking forward to his Army service. He felt secure in the knowledge that by going through training with Bill Marquette and John Renck he would be with two people who would look out for him. I would sorely miss Bob and Bill. Neither needed the direction that I did. They were not going away to find their way, as I soon would.

The month took a good turn in my view when the members of the U.S. Senate voted 67 to 22 to censure Senator Joseph McCarthy for his embarrassing conduct during the spring hearings of the Senate's Permanent Investigations Subcommittee. McCarthy termed it "a lynch party" and called those who voted against him "senile." The incendiary quality of his statements had lost their effectiveness; he was now a broken man isolated from the Republican Party, his colleagues in the Senate, and the press.

Some years later, my neighbor, Edward Bennett Williams, the legendary trial lawyer who had represented McCarthy, told me that the senator took his downfall in stride, steadily increased his daily level of alcohol consumption, and went on a lengthy bender. McCarthy's censure was the chief topic of discussion in most New York bars that week. Irish Catholics put the blame on the commie pinko's. They considered McCarthy's censure an attack against their core beliefs –

everything they stood for. The curse of McCarthy would influence their thinking for many years to come.

Jack Palance

One day after work, moving with the crowd up 32nd Street towards Herald Square, I found myself day dreaming about what Bob Perite, Bill Marquette, and John Renck were doing at Fort Dix and what I would soon be doing at Bainbridge or Great Lakes. As I turned the corner at 6th Avenue, making my way towards the subway entrance, a half step into the turn, I was sent flying by a large man in a blue overcoat, solid as a wall and very tall, who was also making the turn in my direction.

Stunned and embarrassed by my sudden meeting with this hulk of a man and the cold pavement, I grabbed his outstretched hand and was pulled to my feet.

The familiar voice, with the scary smile behind it, asked, "Are you alright?"

"You, you're …"

"Yes, I am," Jack Palance, answered.

"I'm sorry, I wasn't paying attention," I said, not exactly the typical New York response. I was not about to say, "Hey, watch the hell where you're going, buddy!"

He smiled and walked off. Wow, that was exciting, I said to myself. That guy's as big as a house and solid as a rock. Still feeling the sudden jolt of Palance's body and my impact with the pavement, I went down the subway steps savoring another memory for my file. You might describe it as a New York moment.

Planning the Christmas Party

The Christmas Party organizing committee for Equitable's seventh and eighth floors decided that since I would soon be entering the Navy it would be best if I made the hotel arrangements. Their logic was simple – should anything untoward happen and a complaint be made to Equitable Life, I'd be long gone. The assignment required that I don my Easter suit, white shirt and striped tie ensemble, and undertake my first contact with a big-time hotel, our neighbor across 32nd Street, the Pennsylvania Hotel.

I called Pennsylvania 6-5000 and inquired about the rental of a suite of rooms for Friday, December 18th. Within the hour I was passing under the hotel's majestic façade designed by McKim, Mead, and White who had also designed Penn Station. I was soon inspecting a $35 suite with a large parlor, complete with two adjoining bedrooms. The suite was on the inside of the corridor facing an airshaft, but I was not renting it for the view. The commodious parlor contained two large couches and a number of side chairs. If reconfigured, the room could comfortably accommodate 50 people. The hotel sales representative explained the additional charges required for ice and soda, should we decide to supply our own liquor, which we intended to do. The delivery entrance to the hotel was across the street from Equitable Life. We knew the men who worked in the delivery area from the Little Penn Tavern. A few $10 bills would cinch an arrangement to have them purchase the beer and liquor and deliver it to the suite. It was an ideal party venue with a bathroom adjacent to the parlor and separate bathrooms for each of the two bedrooms. As we were leaving the suite, I was asked if I would need the two bedrooms.

"I certainly hope so," I replied. "The party is for senior executives. We'll need the rooms in case a few of them have too much to drink."

"They might have other things in mind," he suggested with a wink of the eye. I booked the room and returned to the office with the good news.

Though parties outside the office premises were not sanctioned by the company, such well-organized events often had management's blessing. It was understood that the rules for such parties were that there were no rules. Every young woman attending an office party knew what every young man had on his mind. The culture and mores of the time, albeit patently wrong, presumed that a young woman participating in such an event did so of her own free will and fully understood the risk inherent in her attendance. The deck was clearly stacked against women, who were begging for trouble if they had too much to drink. The 1950s Christmas Party, as accurately depicted in the acclaimed movie, *The Apartment*, was actually a large-scale sexual encounter that in today's world would be considered a hostile work environment.

The party committee estimated that a ticket charge of $10/guy and $5/girl would cover the cost of the event. This would enable us to put together a kitty of $300 to purchase beer and liquor. In the weeks leading up to the party, the excitement rose. Soon we were oversubscribed since Ace Corcoran was promoting the party throughout the building – it was no longer an exclusive party for the seventh and eighth floors.

It was critical that we observe the capacity limits because of fire department rules. We faced the risk that the hotel's elevator operators could inform the hotel detectives that too many people were visiting our suite – exceeding the capacity limits could shut us down.

I had never seen as much excitement in the Equitable Building as I did on the day of the party. The word was out, "You don't want to miss the seventh and eighth floor party." Seemingly, everyone in the building planned to attend. We decided to collect money at the door from the guys and girls without tickets. At two that afternoon, I signed into the suite. Within the hour, the beer and liquor was delivered. To minimize the service charges, we paid cash to the room service staff assigned to our party, who reciprocated by charging us less than the normal rate. The crowd started arriving at 4:30. We quickly collected another $200. By 5:30, the party was in full swing, the suite jammed with guys and girls, including a few sailors who heard about the party in the hotel lobby.

We were having a great time. There was no trouble, and people drifted in and out in an orderly manner. We even had a few guests on our hotel floor stop by to visit. About 6:30, our Christmas cheer was interrupted by a scream coming from one of the bedrooms. I opened the bedroom door to find a partially dressed couple soaked in vomit and a hapless drunk sitting against the wall continuing to up-chuck his day's consumption of food and beer. The fool managed to target a number of coats, previously stacked on the bed, but moved to the floor by the putative lovers.

Task number one – get rid of the drunk. Two large party attendees were quickly recruited to remove him from the suite.

Task number two – clean up the mess and air out the room. The lovers moved to the bathroom to clean themselves, while a few of us used wet towels to clean the vomit residue from the coats, rug, and bedspread. After some struggle, we managed to open the window to air out the room. The window was our biggest problem – it may not have been opened since the hotel was built by the Pennsylvania Railroad in 1919.

By 7:30, the party was over, the only incident being the drunk's mishap. We split up the additional funds realized from the event while the room service staff cleaned up the parlor and made off with the extra beer and liquor. I set aside enough beer, ice, soda, and a bottle of scotch for later, expecting to maintain the suite and possibly spend the night after visiting the party that the Equitable college crowd was having up the street at the Hotel McAlpin. Just before I locked up the suite, I completed a final inspection to make sure there was no damage and that everything was in proper order.

As I was about to leave, there was pounding on the door. The door lacked an eyehole, requiring me to open the door to determine who was there. Cautiously cracking the door open, I was repulsed by a foul breath. The drunk was back and he was angry. He lunged forward, trying to force his way in, but before he could get his large body through the doorway, I braced the door with my left leg and stopped his advance with my shoulder. He attempted to punch me, but his motion was limited by the un-giving space in the doorway. I countered with a short right jab to his face and uppercut to his nose, triggering a release of snotty blood. His body dropped to the floor with his head jammed in the side of the door. He was barely conscious. Rather than leave him in the hallway, I struggled with his large, limp body and pulled him into the room. Rolling him over, I cringed. He was a mess. I cleaned his face with a wet towel and waited for him to fully revive.

My right hand was throbbing – it was cut, and beginning to swell. I removed my overcoat and jacket and rolled up my shirt sleeve before sitting in a chair and plunging my hand into an ice bucket. That's when it suddenly dawned on me that I had again risked my entire future, this time over a Christmas drunk. Though I had every right to protect myself from injury and the room from damage, I suddenly realized the potential consequences of my actions. Fortunately, my immobilized guest began to move his head and groan. "What happened – what happened?" he slurred through labored breaths.

"You had too much to drink," I said. I offered him a glass of water and helped him into the bathroom, where he soaked his head in the sink. His face bruised and swollen and his clothes askew, he left the room about 20 minutes later, fully understanding that the party was over.

I still didn't know who he was or whether he worked at Equitable, and if he did, what he would do after he sobered up. Would he come after me? Oh, what a mess. I sat down in the chair again and began to reflect on my life. It seemed that I was always going two steps forward and one step back or one step forward and two back. The problem was that the back steps were the ones with severe consequences. As I soaked my hand and sipped a bottle of beer, I decided against any more parties. I'm quitting while I'm still ahead. I gathered up the bottle of scotch, packed it in my small overnight bag, descended to the lobby, paid the bill, and left for home.

Upon my return to work on Monday, I soon learned that many people knew about the brief melee that ensued at the suite, but they were not sure who was involved. I had only mentioned the incident to John McComb, and he was not one to gossip. I was puzzled. How did they find out? I soon learned that the drunken party animal worked on the eighth floor. Upon his arrival at the office that morning he had been called out by Ace Corcoran for spoiling the party. Questioned by Ace about the condition of his face, he told Ace what he remembered, but he wasn't sure who did it. All he said was that he recognized the guy from Equitable. When I got to the eighth floor to look for applications that morning, Ace asked me if I had gotten into a rumble at the hotel. I told him what had happened, and Ace quickly spread the word. People were impressed that I had taken on such a big guy. Yeah, great, I thought, but now that he knows who I am, what will he do to me?

Though I made no attempts to correct people's mistaken impressions of my physical prowess, I understood that it was quick thinking and the use of leverage, namely the door, that saved me from a serious beating. Understandably, I was worried that the big guy would reciprocate. Joe Gianinni pointed the guy out to me in the cafeteria that day. Joe kidded me. "Jesus, he's a big mother. He'll kill you when he sees you."

When I looked over at the guy, I was startled by the damage I had inflicted. I hesitated at first before deciding that it would be a good move on my part to walk over to his table and ask him how he was doing. Luckily, he turned out to be a decent person. He said there were no hard feelings and apologized for screwing up the party. That set things straight and lifted a big load from my shoulders. I walked away from him, still rubbing my sore right hand, thinking how lucky I was that it turned out the way it did. A smarter person would have ignored the pounding on the door and waited for the drunk to go away. I still had much to learn.

Christmas Eve

Early on Christmas Eve, I visited with Dave Richardson and his father in their Matthew's Flats apartment on 52nd Street near Skillman Avenue, where we sat at the kitchen table and drank glasses of Bushmills Irish Whiskey that Mr. Richardson generously poured.

Dave's father was the superintendent and chief maintenance man for a number of the apartment houses on their block. A likeable individual and a good observer of people, he provided fatherly advice about my future, urging me to have the best Christmas I could manage with my family. "Son, your life will never be the same once you leave for the Navy," he cautioned.

Mother was beside herself when I arrived home about 10 that night. Dad, who promised to buy a Christmas tree, had arrived home drunk dragging in a sorry excuse for a tree.

"Look at that tree, Neal. Just look at that tree."

"Mom, he has one eye, he's drunk, and it's late in the evening. What'd you expect him to bring home at the last minute?"

To this day, including trees put out for collection late in January, I have never seen a scrawnier tree more barren of needles.

"I'll get a decent tree," I said.

"I hope you haven't been drinking?"

I ignored her remark as I headed out the door and walked up to Gianinni's Garden Center on 58th Street. No luck there. From Gianinni's I set out on a long journey heading first for Northern Boulevard, then over to Broadway, all the way down to the Ditmars Boulevard-bound elevated line on 31st Street. From there, I walked over to 30th Avenue then up the hill to Steinway Street and down Steinway to 31st Avenue, visiting the empty lots and shuttered stores where Christmas trees were sold in previous weeks, only to find them all empty. I had covered every spot I had seen trees for sale over the years. There were no more trees for sale. Dejected, I began the trek home.

I had walked more than two miles on my futile search when I started down 31st Avenue. Just beyond six corners, where Newtown Road crosses 43rd Street and 31st Avenue, I noticed a few trees propped against the wall of an apartment house. It was next to the empty lot at the corner, just across the street from P.S. 10 on 45th Street. A number of my friends, including Bobby Collins and Brendan Malone lived down the street. Despite the hour, people were coming and going into the walk-up apartments adjacent to the lot.

"Are these trees for sale?" I asked a man unloading his car.

"The guy packed up and left about 9:30. 'See you next year,' he said to me. So, I guess he left them."

"Thanks. I've been looking high and low for a tree."

"Merry Christmas. Pick a good one, son."

To my surprise, I found a decent tree and hauled it home. By 1:30 a.m., Mother and my sisters, Carol, Rose and Patricia, had completed decorating the tree. It may have been the nicest tree we ever enjoyed.

The next morning, Dad was proud of the tree he thought he had purchased. Remembering Mr. Richardson's advice, I complimented him on his selection. Mother, though reluctantly, did the same, while my sisters and younger brother Jimmy managed to hold back their laughter. Thanks to my intrepid journey the previous night and our better judgment that morning, the family managed to enjoy a Christmas devoid of mayhem.

New Year's Eve

My New Year's Eve date was Grace Flori, a neighbor of the Connaughton sisters on 95th Street in Jackson Heights. Grace was an attractive blonde with a great personality. Equally important, she was an excellent dancer. Simply put, she was a great Savoy and an enjoyable person. Dave Richardson and Dottie McQuade, the Connaughton sisters and their dates, Nipper McPartland and Katie Meehan, and a large crowd gathered at a party at a bar on Astoria Boulevard. We enjoyed exclusive use of the bar's back room, dancing the night and the year away to *Sh Boom* and *Earth Angel*, the Penguins new hit song.

I took Grace home in a taxi about two that morning. We chatted briefly outside her apartment house about our great evening, before I walked to the elevated train on Roosevelt Avenue. I never saw Grace again. I hope she got as much out of life as I did.

Waiting on the El platform at Junction Boulevard that clear, crisp night, I reflected on the past year that began in the darkest days of my adolescence, and truly thanked my lucky stars for the friends I had made and the guidance I had received. Rising from the depths of my errant ways I managed to live a year of wonder, enlightenment and levity. It had taken a tough year and the thoughtful advice of caring friends and a very observant teacher to convince me that it was time to shape up and get on with life.

Thinking back to those moments of anguish and self-analysis in Cellblock 'C', I finally began to feel that I could make it in life. 1954 would be hard to forget, but from then on I'd focus on what lay ahead.

For the remainder of my life, I would savor that year that set into motion a series of events that would have a profound effect on the rest of my life.

17

The Notice to Report Arrives

I had been getting anxious about my reporting date. My notice from the Navy finally arrived the first week in January 1955, instructing me to report to 120 Whitehall Street by 8 a.m. on Thursday, January 21st. I called Gerry Andrews and learned that he too was ordered to report that same day making it highly likely that we would go through Boot Camp together. More importantly, we ultimately would be eligible for G.I. Bill benefits, which I would eventually make full use of at New York University and Georgetown University Law School.

The last two weeks at Equitable Life were a series of fond farewells and good-natured lectures on how to properly comport myself. A collection was taken and people contributed over $100, which was presented at a party in the office. My last Friday on the job was spent with a large group in the Little Penn Tavern with me spending some of that money. I went home on the subway with John McComb discussing the good feelings I had for all of the people I had worked with, many of whom became good friends.

Equitable Life was a wonderful employer for me and thousands of others my age. An enduring and rock-solid institution, it provided countless people of my generation and generations to come with a chance to find themselves at critical times in their lives. If I had learned anything at Equitable, it was that working hard, though frowned upon by many including me at the time, would be noticed by those in charge.

The night before I left I had trouble sleeping. When morning finally came on January 21st, I was eager to get on with my life. I was up at the crack of dawn hoping it was not a false dawn, but a genuine new beginning. If I were to succeed, it was crystal clear that I had to go away.

It was strained and quiet at our family breakfast at six that morning. Everyone in the family was tentative. We knew that the family would never be the same. The first of five children was taking his leave. Mother, Dad, Grandpa Jim, my sisters Carol, Rose, Patricia, and my brother Jimmy were all dressed for work and school.

My sisters had mixed emotions. They were sad to see me go, but they were looking forward to the use of my bedroom. We picked away at our food as my Grandfather, who had slept on the plastic covered couch that night, tried to humor me. He slipped me $10, winked, and said, "This should come in handy." Dad spent most of the time convincing Mother that she should let me travel to Whitehall Street on my own.

I left our apartment a few minutes after seven and made it to my induction with five minutes to spare. I lined up with Gerry Andrews and we were sworn in, handed large brown envelopes containing our personal data, and quickly loaded onto one of the three buses bound for the Bainbridge Naval Training Center.

Fateful Journey

Gerry and I made our way to our seats and inspected the contents of the white cardboard boxes awaiting us. Curious, but not yet hungry, I examined the contents. "Jesus – do they expect us to eat this shit?" It was the standard fare provided on all military flights and bus rides – an apple, a small container of milk, and a bologna and American cheese sandwich on white bread wrapped in wax paper. Needless to say, my first impression of Navy chow was not a good one.

Gerry laughed and punched me on the upper arm. "Welcome aboard, sailor. This should be an interesting cruise."

Gerry lived directly across the street from Saint Joseph's Elementary School on 44th Street and 30th Avenue in Astoria. I attended Saint Joseph's for eight long years – eight years of fear-engendering Dominicans, and, until that day, it had accounted for two-thirds of my education and about half of my life. Gerry was handsome, powerfully built, engaging, intelligent, and fun to be with. He was also capable in a fight, a reassuring fact as I knew he would cover my back should push-come-to- shove in the barracks life ahead.

Gerry's passionate relationship with Helen Mack, a high-spirited and gorgeous young woman from Maspeth, had resulted in her pregnancy. He would soon be a father, albeit a reluctant one. The Navy was Gerry's escape from that situation. My reasons for being on that bus were altogether different. In a way, I was escaping from the distractions of the bright lights of a big city, squandered opportunities, and bad decisions. In real terms, the bus trip was all about starting to find a purpose in life, and hopefully to learn about the order of things – the importance of rules, systems, teamwork, focus, effort, character, and trust. After what I had experienced in late 1953 and working through 1954 trying to correct my ways, it was imperative to find my place in life – to have a real purpose in society.

I sat in silence next to Gerry looking out the window, as the chartered buses carried an anxious load of young New Yorkers south through New Jersey and Delaware towards our destination. Once we left the Jersey Turnpike and crossed the Delaware River, the only scenery on Route 40 in Delaware was zoning clutter – small motels, coffee shops, roadhouse cocktail lounges, gas stations, and used car lots. Still, I hoped this journey was my new beginning.

The adrenalin high of the passengers had subsided from its earlier levels and with it their bravado. The cockiness of the guys on my bus was transformed when we crossed over the Maryland line. Sure, there were jokes about their friends who came to Elkton, the first town over the border, for a "shotgun" wedding. Elkton was unique – no waiting – no blood tests. People arrived daily by bus or train, got married, and caught the next train or bus back to New York. I didn't say a word. That could have been the case with me and TG, and I suspected this was where my seatmate had recently celebrated his wedding vows. I glanced at him and the look on his face confirmed my suspicion. Though Elkton was a fresh reminder of escaping the problems back home, like the rest of us, he too was apprehensive of the uncertainty of what awaited us some 20 miles down the road in Perryville, Maryland at the Bainbridge Naval Training Center, high on the bluffs above the Susquehanna River.

The buses arrived at Bainbridge early in the afternoon. When we disembarked, a short and stocky First Class Boatswain's Mate, with numerous red hash marks on his left sleeve, ordered us in a loud voice to line up on the white stripes in the macadam.

"Listen up, you smart-assed, New York, sons of bitches, you belong to me for the next few hours and if you wise off, I'm going to kick your smart-asses. Is that clear?"

The silence was met with another burst from his loud voice, "Did you smart-assed, New Yorkers hear what I just said? Now, tell me in loud and clear voices that, yes, sir, I heard you. Remember, loud and clear."

"Yes, sir. I heard you," we shouted out.

"Fine. Now if you remember to do what I say, then I'll not be angry with you. Do I make myself clear?"

"Yes, sir!"

"Good, now let's get you smart-ass New Yorkers dressed properly."

We all looked at each other in unison, each of us with the same thought - life is going to be different from this day forward. We were formed into separate Companies of 64 men. It was Company 42 for Gerry,

1954 Adventures In New York

me, and Ritchie Drabek from Richmond Hill in Queens, who would later attend radio and Naval Security Group schools with me before we served together on Guam and Okinawa. We marched off in our new ill-fitting uniforms to our barracks. Because of my Naval Reserve service, I was designated Boatswain's Mate of the Watch, provided with temporary Petty Officer's stripes to sew on my jumper, and empowered with the responsibility to assign members of the Company to stand watch from taps and lights out at 9 p.m. until reveille at 6:30 a.m.

In the coming days we were tested, probed, and injected. During the testing and interviewing process I was given a form requesting that I recommend a friend who might be interested in joining the Navy. As a joke, I submitted Dave Richardson's name and much to my surprise he enlisted a month later – about the same time that Bill Marquette, Bob Perite, and John Renck were beginning their Advanced Infantry training at Fort Dix. The Army kept its promise and soon they were serving together in the same Infantry Company in Germany. Bob's wish was granted – he got to see Europe.

Unfortunately, I had an adverse reaction to the numerous shots we received and landed in the hospital for over a week. Ailing "Boots," as we were called, were not given any breaks. Dressed in hospital-issued pajamas and a bathrobe, I was given a crash course in using a buffing machine. I calculated that I polished a few miles of corridors during my one-week stay. Fortunately, a Hospital Corpsman stopped me one morning. "You look familiar. Where're you from?"

"Woodside."

"Where in Woodside?"

"The Boulevard Gardens."

"My name's O'Gallagher. I live on 48th Street."

He was the oldest of the many O'Gallagher brothers. He remembered me from playing in Wanderer's Field, the site of the Woodside Housing Project. He got me relieved from the buffing duty and arranged for my discharge from the hospital. Due to the length of my hospital stay, I was reassigned to a new unit, Company 71.

Almost all the men in my new company were also from New York City. Occupying the adjacent bottom bunk was James Florio, a bright, friendly, determined, and spunky high school dropout from Brooklyn. Florio found the same solid direction that I did in the Navy and would become an officer, a Member of Congress, and the Governor of New Jersey.

My new beginning had begun. Having passed the point of realizing how easy it was to fail, it was now time to determine if I could succeed in life. My Navy training would be another turning point that put me in the right direction for the years ahead. I have followed that course with the help of many fine people along the way, all of whom I thank with profound gratitude, especially those who helped me find my way in that memorable formative year, 1954.

From then on, I continued to look back to that critical year, and all things considered, paraphrasing Sinatra, at 17, I had a very good year.[116] I also knew that it would never be this way again.

***

---

[116] *It Was a Very Good Year* - Lyrics and music by Ervin Drake.

Epilogue

The U.S. Navy surpassed my expectations, provided me with exposure to outstanding individuals from a broad cross section of America, invited me into the Naval Security Group and the elite company of the clandestine communications intelligence community, instilled in me a work ethic, and taught me how to focus, achieve, and advance while taking me to interesting places across the world. Above all, it eliminated any self-doubts I might have held about my ability.

Upon my discharge in 1958 I returned to Equitable Life for a few weeks before joining my father in the construction of the Chase-Manhattan Bank Building before entering New York University in the fall. I quickly adapted to college life and soon had a full plate as captain of the freshman basketball team, senior instructor at the Naval Security Group's Reserve Unit in Whitestone, and in my second semester, part-time work reconciling bank accounts in a brokerage house. I finished college in less than three years by taking full course loads in the summer and attending day and night sessions in my last year. At night during the summers I worked on major New York construction projects including the massive anchorages of the Throggs Neck and the Verrazano Bridges. My most interesting job in construction was driving a diesel locomotive 550 feet under the East River in the boring of the tunnel that now carries waste water from lower Manhattan to a treatment facility on Newtown Creek in Greenpoint.

In 1961, I decided to leave New York for my law school studies at Georgetown University's Law Center. It was a wise choice as I soon met Mary-Margaret Donnelly who was then a senior at Washington's Trinity College. Soon she was a scholarship student and number one in the class behind me at law school. We married in January 1964 when I was attending school in both the day and evening while working at the D.C. Court of

General Sessions. From there, I worked as the assistant director of the Legal Department of the American Automobile Association, where I edited the Digest of Motor Laws and monitored state and federal motor vehicle laws and regulations. It was in that capacity that I provided assistance to the U.S. Senate's Rubicoff subcommittee staff in the hearings on automobile safety, and took an active part and assisted in the drafting and the passage of the landmark auto and tire safety laws enacted by Congress. During this period I was actively involved in the Presidential election of 1964 as an advance man for President Lyndon B. Johnson and Mrs. Johnson and in the 1966 and 1968 elections for President Johnson, Vice President Hubert H. Humphrey, and Vice Presidential nominee Edmund S. Muskie.

In 1966, I was recruited by the U.S. cotton trade to be its representative in Washington where I became involved in myriad issues pertaining to the production, processing, storage, financing, transportation, and marketing of this essential fiber. In the course of almost 45 years I appeared before state, congressional, and foreign parliamentary committees as an expert witness on more than 100 occasions, appeared before state and federal courts and federal regulatory agencies, and participated in two successful cases in the U.S. Supreme Court. In the course of my career in the cotton industry I traveled to more than 50 countries, gave numerous speeches and either chaired or participated in expert panels, served on a multitude of national and international committees, and still serve as the Permanent Representative of the International Cotton Advisory Committee to the United Nations Commission on Internal Trade Law. Upon my retirement as executive vice president and general counsel of the American Cotton Shippers Association, the National Cotton Council of American bestowed upon me its highest honor, the Harry S. Baker Award for distinguished service. I currently maintain a law practice specializing in trade association governance, contracts, agricultural policy, commodity futures trading, trade, and international arbitration.

It has also been my privilege to be blessed with two bright and stimulating daughters, and to participate in numerous civic endeavors, including the presidency of the West Montgomery Citizens Association, coaching AAU girls' basketball, medaling in the Maryland Senior Olympics in basketball and swimming, and participating in the National Senior Olympics as a member of the Maryland basketball team. For an extended period in my 40s and 50s I was a competitive equestrian in combined training (dressage, cross country, and jumping) and active for 20 years in U.S. Pony Club activities with my daughters through the Seneca Valley Pony Club. The University Club of Washington has recognized my endurance in the pool by naming me Athlete of the Year for winning the club swimming championship for 12 consecutive years. As a member of the U.S. Masters swim program, my adventurous nature still prevails in my numerous open water swims, including the Alcatraz to San Francisco swim, which I have successfully completed these last three years as the oldest competitor.

Since I began writing ten years ago, I have been an active board member and officer of The Writer's Center and the American Independent Writers.

But were it not for those who helped in 1954 and in the years that followed, this could have been a very different epilogue.

Acknowledgments

Over the years, I have always looked back at 1954 as the breakthrough year in my life. Things had gone bad primarily because of my lack of focus, inclination to pursue risky conduct, and overall poor judgment.

As you have read, things began to turn in the right direction impelled by the fact that I had learned how life would be if I did not change. These developments came about because of the advice, counsel, and example of many others including my father Patrick A. Gillen, my mother Rose R. McPartland Gillen, my maternal grandfather James McPartland, my aunt Anne Dooley, my great aunts Lilly McPhail and Rose McPartland Ford, my cousins Pat and Bill Dooley and Grace McPartland, retired NY Fire Chief John Hertin, NYPD Chief Inspector Jeremiah Brennan, former NY State Senator and Queens District Attorney Frank D. O'Connor, and Bernie Duffy. Many friends, some of whom were my fellow workers at the Equitable Life, were also helpful including John McComb, Bob Perite, Bob Houlihan, Bill Marquette, Dave Richardson, John Power, Bill Barry, Billy Thomas, Richard Hilliard, Joe Gianinni, Dick Pertrowski, Artie Wassen, John O'Rourke, Andy Rosasco, Pat Shanahan, May Sheridan, Dick Surhoff, Pete Clark, Lester Anderson, Billy "Doc" Doherty, Kennie Reich, Dorothy McQuade, Joan Dean, Maureen Connoughton, Grace Flori, Jack Sherman, Jack Healy, Jack O'Grady, Bill Mackie, Eddie Gardner, Mike Trosie, Dick Donnelly, John Kosnar, Tom Kealey, Father Lyons, and countless others.

In researching and fact checking the events depicted herein I had many face-to-face, telephone, and e-mail exchanges with a number of people with whom I had shared these experiences. Many reviewed the manuscript or parts thereof. I thank them for their assistance, suggestions, clippings, photos, programs, and extraordinary memories. Those who shared with me those times were John McComb, Bob Houlihan, Jack

Kehoe, Bill Marquette, Bob Perite, Howard and Pat Kelly, Kenny Murphy, Billy Thomas, John Power, Richard Hilliard, Billy O'Brien, Emanuel "Manny" Luxenberg, Lester Anderson, Billy "Doc" Doherty, Joe McConnon, Carol Gillen Costello, Jack Schneider, Drew Doyle, Pete Clark, Sean Gallagher, and Tom Kealey. I also thank the resourceful staffs of the Library of the U.S. Military Academy at West Point, the New York Public Library, and the Library of Congress.

I also wish to thank Barbara Esstman and Mia Cortez for their superb edits and suggestions, Don Graul and Martin Tolchin for their perspectives and insights, and above all, Mary-Margaret Gillen for her corrections, salient observations, and her love and counsel.

About the Author

Neal P. Gillen is a Washington area lawyer and author and the Vice Chairman of The Writers' Center

Made in the USA
Charleston, SC
06 November 2012